Y0-ACD-441

WITHDRAWN
UTSA Libraries

ORIGINAL SUBJECTS

RENEWALS 458-4574

DATE DUE			

| GAYLORD | | | PRINTED IN U.S.A. |

HA   RE

FOUNDED BY WILLIAM

WITHDRAWN
UTSA Libraries

Original Subjects

The Child, the Novel, and the Nation

Ala A. Alryyes

DISTRIBUTED BY HARVARD UNIVERSITY PRESS
CAMBRIDGE, MASSACHUSETTS AND LONDON, ENGLAND
2001

Library
University of Texas

Copyright © 2001 by the President and Fellows of Harvard College

All rights reserved. No part of this book may be reproduced in any form or by an electronic or mechanical means, including information storage and retreival systems without permission in writing from the publisher, except by a reviewer, who may quote brief passages in a review.

Printed in the United States of America

FIRST PRINTING

This book is printed on acid-free paper, and its binding materials have been chosen for strength and durability.

Library of Congress Cataloging-in-Publication Data

Alryyes, Ala A., 1963–
 Original subjects : the child, the novel, and the nation / Ala A. Alryyes.
  p. cm.—(Harvard studies in comparative literature : 46)
 Includes bibliographical references and index.
 ISBN 0-674-00257-1 (alk. paper)—ISBN 0-674-00263-6 (pbk. : alk. paper)
 1. Children in literature. 2. Literature, Modern—History and criticism. I. Title. II. Series.

PN56.5.C48 A44 2001
809'.93352054—dc21   2001024559

Library
University of Texas
at San Antonio

To the memory of my parents

Acknowledgments

Original Subjects has benefited from many conversations and much fellowship. I wish to thank my friends in the Department of Comparative Literature at Harvard, where I found a home. I will always remember the fourth floor of Boylston Hall with affection. I am indebted to James Engell, Susan Suleiman, Gregory Nagy, and Marc Shell: for their keen observations and generous belief in the project, many thanks. A year I spent in Paris provided much stimulation and allowed me the time to sharpen my ideas. I am grateful to the Ecole Normale Supérieure for its support; equal thanks to the French Department at Harvard.

For sharing with me their intellectual rigor, broad learning, and love of teaching, I am indebted to my former colleagues in History and Literature at Harvard. I particularly thank Patricia Lynch and Melinda Gray, my co-teachers in the Britain and France Sophomore Tutorial; I am also grateful to Melinda for being generous enough to read much of the manuscript. I am much indebted to my students at Harvard as well. I also wish to thank my friends Lilly Parrot and François Brunet for their wonderful dinners and gracious hospitality in Paris and Burgundy. Sincere thanks for enriching discussions are due to Anthony Appiah, Svetlana Boym, David Bromwich, Peter Brooks, Tom Conley, Philip Fisher, Judith Ryan, Edward Said, Elaine Scarry, Michael Seidel, Werner Sollors, Tzvetan Todorov, and Jan Ziolkowski. I also thank Jan for his invaluable aid with the publication process. I am indebted to Bette Anne Farmer, Eric O'Bryan, and Susan Hayes as well for their help with that process. I am also grateful to my anonymous readers for their helpful comments and suggestions. Finally, a book is a conversation with its predecessors; I heard the voices of their authors and I am grateful.

Contents

ORIGINAL SUBJECTS

ONE

ENIGMATIC RELATIONS: THE NOVEL
AND NATIONAL NARRATIVES

Behind Me—dips Eternity—
Before Me—Immortality—
Myself—the Term between.
Emily Dickinson

His famous scar not withstanding, when Odysseus returns
to Ithaka, only two beings *recognize* him, as it were, without mediation: his protector, the goddess Athena, and his dog,
Argos. The kinds of knowledge available to them are both at
odds with the human knowledge of alterity. Athena is an omniscient knower, whose knowledge of Odysseus encompasses the
changes within space and time that befall him, because she is
aware of these changes. Argos, on the other hand, recognizes
Odysseus by his smell; an essence that is unaffected by
Odysseus' two decades of travel. The identity of Odysseus is, to
Argos, an identity based on the sameness of his body, on a scent
that marks him out from birth to death: it is the scent of nature,
and not culture—independent of time and space.

The two poles of knowledge uponwhich Athena and Argos
rely to recognize Odysseus articulate well with the two poles of
identity which Paul Ricoeur identifies in *Oneself as Another:* "on
one side identity as *sameness* (Latin idem, German Gleichheit,
French mêmeté); on the other, identity as *selfhood* (Latin ipse,
German Selbstheit, French ipséité)."[1] Whereas "sameness is a
concept of relation and relation of relations," selfhood refers to
"permanence in time" (116-8). We can perhaps conclude that

[1] Paul Ricoeur, *Oneself as Another*, trans. Kathleen Blamey (Chicago:
University of Chicago Press, 1992), 116.

Argos recognizes Odysseus' identity because he is incognizant of any gaps between *idem* and *ipse;* whereas Athena, always aware of all the lacunae between them, never fails to recognize him. Both of these types of knowledge, it is important to note, are impervious to time: Argos' because it brackets off time, and Athena's because it encompasses all time. Human knowledge of the *other,* in contrast, has time and history as elements and limitations; in its partiality and contingency, it is narrative in nature. What fills the gap between the two poles of identity, sameness and selfhood, is for each of us, the sum total of human interaction, or, more enigmatically, what we call *culture.* Identity is not formed in isolation, and there is no self that is not defined, in one way or another, in terms of an other.

The limited nature of human knowledge circumscribes belonging. In the *Odyssey,* recognizing the returning but disguised Odysseus requires acts of interpretation of which not every character is capable. Homer deploys what the text refers to as *ainoi* (plural of *ainos,* which translates as "riddling utterance"), and *semata* (plural of *sêma,* one of whose meanings is "sign"). Each of these utterances consists of a narrative code, whose true message necessitates an act of interpretation which in turn, as Gregory Nagy has shown, requires the decoder to possess certain moral, intellectual and emotional ties to the utterer, or encoder of the message.[2] The Homeric narrative sifts the characters within Odysseus' household (Telemachos, Penelope, her suitors, as well as the maids and servants) into two groups: those who can read Odysseus' "language"—his *ainoi* and *semata*—and thus may join the new community he will establish, and those who cannot, and are, therefore, excluded.[3]

[2]Gregory Nagy, *Pindar's Homer: The Lyric Possession of an Epic Past* (Baltimore: Johns Hopkins University Press, 1990), 148.

[3]cf. what Charles Taylor calls "language in a broad sense, covering not only the words we speak, but also other modes of expression whereby we define ourselves." Charles Taylor *Multiculturalism: Examining the Politics of Recognition* (Princeton: Princeton University Press, 1994), 32.

The ability to interpret Odysseus' "language" is predicated upon, as the narrative implies, the knowledge of tradition and the desire for its preservation.[4] It would seem, therefore, that Auerbach ignores this significant point in the famous opening chapter of *Mimesis,* his seminal study of the representation of reality in Western literature, when he says that

> the Homeric poems conceal nothing, they contain no teaching and no secret second meaning. Homer can be analyzed, as we have essayed to do here, but he cannot be *interpreted.*[5] (emphasis mine)

Auerbach makes the above-stated conclusion when he analyzes the scene in which Odysseus' old nurse recognizes him by his scar. Auerbach adduces the fact that the narrative does not launch its flashback or *analepsis* "as a recollection which awakens in Odysseus' mind" to conclude that "any such subjectivistic-perspectivistic procedure, creating a foreground and a background, resulting in the present lying open to the depths of the past, is entirely foreign to the Homeric style" (7). In so arguing, he supports his above-cited belief that the Homeric narrative "cannot be interpreted," and that, also, "the Homeric style knows only a foreground, only a uniformly illuminated, uniformly objective (that is, independent of the subject's position) present" (7). By contrast, Auerbach argues, the Old Testament stories "are fraught with 'background' and mysterious, containing a second, concealed meaning" in need of interpretation (15). Auerbach concludes this analysis of Odysseus' scar, before moving to his comparison with the Biblical story of Abraham and Isaac in Genesis, with the statement that "[since] the excursus does not begin until two lines later,

---

[4]"The *ainos* restricts and is restricted by its audience," Nagy, 148.

[5]Erich Auerbach, *Mimesis: The Representation of Reality in Western Literature,* trans. Willard R. Trask (Princeton: Princeton University Press, 1953), 13.

when Euryclea had discovered the scar ... the story of the wound becomes an independent and exclusive present" (7). Exclusive? Precisely, but not in the sense that Auerbach intends. Auerbach does not attach any interpretive significance to the fact that it is Euryklea who detects the scar. Yet, as the Homeric narrative makes clear, Odysseus' scar is redolent to her of the memory of his visit to his grandfather's house. Reading the sêma of the scar depends on her having been part of the initial experience; and thus on her having preserved it as a *cultural* memory. Auerbach's approach presumes, incorrectly I believe, that the interpretive space is and only is a psychological "depth." But, in fact, the perpetual "present" of the narrative is not available to every one; it is quite exclusive. Unlike the Biblical epic, the interpretive space is not related to a solitary subjectivity, but is rather a function of recognizing oneself and being recognized as belonging to an interpretive community. Like Euryklea, Odysseus' later successful interpretation of Penelope's riddling utterance regarding their marriage bed, confirms his identity as a member of a community which Penelope shares, a community which is more exclusive in this case as it contains only two people: Penelope and her husband. Otherwise, as we know, Penelope's circumspection would not have been satisfied.

The ideology of the narrative is inscribed within the dramatic irony of the narrative technique. The reader/listener, who shares the narrative stance of the omniscient narrator, by "properly reading" the Homeric poetry, will belong to the *community of discourse* that the new Ithaka is. While that reading seems to be—perhaps because of the reader's narrative position—so "natural," it is easy to overlook its ideological import and its cultural construction.

Both narratives then—the Homeric and the Biblical epics—contain utterances in need of interpretation but they are, nevertheless, different in this way: the *Odyssey's* riddles require for their interpretation knowledge that belongs to the memorial past of the community—a past that may be more glorious, but that is of the same "kind" as the present and, hence, repeatable. They are, therefore, riddles whose successful deciphering has the potential to reintegrate the community in the here and now. The latent God of the Bible, however, authorizes an allegorical interpretation of "His" texts, a reading that de-emphasizes the here and now. The eye of the Biblical hero is always oriented toward a transcendent future that is not only superior, vastly superior, to the here and now, but whose attainment requires a break with the past of the community. Abraham must commit an act that is not only striking in its pious cruelty, but also in its radical novelty in a society where the first born son to an elderly father is of great value. In his test, Yahweh's words acknowledge this importance: "Take your son, your only son, your beloved Isaac, and go to the land of Moriah" (Gen. 22). Achilles' glory, his *kleos,* on the other hand, no matter how great it is, old Phoinix gives him to understand, should not make him believe that he is above learning from— and even imitating—Meleagros' example (*Iliad* IX 523 ff.). I shall have more to say about this distinction a bit later.

Because selfhood is narrative in nature, to speak of reading is to speak of community. Charles Taylor, following Heidegger, clarifies this connection in tracing the formation of the self to its "moral sources": the self's narrative is bound with its vision of the good; and, significantly, "this sense of the good . . . woven into my understanding of my life as an unfolding story," is community-dependent.[6] The narrative of the self necessarily unfolds within, and is interpreted by, the community.

How the self is read defines not only how the self lives within the community, but how it "survives" after death. It is precisely in terms of this reaction against death that scholars have recently attempted to explain and justify nationalism. Benedict Anderson trenchantly observes that "No more arresting emblems of the

[6]Charles Taylor, *Sources of the Self: The Making of Modern Identity* (Cambridge: Harvard University Press, 1989), 47.

modern culture of nationalism exist than cenotaphs and tombs of Unknown Soldiers. . . . The cultural significance of such monuments becomes even clearer if one tries to imagine, say, a Tomb of the Unknown Marxist or a cenotaph for fallen Liberals."[7] Anderson states, I believe correctly, that "the nationalist imagining" has a "strong affinity with religious imaginings" (10). And that "the magic of nationalism [is] to turn chance into destiny," unlike "all evolutionary/progressive styles of thought, not excluding Marxism," whose "great weakness" is that questions of suffering and death "are answered with impatient silence." Like "religious thought," Anderson observes, nationalism "responds to obscure intimations of immortality," for the nation transforms "fatality into continuity" (11). Régis Debray also explicitly relates nationalism and death in asserting "We must locate the nation phenomenon within general laws regulating the survival of the human species. This survival is won against death."[8] My disagreement, however, with both of these political philosophers is that I do not believe that this type of survival is, as Debray puts it, "a natural organization proper to *homo sapiens*" (26).[9] Man dies because of his nature; survival, however, has always been in the realm of his culture.

[7]Benedict Anderson, *Imagined Communities: Reflections on the Origin and Spread of Nationalism*, revised ed. (London: Verso, 1983), 9-10.

[8]Régis Debray, "Marxism and the National Question," Interview in *New Left Review*, v. 105, 27.

[9]Ernest Gellner, in his *Nations and Nationalism* (Ithaca, NY: Cornell University Press, 1983), finds the essence of nationalism in the fusion of culture and political power; an aspect of human life non-existent in agricultural life, but which is caused by the industrial homogenization of society through, most fundamentally, the imposition of a standard literacy and education system controlled by the state. Gellner's idea no doubt correctly explains the massification feature of nationalism, though to explain why these masses should become the hordes of wildly cheering, and very frequently, destructive fans, or the soldiers willing to die for a flag, certainly requires going beyond the egalitarianism and homogenization of the Enlightenment and the industrialization of the world.

Arendt: Immortality to Eternity

We find a keener appreciation of the historicity and variability of such desires for "survival" in Hannah Arendt's thought. In *The Human Condition*, Arendt offers an archaeology of the degeneration of the *vita activa*. This is evidenced by an increased valorization of the *vita contemplativa* by Christianity following the decline in value of *action* and *work* to that of necessary *labor* in Greek thought. Arendt traces that decline specifically to Plato:

> However, the enormous superiority of contemplation over activity of any kind, action not excluded, is not Christian in origin. We find it in Plato's political philosophy, where the whole utopian reorganization of *polis* life is not only directed by the superior insight of the philosopher but has no aim other than to make possible the philosopher's way of life.[10]

According to Arendt, both Plato and the Christian tradition converge in emphasizing the superiority of a life of contemplation: "Truth, be it the ancient truth of Being (Plato) or the Christian truth of the living God, can reveal itself only in complete human stillness" (15).

Both Plato and the Biblical narratives are similar in that, in Taylor's terms, the "moral source" they set up for the self is an eternal Truth incommensurate with the world of men, demoting the realm of action. Not only does "Truth" effectively remove action in the world from being principal in accessing the Good, but by consequence, it radically transforms the nature of man's struggle against death. Arendt, in continuing to investigate the difference in "central human concerns" that distinguish "the men of thought and the men of action," concludes her discussion with a superb distinction between two ways of

[10]Hannah Arendt, *The Human Condition* (Chicago: University of Chicago Press, 1958), 14.

imagining survival after death: immortality and eternity. Arendt's discussion is not only fascinating, but also fundamental to our investigation. I shall, therefore, quote from it at length.

Arendt defines immortality as the mode of survival before the discovery of the "Truth" as the ultimate goal of human life:

> Immortality means endurance in time, deathless life on this earth and in this world as it was given, according to Greek understanding, to nature and the Olympian gods. Against this background of nature's ever-recurring life and the gods' deathless and ageless lives stood mortal men, the only mortals in an immortal but not eternal universe, confronted with the immortal lives of their gods but not under the rule of an eternal God. If we trust Herodotus, the difference between the two seems to have been striking to Greek self-understanding prior to the conceptual articulation of the philosophers, and therefore prior to the specifically Greek experiences of the eternal which underlie this articulation. Herodotus, discussing Asiatic forms of worship and belief in an invisible God, mentions explicitly that compared with this transcendent God (as we would say today) who is beyond time and life and the universe, the Greek gods are *anthropophyeis*, have the same nature, not simply the same shape, as man. (18)

Because man is of the same nature as the immortal gods, he achieves his survival through actions, not through an attempt to approach the Good/God:

> The task and potential greatness of mortals lie in their ability to produce things—works and deeds and words—which would deserve to be, and, at least to a degree, are at home in the everlastingness, so that through them mortals could find their place in

a cosmos where everything is immortal except
themselves (19).

When the eternal is discovered, however, as "the true center of
strictly metaphysical thought," "its experience" alters what I
have termed survival. This experience "has no correspondence
with and cannot be transformed into any activity whatsoever,
since even the activity of thought, which goes on within one's
self by means of words, is obviously not only inadequate to render it but would interrupt and ruin the experience itself" (20).

It is clear, then, that these distinct modes of survival, immortality and eternity, have dramatic consequences on the way in
which the relationship between man and the immortal/eternal
objects of worship is conceived (the Greeks imitate and even
compete with their immortal Olympians;[11] Plato contemplates
his eternal Truth; Christians worship their God). Having set the
stage in this manner, we can now analyze the effect of these
respective modes of understanding survival on the relationship
between man and man, or between the self and the other.

Because the Homeric hero achieves immortality through
great "works and deeds and words," he is always acutely in need of
the other to recognize his deed; for immortality always needs an
accounting of it to survive and, hence, to effect survival for the
hero. Greatness cannot be achieved in solitude. Achilles, the swift
runner, though acknowledged to be the "Best of the Acheans,"
seems always to be on the run against being eclipsed by his con-
temporaries, like Diomedes and Ajax, or even his forerunners,
like Meleagros. The discovery of the eternal as the be-all and end-
all of life, however, severely devalues the other as a crucial actor in
the survival of the self. In a society where a one-to-one relationship with the Good (through contemplation) or with God
(through belief) is the source of the highest good, and hence,

[11]No more as aggressively, perhaps, as when Diomedes manages to
injure two gods in one day in the *Iliad*.

with Taylor, of the survival of the self, my connection to the other as the guarantor of my survival is necessarily undermined.

If my relationship with the other loses its rootedness in his being the witness to my deed committed in the here and now, we may perhaps ask what is his place in the new, eternal, cosmic order? Or, looked at from top to bottom, what connections are "required" to create any cohesiveness in a society whose sources of the good are completely separated from the here and now, from the sphere of human activity? In a striking passage in his *Confessions*, Augustine examines his link to his readers, wondering how it is that they can believe him, "Why then should I be concerned for human readers to hear my confessions? . . . And when they hear me talking about myself, how can they know if I am telling the truth, when no one 'knows what is going on in a person except the human spirit which is within' (1 Cor. 2:11)?" This is truly a paradox, but Augustine does not despair: "So as I make my confession, they wish to learn about my inner self, where they cannot penetrate with eye or ear or mind. Yet although they wish to do that and are ready to believe me, they cannot really have certain knowledge. The love which makes them good people tells them that I am not lying in confessing about myself, and the love in them believes me" (181).

In a different context, Stanley Cavell has argued that "What skepticism threatens is precisely irretrievable outsidedness, an uncrossable line, a position from which it is *obvious* that the world is unknowable."[12] Augustine overcomes the problem of skepticism by transmuting doubt into love. Though not the first instance of this kind of affective connection, Augustine's "love" starkly exemplifies this type of human association through which a human being can imagine himself to be kin to, and loving of, a group of people with whom he has no connection anchored in the here and now, in work and action. Love's knowledge, shared

---

[12]Stanley Cavell, *Disowning Knowledge* (Cambridge: Cambridge University Press, 1987), 29.

by the believers in an invisible eternal deity, replaces the day-to-day visibility of words and deeds, which the new community devalues. Augustine makes clear that this love is limited to the group that shares a common transcendent "love" object: he addresses God, stating that "A brotherly mind will love in me what you teach to be lovable, and will regret in me what you teach to be regrettable. This is a mark of a Christian brother's mind, not an outsider's." Belonging and knowing the other are as related in Augustine's *Confessions* as they are in the *Odyssey*, but it is love, not common participation, that provides the exclusive knowledge that renders Augustine's community possible.

Rather than accepting a "mystical" grounding for the nation in a universalist yearning for "survival," we should perhaps locate the nationalist impulse in the desire for connection between self and other, a connection of which survival and transparency are particular manifestations. And, although, strictly speaking, "nationalism" should be reserved for the modern fusion of the nation and the state, the ways in which people within nation-states can see themselves as being related to one another are not novel. The problem of skepticism and its "solutions" are as crucial to the creation of modern nations as they were to the formation of older communities. Whereas the transparency that love ensures is fundamental to one influential type of nationalism, other nationalist traditions seek ties that follow from participation. I would like to stress here, however, that this study will not present a typology of nationalism.[13] I will have little to

[13]For such typologies, see, for example, Liah Greenfeld, *Nationalism: Five Roads to Modernity* (Cambridge: Harvard University Press, 1992); Anthony D. Smith, *The Nation in History: Historiographical Debates about Ethnicity and Nationalism* (Hanover, NH: University Press of New England, 2000); Peter Alter, *Nationalism*, trans. Stuart McKinnon-Evans (London: Edward Arnold, 1989); Hans Kohn, *The Idea of Nationalism* (New York: Macmillan, 1944); Elie Kedourie, *Nationalism* (Oxford: Blackwell, 1960).

say, for instance, of its "genetic" or racial variant, preferring to focus on subtler formulations, on "cultural" conceptions of the nation, whose metaphors and signifying narratives motivate ties between self and other, individual and nation, in terms of the products of man's thoughts and actions, not his blood or genes.[14] Because the ties between one subject and another cannot be taken as given by "biology," they must be invented and propagated. I will employ the term "national narrative" to refer to the constellation of symbolic manifestations of the nation— its political prescriptions, myths of origin, rules of belonging and proper feelings, educational proclamations and policies, and so on—in order to underscore this made (and not found) nature of the nation. What I call "national narratives" will include British and French "social contracts"; I will explain my preference for the former designation a little later.

It might prove helpful, however, briefly to consider the issue of nationalism's taxonomy, tying it to our earlier analysis of identity and recognition. In discussing identity, it should be stressed, we are less interested in how the self plumbs its own makeup than in how it identifies *with* the other, recognizing him/her as a member of the nation. Our differentiation of the two poles of identity, sameness and selfhood, clarifies here that the identification which racial or genetic types of nationalism seek is that of the individual with the *same*. This conception of the compatriot as *same* brackets the value of time in favor of an unchangeable, atemporal knowledge, as Odysseus' body was/is known to Argos: all Aryans in the Nazi formulation, for instance, are members of the German nation. Such a view, of course, may take the form of a narrative, as when it becomes part of the regime's propaganda, promoted in literature and film. Still, it is a narrative that purports to deliver a non-narrative "fact": that Aryans are related through biology. In its pretension to

[14]I regard "civic" nationalism as part of this cultural formulation.

"scientific" status, this racial nationalism negates the dynamic essence of narrative.[15]

The other pole of identity, the reader may recall, is that of "selfhood," a narrative of the actions and thoughts of a person: "Unlike philosophical syllogisms," observes Peter Brooks, "narratives are temporal syllogisms, concerning the connective processes of time."[16] Still, it is precisely because time is a constituent of selfhood that this pole of one's identity is not identical with another subject's account of it, the knowledge that would allow or hamper an identification with the other as a member of one's community. Unlike Athena's, the self's knowledge of the other's selfhood is never complete. Human knowledge of the other is a special type of the "selfhood" narrative, an *enigmatic* narrative in which, because all time can never be encompassed, knowledge and accounts of the other are always partial and incomplete.

This enigmatic account, in which narrative desire is the result of incomplete knowledge, subtends two discourses that this study seeks to connect: the "private" novel and "public" nationalism—though these oppositions will not hold when we examine them more closely. Two general similarities between them are noteworthy here. Being as they are modern reformulations of inherited forms of conceiving and representing human association, both the novel and national narratives narrate and attempt to effect new views of societal ties. Both unfold plots of human interaction, exploring given rules of interlocution, contact, and hierarchy among their subjects—and improvising new

[15]There were, to be sure, other national socialist narratives that were more temporal and historical; after all, the era was seen as that of the Third Reich. Such archetypal schematics of history, however, are based on the allegorical identity of epochs, an identity that occludes the importance of time's passage.

[16]Peter Brooks, *Reading for the Plot: Design and Intention in Narrative* (New York: Vintage, 1975), 21.

ones. Second, both discourses relate human communication to a desire for knowledge of the other's mind, access to his hidden thoughts. In the case of national narratives, this yearning is evidenced in both Augustine's rhetoric and in the widespread nationalist obsession with the display of loyalty, be it via flags, oaths, festivals, or portraits of leaders. The novel is another kind of an epistemological legerdemain that eschews narrative's older delight in fantasy for the conceit of "truthfully" motivating the knowledge it displays of its characters. As Hayden White observes, "To be a 'realist' meant both to see things clearly, as they *really* were, and to draw appropriate conclusions from this clear apprehension of reality for the living of a possible life on its basis."[17]

For the great realist pioneer Daniel Defoe, for example, the tension associated with the novelistic violation of journalistic "truth" is allayed by the involvement of his first-person narrator in a community of rebels (Puritans, prostitutes or colonial adventurers) with extraordinary experience. The narrator often claims an experiential knowledge that is personal and, therefore, authentic—Crusoe is wrecked on an Island; Moll is "left a poor desolate Girl without Friends, without Cloaths, without Help or Helper in the World"; Roxana "leave[s] anyone that is a Mother of Children, and has liv'd [as she has, before her husband abandons her] in Plenty and good Fashion, to consider and reflect what must be my condition to have my children starve before my face." In addition, Defoe's narrator's experience falls outside the social pale of accepted behavior and destiny—Crusoe observes cannibalism on the island; Moll sleeps with her brother; Roxana nearly goes mad when she discovers her own culpability in the murder of the daughter she abandoned— making that very experience of interest, reportable, novel.

The novel and national narratives are symbolic and social discourses. Echoing, *mutatis mutandis,* Augustine's linkage of

[17]Hayden White, *Metahistory: The Historical Imagination in Nineteenth-Century Europe* (Baltimore: Johns Hopkins University Press, 1973), 46.

community and the skeptical problematic, Hans Aarsleff writes following Humboldt, that language "develops only socially as we keep testing the rightness of our words by adjusting them, so to speak, by trial upon others . . . a trial made necessary by the radical impossibility that others can have access to what goes on in our minds."[18] The two affinities of the novel and national narratives—the search for rules of association and the longing for transparency—resemble pendulum swings between the poles of language's limited capability and that of the human yearning for Adam's perfect language: the desire for transparency is itself a corollary of the search for rules of contact, an overreaching that rejects barriers and limits in search of an unlimited visibility.[19] Both enigmatic narratives, as I called them, are propelled forward by a desire born of the limited knowledge of the other's selfhood.

These two similarities between the novel and national narratives, I submit, render a child's story an original subject of both discourses. Because children represent both the promise of and resistance to continuity, they acquire a particular value in these narratives' symbolic constructions. In both discourses, the child is an actor in an original discursive condition and also an excluded cipher; he/she is both out of place and a place of beginning. Why and how do children become implicated in

[18]Hans Aarsleff, intro. to Wilhelm von Humboldt, *On Language: the Diversity of Human Language-Structure and its Influence on the Mental Develpment of Mankind*, trans. Peter Heath (Cambridge: Cambridge UP, 1988).

[19]Perhaps the supreme examples of a tentative and subtle exploration of the rules of human interaction and speech are the novels of Jane Austen. On the other hand, the most unabashed practitioners of the overreach for transparency are Robespierre and the other Revolutionary orators, who ordained festivals, most famously the Festival of the Supreme Being of 8 June 1793, directed by David, in which national sentiment and fusion were put on display. Citizens embraced openly and exhibited their patriotism in dress, mutual singing and oath taking.

national imaginings? What are some of the intellectual moves and historical changes that cause such a shift? How do "childhood" and "children" figure in the novel, influencing its form and affecting its genesis? These are some of the questions that this book seeks to address. I do not, however, intend to investigate the nature of childhood or young age in itself—as though that nature can be investigated—or the writings or opinions of children. Rather, my main emphasis is on the construction and use of young age in modern European novels and national narratives.

I will return to these themes later. At this point, however, a few general observations will suffice. The nascent novel and modern national narratives resisted fictional and political representations in which nature and God, duty and happiness, were firmly on the side of the father and of the Father. Seventeenth- and eighteenth-century national narratives combated absolutist myths of the state, providing alternative accounts of political authority and subjecthood, and acting as "both entrie[s] into and deflection[s] of existing strategies of representation."[20] Because the king's authority was portrayed as being immemorial, the beginnings of the commonwealth or the nation, the childhood of man and society, became the sites on which that allegedly immutable authority could be contested. Furthermore, since royal dominion was figured in terms of fatherhood, defining the borders and duties of "childhood" became fundamental to these narratives' resistance. For related reasons, the child was also a place of beginning for the realist novel, in which the young inscribed the struggle for forbidden happiness beyond the father's house and allegorized the struggle of the rising bourgeoisie.

---

[20]Stephen Greenblatt, ed. *Allegory and Representation* (Baltimore: Johns Hopkins University Press, 1981), xiii.

Childhood and National Myths

In my second and third chapters, I explore the contrasting uses and conceptions of "children" and "childhood" by several eighteenth-century political philosophers, tying their conceptions to these philosophers' views of the relation between the individual and the nation-state. The national narratives these two chapters examine closely include Locke's *Second Treatise of Government*, Rousseau's *Discourse on the Origin of Inequality*, *The Social Contract*, and *Emile*. While a few of these political discourses are more commonly called "social contracts" especially the *Second Treatise* and *The Social Contract*, I prefer to use the term "national narrative" for a number of reasons. First, it does not set arbitrary distinctions between similar discourses: both Rousseau's *The Social Contract* and *Discourse on the Origin of Inequality*, for example, are anatomies of past and future utopias intended as national and social critiques. *Emile*, not considered a social contract, is both an educational treatise and a political prescription: Rousseau, for example, diagnoses the child's tears as evidence of his dependence on adults, a link "in that long chain of which the social order is formed."[21] I favor the term for more than linguistic uniformity, however. This book studies the rise and development of the realist novel; such an aim is necessarily historical. By calling the political discourses that accompanied the novel "national narratives," I stress the necessary historicity of these discourses, their involvements in the national developments that influenced and were affected by them. Far from being a convenient label, much can be learnt from apprehending these "social contracts" within their historical settings and not merely as procedural agreements or prescriptions. Of course these visions might prove so

[21]Jean-Jacques Rousseau, *Emile*, trans. Allan Bloom (New York: Basic Books, 1979), 65.

just and conducive to the good life that one would hope they might be adopted universally as contractual civic arrangements. Yet their beginnings are particular and historical, a significant point since my own narrative is concerned with origins.

Furthermore, recognizing these social contracts as narratives draws our attention to their own, sometimes careful, sometimes obsessive, attempts to overcome the epistemological obscurity inherent in the recognized limitations of human knowledge. In some (Locke's *Second Treatise*), procedure and participation supplant transparency; in others (Rousseau's *Social Contract*), a mythological figure restores the openness of souls. In all of these accounts, however, the essential problem of how to get from point A to point B, from the state of nature to the commonwealth or the republic, is described in terms of a beginning, middle, and end, obeying the Aristotelian definition of plot. By way of a brief example here, Locke's *Second Treatise* has a beginning in the "State of Nature," one middle in the consensual establishment of the "Commonwealth" and one possible end in Locke's discussion of the "Dissolution of Government," a plot vitally related to Locke's taking part in a historical struggle against a tyrannical restored English monarch. But, as we shall see, there are other possible plots within this national narrative. My objective, then, is to analyze these political discourses, to emplot them as national narratives, emphasizing both their historicity and the relevance of the child's story they unfold to the rising novel.

Augustine's yearning for connection finds an echo in the eighteenth-century genesis of nationalism. Thinkers like Hamann, Herder, and Rousseau strongly opposed the Enlightenment's atomistic notions of human association and advocated instead a "natural," organic link, a shared history, between the individual and the nation. Chapter three examines the consequences of Rousseau's profound discontent with the distance between self and other, which he blames on modern society.

Rousseau's own social contract, as well as his other national narratives, attempts to re-enchant the relation between the individual and the state, belying Ernst Cassirer's contention that, with the foundation of the state in a social contract, "the myth of the state is gone."[22] Rousseau rues the passing of coherence and fusion that myth embodies, for, as Peter Herbst puts it: "Myths are teachable and professable, and they can therefore serve as the foci of coherence of social and political and religious groups and movements."[23] The power of the myth, be it that of the Chain of Being or of Rousseau's Legislator, is that it acts as a guarantor of the mind of others. All believe in the myth; hence, I know what others think and believe: their minds are transparent to me. Rousseau's Lawgiver, the architect of the nation in *The Social Contract*, for instance, becomes a "superior intelligence," an avatar of Lycurgus or Moses, who will "denature" men, fusing them into the General Will.

Although Rousseau did not see his beliefs in a nationalist vein, his writings fundamentally influenced the debates and representations of the French Revolution. Hence, I believe it is appropriate to refer to his accounts as "national narratives." Yet, the extent to which some of his most influential political views were intertwined with his personal life is remarkably ironic. Thus, for instance, it is tempting to link the death of Rousseau's mother in childbirth to his near obsession with transparency, a persistent metaphor and ideal of human communication in his *oeuvre*, that comes to underlie his national narratives. In his *Confessions*, Rousseau echoes Augustine, avowing that he has revealed his "secret soul" just as "Thou thyself hast seen it, Eternal being!" Later, describing his father's abiding memory of Jean-Jacques's dead mother, Rousseau relates that he "died in

[22]Ernst Cassirer, *The Myth of the State* (New Haven: Yale University Press, 1946), 173.
[23]Peter Herbst, "Myth as the Expression of Collective Consciousness in Romantic Nationalism," in *Romantic Nationalism in Europe*, ed. J. C. Eade (Sydney: Humanities Research Centre, 1983), 24.

the arms of his second wife, but with his first wife's name on his lips, and her picture imprinted upon his heart."[24] Transparency not only authenticates Jean-Jacques's own heart to his reader, but also, despite appearances to the contrary ("in the arms of the second wife"), his father's, saving Rousseau's mother, if only as a picture upon a dying heart.

Transparency, the openness of souls, is a central mythic element in both Rousseau's archaeology of the lost state of nature and his national utopias where transparency is restored. Rousseau finds a unique emblem of the possibility of transparency in the child and "childhood," sowing the seeds of a new political myth, that of the national child. In *Emile*, Rousseau praises Plato's *Republic* as "the most beautiful educational treatise ever written."[25] Yet, Rousseau, in fact, reverses Plato's priorities. Plato links justice in the soul and in the *polis*, but begins with an account of justice in the *polis* because, although both accounts are written in the "same letters," what is written in "small letters" in the individual soul is more easily discerned in the larger letters of the *polis*.[26] Rousseau's thought experiment in *Emile*, on the other hand, uses the education of a sequestered child to reflect on the possibility of societal virtue. If, in the words of Cassirer reading Plato, "Not only the individual man, but also the state has to choose its daimon," Rousseau chooses the child.

Rousseau's secularization of a religious nostalgia for a lost unity and his views concerning the child resemble the Romantic *Universalgeschichte*, allegorical narratives in which the history of humanity is imagined in terms of the life story of a "single man who lives perpetually on and learns something all

[24]Jean-Jacques Rousseau, *The Confessions*, trans. J. M. Cohen (London: Penguin, 1953 (1781)), 17–9.

[25]Jean-Jacques Rousseau, *Emile*, 40.

[26]Plato, *The Republic*, trans. Paul Shorey, in *The Collected Dialogues*, ed. Edith Hamilton and Huntington Cairns (Princeton: Princeton UP, 1994, 615).

the time."[27] The shift from humanity to the nation follows only too easily: the life of one man comes to stand for the history of the nation, and the child comes to allegorize both privileged past periods of national history and the promise of a happier future. Analyzing the shape of these *Universalgeschichte* in his *Natural Supernaturalism*, M. H. Abrams argues that they are secularized versions of the Christian narrative of the Fall and Redemption. Adam falls, losing his original happiness. His fall, however, is paradoxically a *felix culpa,* since he later earns not only God's "abounding grace," but also a "Paradise, far happier place/ Than this of *Eden,* and far happier days."[28] Adam's journey is, therefore, not an odyssey since the place he "returns" to is higher than his lost home. The Romantic secular journey follows the shape of Adam's journey; it has the shape of a spiral, not a circle.

Almost all the Romantic spiral narratives open with the happy Greeks who lived in an unconscious fusion with nature and other men. That Arcadia is, however, lost to modern man, who is severed from nature, other men obscure to him. Yet, this fall is a good one, for man in the here and now, the second stage of the spiral, has become self-concious and morally free. The third stage—Schiller saw art as its harbinger—is that of a new spontaneous union with nature and other men: "The way back to Arcadia is closed forever, onward toward Elysium," admonishes the philosopher.[29] The child allegorizes—in this Romantic scheme— the happy Arcadia of transparency and fusion. He is also the promise of a national Elysium brought about by proper education. A conflict is often unavoidable in this scheme between the

[27]Blaise Pascal, Preface to *Le Traité du vide: Opuscules et lettres,* ed. Louis Lafuma (Paris, Editions Montaigne, 1955), 54. Lessing, Schiller, and Kant all wrote examples of this genre.

[28]Milton, *Paradise Lost,* quoted in M. H. Abrams, *Natural Supernaturalism: Tradition and Revolution in Romantic Literature* (New York: Norton, 1971), 208.

[29]Quoted in Abrams, 215.

family and the nation. The nation adopts the homeless child and takes charge of his education; it assumes the shape of his family. This metaphor was literalized after the French Revolution when the state ritualistically adopted orphans whose parents were executed during the Terror. National education has its symbolic manifestations as well: If the child allegorizes national history, the citizen also becomes a "child" of the nation.

If Arendt's "eternity" model of interconnection undergirds Rousseau's obsession with national transparency, does the communal glory of "immortality" come into play in modern European national narratives?[30] Trusting the other might take the shape of sharing with him/her a noble story of origins that would dictate a certain code of behavior ostensibly partaking of that past glory. Thus it may be true, as Cassirer suggests, that social contracts disenchant the state, but the narrative of their "origin" is rarely devoid of the mythic. If the Lockean social contract reduces ties among citizens and the state to consensual civic actions and mutual self-interest, it is no less true that the "original moment" of contracting is not only awe-inspiring but also infused with myth's symbolic power. This power is unmistakable in Locke's account of the creation of the commonwealth, when "free and equal" individuals assembled and "by the consent of every individual made a *community,* [and] have thereby made that community one body."[31] Such an assembly and its originary actions, are not descriptive but constitutive, not historical but mythic. Though the here and now of the Lockean contract is predicated on common beliefs in "universal" values (notably liberty) and shared interests in these values' rewards (such as property and economic self-making), the contract's mythic point of

---

[30]Rousseau's advocacy of Greek-type athletic festivals has little to do with the competitive glory of Arendt's analysis. It is motivated by the desire for public transparency.

[31]John Locke, *Second Treatise of Government,* ed. C.B. Macpherson (Indianapolis: Hackett, 1980 (1690)), 52.

national origin is reminiscent of the collective glory of the Greek example. It is worth emphasizing however, that this particular myth of a civic origin of national ties reduces the symbolic value of childhood. Locke sees the child as an irrational "adult-in-waiting." In fact, the child mars, so to speak, the metaphor of the consent of all to the rational civil contract.

Another view of the origin of British freedom, by contrast, is one which is more wary of innovation and stories of consent, grounding liberty explicitly in a mythical golden age. Edmund Burke, rejecting the argument that the French Revolution merely repeated what its English analogue had done a century earlier, insisted that "The [Glorious] Revolution was made to *preserve* our ancient, indisputable laws and liberties and that *ancient* constitution of government which is our only security for law and liberty."[32] In a treatise written for the benefit of George I's grandson, the Prince of Wales, another brilliant Tory, Lord Bolingbroke, rues that "the *British spirit,* that *spirit,* which has preserved liberty hitherto in one corner of the world at least, [will not] be so *easily* or so *soon* reinfused into the *British* nation."[33] A new type of monarch, the "PATRIOT KING," is needed, Bolingbroke enjoins, whose authority follows not from any antiquated divine right, but from his capacity to redeem the nation, restoring its "free constitution," which, unlike "the law given immediately to all men by God," is a "particular . . . constitution of laws," a specific historical grounding of the now lost "British spirit" (52). The child is more significant symbolically within this view of "Britishness" than in the Lockean consensual variant. Not exactly the emblem of the nation that Rousseau created him, the child still symbolizes both the young age of the nation, when its ancient laws were sacred; and, as Bolingbroke's rhetoric illustrates, the national utility of education and hope in the young.

[32]Edmund Burke, *Reflections on the Revolution in France* (New York: Penguin, 1973 (1790)), 27.

[33]Henry St. John, Viscount Bolingbroke, *The Idea of a Patriot King* (Oxford: Oxford University Press, 1931 (1738)), 44.

This persuasion of civic freedom as an inheritance, emphasizing the continuity of old and new liberty, resonates with a
strong current of American national identity, which identifies
being American with being free, linking this very liberty to an
ahistorical mythologizing of the Founding Fathers' inaugural
acts. This individual "freedom" is seen as a heritage—the current embodiment of an initial collective deed, for instance, the
ratification of the Constitution, or a common attribute, such as
belonging to a country of immigrants. In other words, this
model offers an "immortal" type of story—in Arendt's formulation—a story of "works and deeds and words," and grounds
the ties between subjects in an allegorical folding of that glorious narrative onto the nation's shared goals today. An essentially Lockean formulation, this national connection prefers
shared "values" and interests to transparent souls.

Often, however, this shared memory/fantasy might need
some jogging. Analyzing the recent "privatization of U.S. citizenship," Lauren Berlant incisively proposes a "theory of infan-
tile citizenship," in which a young person is "a *stand-in* for a
complicated and contradictory set of anxieties about national
identity."[34] Berlant identifies a recurring plot, a "pilgrimage-to-
Washington narrative," in which either a child or a child-like
adult goes to Washington. Unschooled in the political realities
and behavior codes of the capital, the child-citizen elicits "scorn
and derision from 'knowing' adult citizens but also a kind of
admiration from these same people, who can remember with
nostalgia the time that they were 'unknowing' and believed in
the capacity of the nation to be practically utopian" (28-9). I
would suggest that part of Berlant's narrative's symbolic power
lies in its ability to activate a "repressed" element of the American national narrative. The naïveté of the child-citizen in
Washington, where the glorious past is evoked by monuments

[34]Lauren Berlant, *The Queen of America Goes to Washington City*
(Durham: Duke University Press, 1997), 6.

and national institutions, reanimates a time when the "glory" was actual; it unearths the supposedly shared passions—such as civic virtue and public concern—that are then forgotten in order to allow, in Berlant's words, the citizen adults "to be politically happy and economically functional" (29).

These connections between nations and children, it will turn out, are also apposite to an analysis of the form and content of the novel in the eighteenth and nineteenth centuries, an analysis central to my arguments in chapters four and five. Not only is the suffering of the homeless child a central element in nationalist narratives but also, I will advocate, it underpins the rise of the realist novel in the eighteenth century. I shall argue that the rise of the novel, familiarly related to the new middle-class experience, is also fundamentally linked to the experience of homeless children. Most scholars agree that—concerned with the experience of modern personal time—the nascent realist novel of the eighteenth century turned away from received forms and plots. Yet, a paradox, I find, associated with the rise of the novel is that it often narrates a neo-archetypal story of an often unhappy child who leaves her/his father's house for a place in the world. Staging his Lockean freedom, the child sets forth into the world, losing a home, acquiring narratable experience, and becoming the hero of the novel. But the child remembers his/her father's tears, and often his curse. The child's experience in the world narrated in the novel is also a dialogue with the lost home.[35]

[35]The model I advance provides a complementary thesis to the association of the rise of the novel and women's experience, eloquently expressed by Nancy Armstrong, who sees a "new form of political power" wielded by "the domestic woman" and a "specifically modern form of desire." She does not, however, make the connection between the novelistic privileging of the domestic sphere—which profoundly affected male writers as well—and nationalism, though she recognizes that shift as "political." See Nancy Armstrong, *Desire and Domestic Fiction: A Political History of the Novel* (Oxford: Oxford University Press, 1987), 3.

A nation predicated on Lockean enlightened self-interest may not value transparency as Rousseau's national vision did. Yet, transparency can return in surprising ways. Asserting that "Nothing is more certain, than that men are, in a great measure, govern'd by interest," David Hume wonders why "any disorder can ever arise in society," if it is clear to even "the most rude and uncultivated of human race" that their interest lies in "the upholding of society, and the observation of the rules of justice." His answer lies in the limited "imagination" of individuals:

> It has been observ'd, in treating of the passions, that men are mightily govern'd by the imagination . . . What strikes upon them with a strong and lively idea commonly prevails above what lies in a more obscure light.[36]

Governments, Hume contends, are instituted since imagination makes men value the intense affect of present sensations and ideas over the long-term benefit of distant goods, preferring "any trivial advantage, that is present, to the maintenance of order in society, which so much depends on the observance of justice." Hume concludes, "Here, *then is the origin of civil gov't and allegiance*. Men are not able radically to cure, either in themselves or in others, the narrowness of soul, which makes them prefer the present to the remote" (537). Hume's use of optical metaphors evokes his fundamental epistemological skepticism, which complicates the stability of a collective composed of separate individuals. His argument above regarding the obscurity of remote interest mirrors Rousseau's rhetoric of transparency. Common interest, however, not the ability to read the hearts of others, solves the problem of skepticism. Hume maintains that cooperation is easier

[36]David Hume, *A Treatise of Human Nature* (Oxford: Oxford University Press, 1978 (1739–40), 534–9.

among people who are related through the contiguity and relation that common property engenders:

> Two neighbours may agree to drain a meadow, which they possess in common, because 'tis easy for them to *know each others mind* [my emphasis] . . . But 'tis very difficult, and indeed impossible, that a thousand persons shou'd agree in any such action (537).

In the absence of property's knowledge, governments remedy the essential human failure to know the minds of others because "Magistrates," not myopically preferring the ephemeral, "find an immediate interest in the interest of any considerable part of their subjects . . .

> Thus bridges are built; harbours open'd; ramparts raised; canals form'd, fleets equip'd; and armies disciplin'd; everywhere by the care of gov't, which, tho' composed of men subject to all human infirmities, becomes by one of the finest and most subtle inventions imaginable, a composition, that is, in some measure, exempted from all these infirmities (539).

Governments guarantee the long-term interest of a majority of the citizens, turning the discordant desires of the many into a harmonious "composition." Hume's shift to the musical metaphors of the last passage underscores how governments do away with the need for individual transparency. Yet it is governments' unobscured vision which makes national progress, indeed existence, possible, and both in peacetime and wartime.

This connection between national evolution, property, and transparency is crucial to Walter Scott's fiction, which, in the age of French national tumult and British peace, performs an archaeology of British history, uncovering past violence in the national struggles between Scotland and England, the birth pangs of Britain. Walter Scott's Waverley Novels narrate the formation of the British nation through the clash of opposing forces: the absolutist Royalists and the Covenanter Calvinist fundamentalists in *Old Mortality,* for example. Scott's hero is not a child in age, but the novels mark him as a child who survives the national turmoil and stands for the citizen. Scott, as I show in chapter five, invents a new form of the novel predicated on the separation between the omniscient knowledge of the national narrator and the limited knowledge of his hero. The narrator unfolds the child's life story, and in the process, narrates national history.

TWO

"TILL REASON SHALL TAKE ITS PLACE":
Locke, Consent, and the Problem Child

> Brutus: "Remember March, the ides of March remember.
> Did not great Julius bleed for justice' sake?
> What villain touch'd his body, that did stab,
> And not for justice?"
>
> Anthony: "O mighty Caesar! Dost thou lie so low?
> Are all thy conquests, glories, triumphs, spoils,
> Shrunk to this little measure? Fare thee well."
>
> Shakespeare, *Julius Caesar*

In his defense of Stuart orthodoxy against the populism of the Puritan Revolution, Sir Robert Filmer insisted that political obligation to obey the king was the same as the duty to obey one's father since the king's authority devolved to him from Adam, the original father/king: "I see not then how the children of Adam, or of any man else, can be free from the subjection to their parents. And this subordination of children is the fountain of all regal authority, by the ordination of God himself."[1] Filmer was hardly inscribing the manifesto of a new political theory. "Children," in the Stuart family, observes Gordon Schochet, in his seminal study of patriarchalism, "who previously had no conception whatever of politics were introduced to the state and told that it was identical to the household."[2]

[1] Sir Robert Filmer, *Patriarcha and Other Political Works*, ed. Peter Laslett (Oxford: Blackwell, 1949), 57.

[2] Gordon J. Schochet, *Patriarchalism in Political Thought: The Authoritarian Family and Political Speculation and Attitudes Especially in Seventeenth-Century England* (New York: Basic Books, 1975), 73.

In his *Second Treatise*, Locke argues against Filmer's natural subjection precisely on the ground that, though that condition is acceptable to children in families under the rule of their fathers, adults form political associations that are based on consent. Children, however, present a serious challenge to the contractarian since their dependence means that at the hypothetical point of the establishment of the contract, the population could not have consisted of "free and equal individuals."[3]

Jeremy Waldron perceptively observes that the *Second Treatise* "appears to tell not one but *two* stories . . . about the development of politics and civil society. . . . The first and most familiar is the classic story of the state of nature, the social contract, and the deliberate institution of political arrangements. . . . The other story has an utterly different shape. It is based on what we may term Locke's speculations in political anthropology. This is the story of the gradual and indiscernible growth of modern political institutions, modern political problems, and modern political consciousness out of the simple tribal group."[4] It will turn out, however, that children, or the existence of the class of persons that Locke defines as children, are quite inimical to his goals. They act to weaken the universality of the first story, that of the consent of all, and to give credence to the second, that of the growth of the power of the father. We will attend to the anthropological tale a bit later, but first, the first story.

In the text, Locke adduces the first story, that of the free and equal individuals in the "state of nature" assembling and creating a consensual state as his response to Filmer's authoritarian assertions. "For when any number of men have," Locke writes

[3]All references are to John Locke, *Second Treatise of Government*, ed. C. B. Macpherson (Indianapolis: Hackett, 1980 (1690)).

[4]Jeremy Waldron, "John Locke: Social Contract versus Political Anthropology," in *The Social Contract from Hobbes to Rawls*, ed. David Boucher and Paul Kelly (London: Routledge, 1994), 52.

in the chapter entitled *Of the Beginning of Political Societies*, "by the consent of *every* [emphasis added] individual made a *community*, they have thereby made that community one body" (52). In the state of nature, that is, before they contract, these individuals are in a "state of perfect freedom" and "also of equality" (8). But the requirement of universal equality proves problematic for Locke, as, of course, it will for Rousseau, only more so. And the difference in manner with which these two theorists of the social contract deal with the difficult position of children will point to the growing valence that children have in nationalist views of the state.

Regarding the equality which is inherent in the "state of nature," Locke confesses that

> Though I have said above, Chap 2. that all men by nature are equal, I cannot be supposed to understand all sorts of equality: *age* or *virtue* may give men a just precedency . . . *birth* may subject some, and alliance or benefits others, to pay an observance to those whom nature, gratitude or other respects, may have made it due: and yet all this consists with the *equality*, which all men are in, in respect of jurisdiction or dominion one over another; which was the equality that I there spoke of . . . that every man hath, to his natural freedom (31).

Locke is less exacting in his definition of equality than Rousseau. According to his view, a legitimate civil society is fully compatible with the distinctions and privileges, even inherited, that set men apart. In the category of children, Locke, however, confronts the same problem which Rousseau was later to universalize,[5] the problem of other-dependence:

[5]"L'Homme est né libre, et par-tout il est dans les fers" J. J. Rousseau, *Du Contract Social.*

> *Children*, I confess, are not born in this [refers to
> above quote] state of equality, though they are born
> to it. Their parents have a sort of rule and jurisdic-
> tion over them, when they come into the world, and
> for some time after . . . (31).

Locke, who had written a tract on education, which shows
some authoritarian ideas of his own when it comes to raising
children,[6] was aware, as we saw above, of the difficulty that children represent to his account of the consensual society. He
therefore tackles this problem immediately to immunize his
tract against any possible attack by the Filmerians who are
strengthened by the indisputable authority of the father over his
children. Locke, of course, does not dispute this power. But he
limits it both in extent and in duration. Most importantly, he is
explicit about distinguishing the type of authority that fathers
have over children from the political power of the "magistrate"
and the "despotical" power of "absolute dominion" (90). Locke
uses a number of analytic strategies to separate the child from
the Filmerian subject. Interestingly, since Filmer invests the
absolute monarch with the inherited power of the Christian
ur-father, Adam, Locke ungenders paternal power by insisting
that it properly be termed "parental" and not "paternal," (30)
though English law at that time clearly gave it to the father.
Locke also argues that the parents' power ends when the child
reaches maturity "at the age of one and twenty years." He also
carefully distinguishes this power "that parents have over their
children, [that] arises from that duty which is incumbent on
them, to take care of their off-spring, during the imperfect state
of childhood," (32) and that is tempered with "inclinations of

---

[6]"I imagine everyone will judge it reasonable, that their children,
when little, should look upon their parents as their Lords, their absolute
Governors; and as such stand in awe of them." John Locke, "Some
Thoughts Concerning Education," in *The Educational Writings of John
Locke*, ed. James Axtell (Cambridge: Cambridge University Press, 1968),
145.

tenderness and concern" from the "absolute arbitrary dominion" of Filmer (35).

Locke succeeds to a certain extent in limiting the power of parents over children. He is perhaps most successful when he demonstrates that the parental power is limited in duration. Clearly a power that is limited in time cannot be absolute, and therefore, cannot lend credence to an absolute authority vested in the monarch as *pater patriae*. He seems to me to be less successful when he distinguishes this kind of power from the absolute type. He situates the locus of this difference, the "inclinations of tenderness and concern," in the parents; thus making it a duty of the parents, and not a right with which the child is endowed as a *subject*.

In arguing that the power be termed "parental," and that the father shares it with the mother, Locke bolsters his insistence on the distinction between this power and that of the magistrate, for "If the father die whilst the children are young, do they not naturally everywhere owe the same obedience to their *mother* during their minority as to their father were he alive? and will any one say, that the mother hath legislative powers over her children? that she can make standing rules . . . [which she can] inforce the observation of with capital punishments? for this is the proper power of the magistrate, of which the father hath not so much as the shadow" (36). The answer to the first rhetorical question would be "yes," to the second "no." Thus, that the mother's power is limited proves Locke's conclusion regarding the limitation on the father's since he postulates the parents to share equally the power over the children. But why the roundabout proof? Why does not Locke argue directly that a father cannot enforce "capital punishments" against his children? No doubt, because Filmerians extend the power of the father in the family to that of the King in the Commonwealth who does very much impose capital punishments. But also, and this is an important point, Locke's circuitous argument points to an early awareness—too rational, perhaps, to be called unconscious—of the conflict between father and children (son) in the family which might precipitate violence.

The reliance on the parents' love and mercy for the protection, and certainly the preservation of the very life of the children is not a situation the major proponent of "subjective right" theory should have accepted without concern. The rights of the children come dangerously close to being "natural" rights. According to Charles Taylor, "a subjective right is something which the possessor can and ought to act on to put it into effect. To accord you an immunity, formerly given to you by natural law, in the form of a natural right is to give you a role in establishing and enforcing this immunity."[7] But children, unable because of the lack of reason, and hence freedom, to participate in the establishment of the structure, the commonwealth, are under natural law. They are, in other words, precisely where the Filmerians would want the entire population to be vis-à-vis the king.

The existence of a class of persons inherently incapable of consent makes it clear that Locke's narrative of the universal creation of the body-politic cannot be satisfied. The children of those "individuals"—who consented to make the "community"—could not have consented at that moment, and will need up to twenty-one years to reach the age of consent.[8] Not *every* individual could have consented to the establishment of the "one body." That is a problem for Locke's first story, for our mind's eye is now cognizant of a significant number of individuals who have to be, or are excluded form the great metaphor of the assembly consenting to the community.

An objection to our conclusions can be raised on at least two accounts: First, Locke himself excludes the children from being free precisely because they do not have the *reason* required to be under law, where law itself is freedom, and not its

[7]Charles Taylor, *Sources of the Self*, 11.
[8]Locke defines twenty-one as the age of consent (Ch. VI, sec. 59).

curtailment (32). They, therefore, could not have figured in the consensual establishment of the commonwealth. "Thus we are *born free*, as we are born rational; not that we have actually the exercise of either: age," argues Locke, "that brings one, brings with it the other too" (34). Clearly, one cannot accept that premise without diluting the metaphorical power of the universal contract which ends the state of nature. A snapshot of the assembly at the moment of the contract will, as we mentioned above, discover a sizable group of 'persons,' or at least, sentient beings, who are excluded.

Locke could not have ignored, in formulating his model of the creation of civil society from the state of nature, the presence of children, who could not have consented. His solution, as we mentioned above, consists in excluding the children from the formation of the community until they attain reason and freedom at twenty-one at which time they may *explicitly* consent to the community, and by doing so, we presume, belatedly participate in that awesome moment of creation. As adults, the children are fully enfranchised, but in Locke's contract, their *childhood* is figured as absence:

> The *power*, then, that *parents have* over their children, arises from that duty which is incumbent on them, to take care of their off-spring, during the imperfect state of childhood. To inform the mind, and govern the actions of their yet ignorant nonage, *till reason shall take its place* [emphasis mine], and ease them of that trouble, is what the children want, and the parents are bound to (32).

Locke emphasizes the *growth* of children: what matters to the state is what they become at twenty-one, not any essence of their childhood *per se*. But his emphasis on growth underscores the negative valence which children, or more precisely childhood, has for him. The nationalist outlook, as we shall see, will prove very different.

Locke's jaundiced view of childhood is quite consistent with his famous view of the mind as a *tabula rasa*,[9] and his view of the self as an object. Taylor calls his view of the self "punctual":

> The disengagement both from the activities of thought and from our unreflecting desires and tastes allows us to see ourselves as objects of far-reaching reformation. . . . The subject who can take this kind of radical disengagement to himself or herself with a view to remaking, is what I want to call the "punctual" self. To take this stance is to iden-tify oneself with the power to objectify and remake, and by this act to distance oneself from all the par-ticular features which are objects of potential change. What we are essentially is none of the latter, but that which finds itself capable of fixing them and working on them. This is what the image of the point is meant to convey, drawing on the geometri-cal term: the real self is "extensionless"; it is nowhere but in this power to fix things as objects (171-2).

Because the Lockean self is that extensionless center of con-sciousness and control, there is no inherent value to the story of the self, no historicity, that is embedded in childhood, and hence in the child. The self is not something that you lose, and spend your life trying to find, as Rousseau esteemed the "authentic" self of the child that is falsified both by the pressure to conform to society and by bad education. Nor is the self defined by the narrative, even if futile, or infinite, of that search,

[9]But cf. James Engell who carefully observes: "How far too much of a stock notion about Locke this is, because he also states that the mind rapidly loses its mental virginity . . ." *The Creative Imagination: Enlight-enment to Romanticism* (Cambridge: Harvard University Press, 1981), 18. His observation, however, does not contradict mine for he also observes that Locke "does not use the words 'original' . . . [nor] talks about genius . . ." (19).

remembered or imagined as self-constitutive memory.[10] For Locke, the child is certainly *not* the father of the man.

The position of the child in Locke's contract also suffers because of his challenge to prevailing theories of the connections between man and cosmos. In his seminal *The Great Chain of Being*, Arthur Lovejoy argues that the "vogue" of that conception in the eighteenth century is attested to by the fact that the two most influential philosophers of the late seventeenth century, Leibniz and Locke, insisted upon "the ancient theses." Lovejoy adduces a passage from the *Essay Concerning Human Understanding* in which Locke seems to accept what Lovejoy calls the concept of "plenitude": that, in Locke's words, "In all the visible corporeal world we see no chasms or gaps . . . [And] that the species of creatures should also, by gentle degrees, ascend from us towards his infinite perfection, as we see they gradually descend from us downwards."[11] Certainly, Locke accepts the superiority of humans to all other animals and plants; and their inferiority to God and whatever creatures "ascend upwards." But he rejects a crucial element of the "Great Chain of Being": the concept of "correspondences" that dates back to Plato's *Republic*. It is the notion that ideas must manifest themselves in all domains. Every being in the cosmos not only fills its place in the Great Chain, but also exhibits its ontological being, which is interchangeable with others who share its kind. For example, the king among men corresponds to a lion among animals and an eagle among birds. Locke rejects this idea of natural power.

The correspondence of power was not, however, limited to the political sphere. With the decline of feudalism, and the growth of domestic patriarchy, it extended to the family. Thus,

---

[10]See M. H. Abrams, *Natural Supernaturalism*, on the value of the "infinite" search for the Romantics.

[11]Arthur Lovejoy, *The Great Chain of Being: A Study of the History of an Idea* (Cambridge: Harvard University Press, 1936), 184.

the paterfamilias was its king and lion. But the child, like any other link in the chain, was endowed with an allegorical essence that corresponded to the subject among men and, say, the lamb among animals. Locke removed the natural power of the king and the father. But by insisting that the nature of the newborn child is essentially a *tabula rasa*, he reduced any inherent symbolic value that accrued to the child. To sum up, the child was dead as the signifier that he/she had been in the old cosmological system, and not yet born as a signifier in the new ontology, first fully expressed by Rousseau.

Locke's view of childhood as the "ignorant nonage" to be replaced by reason supposes a uniformity of development, an identical growth, which, significantly, he contradicts in his educational manual *Some Thoughts Concerning Education* (1693).[12] In this enormously influential work Locke is quite aware not only of the differing "characters" of children, but also of the residual effect of these inborn "natural" characters on the adults the children will grow to:

> Begin therefore betimes nicely to observe your Son's *Temper*; and that, when he is under least restraint, in his Play, and as he thinks out of your sight. See what are his *Predominant Passions,* and *prevailing Inclinations;* whether he be Fierce or Mild, Bold or Bashful, Compassionate or Cruel, Open or Reserved, etc. For as these are different in him, so are your Methods to be different. and your authority must hence take measure to apply it self [sic] different ways to him. . . . But this, be sure, after all is done, the Bypass will always hang on that side, that Nature first placed it: And if you carefully observe the Char-

[12]First published in 1693, *Some Thoughts* went through fifteen editions and twenty-six printings in Britain by 1800 and inspired an enormous volume of commentary. It was translated into French in 1695, and by 1874 had editions in Czech, Dutch, German, Italian, Spanish and Swedish. By 1959, it was printed in Poland and Romania.

> acters of his Mind, now in the first Scenes of his Life,
> you will ever after be able to judge which way his
> Thoughts lean, and what he aims at, even hereafter,
> when, as he grows up, the Plot thickens, and he puts
> on several Shapes to act it.[13]

For the purposes of the contract, however, this potential multi-plicity and variety is ignored. Locke's account of childhood is the absence that is filled by growth and education. According to Locke, the child *qua* child has nothing to contribute to the commonwealth except to grow up without causing too many problems in the interim, in order to become the rational adult. The "reason" that will erase the "trouble" of childhood will produce, so to speak, an adult person who will ratify the original contract—created by those who preceded him to adulthood—by *explicitly* consenting to it. The more nuanced, and realistic, account of the variety of characters possible when children grow up in his educational tract poses dangers to the consensual account of the first story for it is possible that some of the "thoughts" and "aims" of the new adults do not "lean" in the direction of ratifying or maintaining the commonwealth. I will develop this point further in discussing Locke's second story of the growth of the community out of the tribal group.

A second objection to the premise that children present a problem for Locke's account of the state of nature is that Locke himself, not withstanding his statements in the *Second Treatise* to the contrary, did not regard the state of nature as historical.[14] The position is best expressed by one of the major interpreters of Locke, John Dunn, who argues that "the state of nature, that state that 'all Men are naturally in', is not an asocial condition but an ahistorical condition. It is that state in which men are set

---

[13]Locke, *Some Thoughts*, 206–7.

[14]Cf. Locke's discussion of the objections that may be raised to his view of the state of nature, *Second Treatise* (Ch. VIII, sec. 100).

by God."[15] The proposition that Locke did not regard the "state of nature" as historical is a commonplace of Lockean criticism, and, therefore, raising the "realist" detail of the children is, according to that view, not relevant. Let us, however, delay our response to this objection until after moving on to the second, "anthropological" story.

The presence of children in the commonwealth, and the fact of their parents' power over them not only weaken the first story of consent, but also are evidence of an undesirable story which Locke's precision and powerful understanding of the Filmerian position force him to relate and consider. Having attempted to undo the damage that the unfree children cause to his great account of the consensual commonwealth by arguing that once the children reach the age of reason, the power of their parents over them ceases, Locke concludes this chapter with the second story, namely, "how easy it was, in the first ages of the world . . . for the *father of the family* to become the prince of it; he had been a ruler from the beginning of the infancy of his children . . ." (40–1). This is the account of the growth of the extended family into the tribe, and the creation of what Freud, following Darwin, refers to as the "primal horde."[16]

Again, this story seems awfully close to Filmer's and Locke deftly outmaneuvers him by arguing that the power of the father over his extended family is not naturally political, but becomes so through the "tacit consent" of his children: "Thus it was easy, and almost natural for children, by a tacit, and scarce *avoidable* [emphasis added] consent, to make way for the *father's authority and government*" (41). The children, enjoying "paternal affection" (56) and "the easiness and equality of it" (59), and "accustomed in their childhood to follow his direc-

---

[15]John Dunn, *The Political Thought of John Locke: An Historical Account of the Argument of the "Two Treatises of Government"* (Cambridge: Cambridge University Press, 1969), 97.

[16]Sigmund Freud, *Totem and Taboo,* trans. James Strachey, Standard Edition (New York: Norton, 1989), 156.

tion" tacitly consent to the political rule of the father, until the "ambition and luxury in future ages [after the "*golden age*"] would retain and increase the power, . . . and aided by flattery, taught princes to have distinct and separate interests from their people [the descendants, presumably, of the Prince's sons], men found it necessary to examine more carefully *the original* and rights *of government*; and to find out ways to restrain the *exorbitances*, and *prevent* the abuses of that power . . ." (60).

The chapter in which Locke makes the above-mentioned observation is entitled "Of the Beginning of Political Societies" and we presume that examining "the original and rights of government" is precisely what he is engaged in, the text being self-referential. That narrative, of the growth of the family into the tribe and eventually into the commonwealth; and of the biological father into the paterfamilias and to the good prince and finally the abusive king, is based not only on what Waldron calls "political anthropology" but on history as well. It is the interlaced history of the growth of absolutist power *and* the emergence of the "men [who] found it necessary to examine" that malignant power and its "flatter[ers]." It is the story of the Stuart dynasty, its sycophants led by Sir Robert Filmer, and the attack led by John Locke.[17] This second story is historical in a sense in which the first story, that of the establishment of the commonwealth from the state of nature through the consent of all is not, even according to Locke as we mentioned above. Locke postulates the state of nature, according to Dunn, because it allows him "to find some criterion for human morality which is outside history." Nature, in the Lockean usage, is quite different from the Hobbesian nature," argues Dunn, "since it includes an 'intruding term' which is 'God.'"[18]

[17]It is now generally accepted, mostly through the scholarship of Peter Laslett, that Locke wrote the two *Treatises of Government* to attack Filmer's, and not Hobbes's, absolutism.

[18]Dunn, 68.

Perhaps we may term Dunn's "state of nature" a model for the commonwealth. Thus, its establishment with the consent of all is not a historical description of how things really are, but how, ideally speaking, they could have been. It is then, according to the familiar Aristotelian observation, more philosophical. We can now turn to our imaginary reader's second objection: Since the state of nature is a hypothetical and not historical condition, why should we raise the realistic issue of the subjection of children? That the model is not historical, however, does not excuse it from being judged by the criterion of consistency. Freud's theory of the mind, for example, is, according to the physiological knowledge of our day, not biological or descriptive and yet it endures because of the fit that it has with the "reality" it models—the diagnosis and sometimes treatment of neuroses. In order for Locke's model to fit with reality, in order that his metaphor of the "state of nature" acquire the power of description that Freud's metaphor has, it is essential to address the issue of children in the "ahistorical" model. This perhaps answers the second objection mentioned above, regarding the legitimacy of raising the problem of children in Locke's first story notwithstanding the ahistoricity of the state of nature. If, as Dunn argues, "The state of nature is not of course in itself a specific historical stage; it is intended to specify the continuing moral order within which human beings live and make their history,"[19] then the fact that the human race propagates itself by having children who are by nature, at least for a while, "inferior" to adults must figure in Locke's first story.

It figures even more, naturally, in the second story where children cannot be so easily excluded from consideration. What difficulties do children and childhood present in this anthropological, historical, story? First, as mentioned above, children *necessitate* this second story. They are indeed born weaker than their parents, and as is well known, need proportionally the longest period of

---

[19]Dunn, 68.

dependence on their parents for basic survival in the animal kingdom. Second, children raise the crucial and complex issue of freedom—material and psychological—and the connection of their freedom to political liberty. I shall examine later—in chapter four—how Locke was more aware of financial than psychological bondage. For the moment, however, it is hard to overemphasize his ambivalence regarding the possible freedom of children in the second story: the qualifier "scarce avoidable" says it all.

The second story to which Waldron refers actually lies at the center of Freud's discussion of the birth of a 'civilized' post incest-prohibition society in *Totem and Taboo*, where, Freud argues, the taboo on incest resulted from the sons' guilt over their murder of the all-powerful father, who monopolized the women of the tribe. It is also the account that recent feminist reinterpretations of the social contract, such as Carole Pateman's influential *The Sexual Contract*, center on. Pateman argues that Locke's contract, far from creating the universal "public sphere of civil freedom" and ending patriarchy, enacted a "fraternal patriarchy" in which the sons simultaneously seized both "dimensions of the defeated father's political right, his sex right as well as his paternal right."[20] The "sex-right," which the brothers exercise over their wives is what Pateman calls "the sexual contract": the private, ignored, other half of the story (her elaboration is a continuation, in essence, of Waldron's "anthropological story above). In presenting this Freudian twist into her reading of Locke's *Second Treatise*, Pateman offers a marvelous rapprochement of the domestic-sexual and the political spheres. Pateman's argument applies *a fortiori* to children. For, in theory, nothing essential prevents women from achieving equality with men in a civil society. Children, however, by biological necessity, are totally dependent on their parents for a long time, and are under their power—mothers' and fathers'—during that period.

[20]Carole Pateman, *The Sexual Contract* (Stanford: Stanford University Press, 1988), 33.

And that dependence indeed defined the very category of "children." For the association of childhood and dependence was widespread in England during the sixteenth and seventeenth centuries. In his account of patriarchalism's genesis and its various manifestations, especially during the seventeenth-century controversies, Schochet relates that "Thomas Cobbet urged his 'Courteous Reader' to 'remember . . . that under the notion of children in this discourse, are understood, all such as are in relation of children, whether Adult persons, or children in Age.'"[21] Servants also were urged to obey the Fifth Commandment by obeying their masters. Enjoining this duty in a tract whose title conflates the religious, the political, and the domestic, John Dod and Robert Cleaver wrote, "The householder is called *Pater Familias,* that is, a father of a familie; because he should have a fatherly care over his servants, as if they were his children." All "godly servants," they further instructed "may in a few words learne what dutie they owe their masters, mistresses, and dames: namely to love them, and to be affectionated towards them, as a dutifull child is towards his father . . ."[22] These views expounded in conduct books and preached from the pulpit were social variants and precursors of Filmer's, more explicitly political, national narrative. The child's carrying out his duty was not only being pious, these guides emphasized, but also patriotic. Society consisted of "severall houses, and if the several houses which are so many members be not well ruled," William Jones wondered, "how can the whole body be well ordered?"[23] As we shall see a bit later, however, servants and apprentices did not always prove willing "children."

[21]Thomas Cobbet, *A Fruitful and Usefull Discourse Touching the Honor Due from Children to Parents* (London, 1656), quoted in Schochet, *Patriarchalism in Political Thought,* 67.

[22]John Dod & Robert Cleaver, *Godly Forme of Household Government, for the Ordering of Private Families* (London, 1598).

[23]William Jones, *Briefe Exhortation to All Men to Set Their Houses in Good Order* (London, 1631), 11.

Versions of Patriarchal Rule

Patriachalism of course did not start with the Civil War and its repercussions; one can trace the lineage of patriarchal political theories in Western thought as far back as Plato. Indeed, the patriarchal-familial conception had become the chief view of political origins by Filmer's time. Schochet persuasively argues that the need to set the widely-accepted ancient beliefs explicitly in writing arose from the recent attacks by the advocates of the voluntary contract theories: "The patriarchal doctrine, in response, was transformed from a vaguely articulated societal theory into an intentional political ideology."[24] By Locke's time there were many strands and variations of patriarchal theories, but Filmer's supposes first that the power of the father is *ab initio* political, and, second, that it is an inheritance that the current king has received from the first Father/King Adam. Like Locke, Filmer's political formulations were interventions in the seventeenth-century national political struggles between king and parliament. His new patriarchal views "transcended the traditional idea of order and radicalized the innovative concept of divine right monarchy," rejecting the naturalness of hierarchy and asserting that "the difference between a Peer and a Commoner, is not by nature but by the grace of the Prince."[25]

In a comical footnote to the history of political philosophy, Filmer piously, but condescendingly, observes for the benefit of his readers that "We cannot much blame Aristotle for the uncertainty and contrariety in him about the sorts of government, if we consider him as a heathen; for it is not possible for the wit of man to search out the first grounds or principles of government (which necessarily depend upon the original of

[24]Schochet, 55.
[25]Stephen L. Collins, *From Divine Cosmos to Sovereign State* (Oxford: Oxford University Press, 1989), 153.

property) except he know that at the creation one man alone was made, to whom all the dominion of all things was given and from whom all men derive their title."[26] What Filmer "blames" Aristotle for is hardly the absence of patriarchal rule, nor even the lack of linkage in Aristotelian thought between the household and the *polis,* but that Aristotle distinguished between the public and the private realms of dominion.

In a view breathtaking in its elegance and complexity, Aristotle separates the chronological linkage between the two realms—family and *polis*—from the "natural" linkage, in-born in man.[27] Aristotle in *The Politics* asserts that the household is chronologically prior to the *polis:* "First, then, there must of necessity be a conjunction of persons who cannot exist without one another: on the one hand, male and female, for the sake of reproduction . . . on the other, the naturally ruling and ruled [i.e. masters and slaves], on account of preservation. . . . From these two partnerships, then, the household first arose . . ." The households form villages and finally "The partnership arising from [the union of] several villages that is complete is the city" (36). But because, famously, "man is by nature a political animal," Aristotle asserts that "The city is thus prior by nature to the household and to each of us" (37). The *polis,* although it comes last in the chronology of human association, is first in man's nature; in fulfilling that nature, man strives toward a teleological perfection.

Aristotle's view of the teleological, and not genetic, linkage between the power of the father in the household, and that of the *politikos* in the *polis* is what irks Filmer—he, I believe, would call man "by nature, an obedient child"—for it does not support the "inherited power" theory, and in fact keeps the door open for the contractualists to argue for the separation of polit-

---

[26]Filmer, *Patriarcha,* quoted in Dunn, 62.
[27]Or what Schochet in *Partriarchalism* calls "genetic." *See* Schochet, 21.

ical and paternal power. Inherent to their argument is the claim that political obligation did not follow naturally from filial obedience but was contracted by parties sufficiently free to enter into a compact.

I must emphasize here that Aristotle's view is far from unpatriarchal: my choice of "man" above is intentional for, as is well known, Aristotle consigned women and slaves to the private realm: that is, the realm of deprivation and lack of freedom. In fact he uses the distinction between the rule of the father and master over his household—wife, children, and slaves—and "political" rule to prove that "Those [read Plato in the *Statesman*] who suppose that the same person is expert in political [rule], kingly [rule], managing the household and being a master [of slaves] do not argue rightly. . . . For the one sort is over those free by nature [i.e. fellow male citizens], the other over slaves" (43). The public realm, the realm of freedom, is limited to heads of households—male citizens of the *polis*. As Arendt argues, "According to Greek thought, the human capacity for political organization is not only different from but stands in direct opposition to that natural association whose center is the home (*oikia*) and the family," the latter being the realm of necessity, birth and death—the domain of women, slaves, and children.[28]

Aristotle's patriarchy, however, differs considerably from the genetic view of Filmer in which all persons are subjugated to the king who has inherited his rule from Adam; Filmer's theory is clearly based on the identity of paternal and political power. Aristotle's *politikos*, however, could not be a *pater patriae*. In fact, Aristotle saw the identity of the two realms— what Plato suggested—as a characteristic of barbarians who lacked freedom.

As was discussed earlier, Locke's second story—the patriarchal narrative—has both anthropological and historical

[28]Arendt, *The Human Condition,* 24.

dimensions. Locke's view of the naturalness of the children's submission to the father's political power, underscored in his reference to the children's "scarce avoidable" consent, is surely not a welcome surmise for the great contractualist, for it strikes at the heart of the voluntarist argument: the freedom to contract political obligation that is not preempted by natural-genetic filial obedience. That Locke could not avoid mentioning that story points out the great power of the father in Stuart society to whose rise, since the Middle Ages, two related factors contributed: centralization of royal power and the Reformation.

The decline of feudalism and the rise of powerful centralized states in Europe meant that the state ceased to view "good lordship"—the dominance over kin and clientage—as a threat. Patriarchy, hitherto under attack by the state, was supported by it "in the much modified form of authoritarian dominance by the husband and father over the woman and children within the nuclear family. What had been previously a real threat to political order was thus neatly transformed into a formidable buttress to it."[29] "Magistrates and ministers," notes Paul Griffiths, "perpetuated a patriarchal fiction in which the family was presented as a 'little commonwealth', 'the picture of the commonwealth', or a 'little' and 'lesser church'."[30] The Fifth Commandment that enjoins one to "obey thy father and thy mother," was used to justify the dominance of father and king—with the part about the mother largely forgotten. "All kings were fathers and all fathers ruled." The church, enormously influential in a largely illiterate society, preached from the pulpit and in catechism books that the Fifth Com-

[29]Lawrence Stone, *The Family, Sex, and Marriage: In England 1500–1800,* Abridged ed. (New York: Harper, 1979), 111.

[30]Paul Griffiths, *Youth and Authority: Formative Experiences in England 1560–1640* (Oxford: Oxford University Press, 1996), 65.

mandment imposed the duty of obedience to father, magistrate and king.[31]

Not only did the identification of kings with fathers contribute greatly to the rise of patriarchal power, but so did the Reformation. The denigration of religious chastity and the celebration and moral elevation of marriage and the begetting of children by English Protestants, most famously Milton,[32] placed a greater emphasis on the family. Further, the doctrine of the priesthood of all believers, coupled with the attack on ordained priests, meant that the father became the spiritual, as well as the temporal, head of the family. As Michael Walzer observes, "Calvin radically deemphasized the natural and affective aspects of fatherhood, and dramatically stressed its authoritarian features." He transformed "Fatherhood . . . into a religious office, with its duties and its obligations prescribed in the Word. . . ."[33] "God calls himself throughout the Scriptures our Father," admonishes William Fleetwood, "and from that Title and Relation calls for our Obedience."[34]

Lawrence Stone argues that "The shift to Protestantism meant the loss by the wife of control over the domestic rituals of religious fasting and feasting on the appropriate days . . . More-

---

[31]"The catechism is a series of questions and answers designed to demonstrate the basic tenets of faith through explication of its primary documents—the Apostles' Creed, the Ten Commandments, and the Lord's Prayer—with an explanation of the Sacraments appended." Stone, 75.

[32]*Paradise Lost* was one of the earliest literary celebrations of married love, even though it adopted the conventions of strictly adulterous courtly love.

[33]Michael Walzer, *The Revolution of the Saints: A Study in the Origins of Radical Politics* (Cambridge: Harvard University Press, 1965), 49.

[34]William Fleetwood, *The Relative Duties of Parents and Children, Husbands and Wives, Masters and Servants* (New York: Garland, 1985 (1705)), 7.

over, the identity of the husband and father with the family religious confessor placed severe strains on many wives and children, who found themselves trapped in a situation where they
had no one to turn to for escape or alternative counsel."[35] The
paternal grip on purse and soul must give pause to the contractualist who believes in the freedom of the parties. Locke, not surprisingly, finds it easier to deal with financial bondage than
psychological chains. My figuring of these accounts of political
association as national *narratives*, however, emphasizes that we
must pay attention to the repercussions of affective bonds among
the accounts' actors. We will indeed discover that both individualism and the subjective chains of childhood were fundamental
to the rise of the novel, to Defoe, Fielding, and Richardson.[36]

Youth and the Nation

As we saw, in Locke's version of the national narrative—particularly his consensual story—children could not be proper
political subjects; in Filmer's, by contrast, all the king's subjects
were in fact children. It bears stressing that not only the duty of
childhood but also its duration proved both socioeconomic
and political. Childhood transgressed into what today we
would call "youth" or "adolescence"; it did not end, for instance,
with the child leaving home for domestic service or apprenticeship. I will examine these distinctions briefly below and, more
elaborately, later in chapter four.

[35]Stone, 111.
[36]Masculine bias favored the sons as well; and was reflected in the
gendered language of the guidebooks. Whereas young men were directed
to obey in order to grow up into fathers and heads of households, a
young woman's obedience prefigured her later silent and passive role as a
wife and mother. Books addressed to women, according to Suzanne Hull,
enjoined them to be chaste, silent, and obedient. See Suzanne Hull,
Chaste, Silent and Obedient: English Books for Women 1475–1640 (San
Marino: Huntington Library, 1982)

In a time of great change, childhood acquired a symbolic and practical value for the nation. C. John Somerville argues that Puritans had a particular interest in their children because Puritanism was essentially a "reform movement," for which the loyalty of the younger generation was crucial. Future-oriented, Puritanism looked to its children for belief, defense, and continuation.[37] The child's symbolic value depended on the appraiser: whereas, as Leah Marcus stresses, "For seventeenth-century Puritans, their children were the best hope for a better England to come," for "conservative Anglicans, childhood was a symbolic link with a idealized England gone by."[38] Still, adults always had the duty to guide the young. In his essay on the "Guide" tradition in Puritan literature, J. Paul Hunter emphasizes that "During the moral crisis of the late seventeenth century, guide literature increased in both bulk and intensity." Guide literature had always been "more or less aimed at youth" but "shortly after the Restoration youth became a more explicit center of attention."[39]

In *God the Guide of Youth*, Timothy Cruso, a fellow student of Defoe's at the Dissenter's Morton Academy, warned that "We see such Crowds and Swarms of *young ones* continually *posting down* to Hell, and *bringing up* so much of Hell in the midst of us, that both in compassion to them and to our Native Countrey, we cannot but use some Christian endeavors to open the eyes of these *Mad Prodigals*, and to fetch them home."[40] Despair

[37]C. John Somerville, *The Discovery of Childhood in Puritan England* (Athens, GA: University of Georgia Press, 1992), 10.

[38]Leah S. Marcus, *Childhood and Cultural Despair* (Pittsburgh: University of Pittsburgh Press, 1978), 43.

[39]J. Paul Hunter, *The Reluctant Pilgrim: Defoe's Emblematic Method and Quest for Form in* Robinson Crusoe (Baltimore: Johns Hopkins University Press, 1966), 31.

[40]Timothy Cruso, *God the Guide of Youth* (1695), quoted in Hunter, 32.

that bad youth corrupted the nation was somewhat balanced by the regenerate young auguring national hope: "If we recover our youth, we may hope [God will] yet continue amongst us. Young ones, I would be earnest with you; for God indicates his mind to England by you."[41]

A century earlier, ardent Catholics were equally fearful of the insubordination of youth and as convinced that the youth of England had been instrumental to the rise of godlessness. This time, however, they blamed the young for the spread of the Reformation. As Susan Brigden notes, "Sir Thomas More blamed the Reformation upon a conspiracy, a conspiracy in which 'lewde laddys' took concerted action to spread their heresy."[42] During the Civil War, Griffiths observes, "Both royalists and parliamentarians derived much value in accusing the other side of conscripting young people who should have remained in safe and close dependency."[43] Young people, however, did not only fight on the battlefields. Christopher Hill links youthful disobedience to the inversions of authority that racked England during the Civil War: "We think of refusal of 'hat honour' and the use of 'thou' by Quakers as gestures of social protest, and so they were. But they also marked a refusal of deference from the young to the old, from sons to fathers. . . the fiercest and most anguished battles were those waged within the home, between the generations."[44]

Adults recognized youth's difference. A widespread strand of belief, relying on Galenic physiology, ascribed the rebelliousness of the young to the dominance of red choler. The "humour" of most young people, Fleetwood explained, made them "grow

[41]Daniel Williams, *The Vanity of Childhood and Youth* (London, 1691), quoted in Hunter, 32.

[42]Susan Brigden, "Youth and the English Reformation," in *Past & Present*, 95 (1982), 37.

[43]Griffiths, 72.

[44]Christoher Hill, *The World Turned Upside Down: Radical Ideas During the English Revolution* (London: Penguin, 1972), 189.

wanton, insolent and head-strong upon the least indulgence."[45] In his *A Young Man's Inquisition or Trial*, William Guild warned that most young people "walketh and loveth to walketh in that broad byway of liberty, where there is no restraint or curbing of the affections and lusts of the flesh . . . [and therefore] hath need of straiter discipline, more carefull watching . . . harder brydling, and more diligent instruction by the word of God."[46] Such attention to the willfulness of the young and the danger of youthful energy is quite at odds with the images of "children" we saw in Locke and Filmer. For what Filmer's and Locke's children share is their passivity; despite their great differences, the two political theorists unfold national narratives in which "childhood" is marked by either obedience or exclusion. Yet, of course, young people have not always been either submissive to authority or content to absent themselves from politics. In a certain sense, the prescriptive view of childhood delineated above is influenced by a long tradition of emphasizing the propensity to sin, disobedience, and insubordination of the young.

I will argue in chapter four for a close connection between homeless children and the nascent eighteenth-century novel; I should like, therefore, to devote some attention to what historically constituted the largest group of young people who left home. As the population of London swelled from around 60,000 in 1500 to about 200,000 by 1600, powerful economic and social upheavals added to the convulsions of the Reformation and the perceived threat of the young. Perhaps no other group in English society, besides masterless men, elicited more anxiety than the large class of young men who left their homes and flocked to the capital to be bound as apprentices. "One of the oldest [labour] devices known to man," as the historian Steven Smith describes, apprenticeship supplied labor to the market and training to the

[45]Fleetwood, 16.
[46]William Guild, *A Young Man's Inquisition or Trial* (London, 1608), 20–1.

labor force, while strictly controlling admission into the freedom of London. It was a formal process in which the apprentice and the master signed indenture papers that named the apprentice, his father, their hometown, and then the master. The papers also specified the length of the apprenticeship term, normally seven years, during which term "the said apprentice his said master well and truly shall serve, his secrets keep close, his commandments lawful and honest he shall willingly do: hurt nor damage to his said master he shall non do."[47]

The injunction to secrecy highlights the domestic relation of apprentice and master, for "apprenticeship was seen as a type of family relationship rather than labor relationship, and the apprentice was viewed as a child, rather than a trainee, an assistant in a shop, or a skilled worker."[48] The apprentice relied on his master for food and shelter, becoming part of the master's household. His expected child-like subjection is underlined by some moral commitments: the apprentice promised not to drink or fornicate, not to get married or run away, and to obey his master. In reality, apprenticeship placed a burden not only on the apprentice, but also on the master, who, obliged to feed, clothe and house his apprentices even if they were sick or unproductive, was "tempted to take outrageous steps to get rid of an unwanted apprentice. Sometimes he would contrive to get him taken by a press-gang . . . [or] dispose of him to the master of a ship to be sold in the colonies."[49] The ideal master-apprentice relationship did not always work, then; and its occasional failure is attested not only by the numerous cases of apprentices suing their masters for abuse or failure to provide

[47]Steven R. Smith, "The London Apprentices as Seventeenth-Century Adolescents," in *Past & Present*, 61 (1973), 150.

[48]Ilana K. Ben-Amos, *Adolescence and Youth in Early Modern England* (New Haven: Yale University Press, 1994), 85.

[49]M. Dorothy George, *London Life in the Eighteenth Century* (Chicago: Academy Chicago, 1984 (1925)), 227.

the sought training, but also by competing literary images of apprentices.

In fact, the two nationally-weighted views of childhood adumbrated above—its duty to obey authority and the troublesome energy it menaces—are best unfolded by examining the variety of texts addressed to apprentices and to those with supposed dominion over them. That apprentices were required to obey their masters is preached by the great many domestic guidebooks—some examples of which we encountered above—that depicted apprentices and other dependents as children. Others that represented this ideal master-apprentice relationship included William Gouge's *Of Domestical Duties*, Thomas Carter's *Christian Commonwealth*, Robert Abbot's *A Christian Family Builded by God*, and Richard Allestree's *The Whole Duty of Man*. Such guides "accepted the patriarchal nature of the servant-master relationship, the master's duty to provide moral and religious instruction as well as vocational training, the master's responsibility for disciplining his apprentices, and the apprentice's obligation to render complete obedience and faithful service."[50]

If court cases against abusive masters give the view of apprentices as victims, and guidebooks depict them as obedient children, other texts represent them as vigorous, plucky, and troublesome. A particular theme occupied both religious and secular writers as an emblem of disobedience. "As for you, Master Quicksilver," Touchstone admonishes his disobedient and wasteful apprentice in *Eastward Ho*, "think of the husks, for thy course is running directly to the hogs' trough; husks, sirrah."[51] The reference to husks images the disobedient apprentice as a prodigal son, drawing on a long tradition of using the theme of

[50]Smith, 152.
[51]George Chapman, Ben Jonson, and John Marston, *Eastward Ho*, ed. R. W. Van Fossen (Manchester: Manchester University Press, 1979), 75.

the prodigal, based on St. Luke, in both sermons and more "secular" literary works.[52]

The Prodigal "Son"

In the biblical parable, the younger son asks for his portion of goods and leaves his father's house. Wasting his money in "riotous living," the prodigal is brought low and reduced to almost filling "his belly with the husks the swine did eat." He repents and returns home to his father's welcoming forgiveness. Though the original lesson of the parable teaches the prodigal's rebellion, repentance, and return to the father as an allegory of Christian salvation, this parable became the most popular by far of the biblical parables, I believe, because it both threatens and confirms, in remarkably terse and visual prose, the power of patriarchy—society's ruling political fiction.[53] The theme of the

---

[52]The theme is prominent in medieval morality plays, ballads, prints, and sermons. An example of a dramatic treatment is the Tudor interlude *Youth* in Ian Lancashire, *Two Tudor Interludes* (Manchester: Manchester University Press, 1980). For other plays dramatizing the theme of the prodigal, see F. P. Wilson, *The English Drama 1485–1585* (Oxford: Oxford University Press, 1969), 96–101 and Peter Ure, *Elizabethan and Jacobean Drama*, ed. J. C. Maxwell (Liverpool: Liverpool University Press, 1974), 187–221. For the theme in broadside ballads, woodcuts, and chapbooks, see Tessa Watt, *Cheap Print and Popular Piety 1550–1640* (Cambridge: Cambridge University Press, 1991), 120, 202–10 and Natascha Würzbach, *The Rise of the English Street Ballad 1550–1650*, trans. Gayna Walls (Cambridge: Cambridge University Press, 1990(1981)), 126–9.

[53]"Depictions of the parable rarely occurred before the thirteenth century, but increased thereafter in illuminated manuscripts, Bibles, and gospel texts . . . [It also appeared in] sculpture and stained-glass windows . . . Similarly, narratives in four or more scenes were woven into tapestries and painted on wall hangings, furniture, and other decorative objects, testifying to the parable's ubiquitous presence among the artifacts of daily life." Ellen G. D'Oench, *Prodigal Son Narratives: 1480–1980* (New Haven: Yale University Press, 1995), 3.

prodigal is of some interest to the eighteenth-century novel and will occupy me in chapter four; I should like to examine its aforementioned Jacobean representation in more detail.

Eastward Ho, a comedy by George Chapman, Ben Jonson, and John Marston noteworthy for the seamlessness of its collaborative writing, is one of the most sophisticated dramatizations of the theme of the apprentice as prodigal. First performed at the Blackfriars Theatre in 1605, it features a wise and jovial London goldsmith, Touchstone, who acts to reform the wayward and extravagant Quicksilver and to reward his other apprentice, the temperate and virtuous Golding, the "elder brother" of the biblical parable. In fact, the play's plot is structured, as A. Caputi puts it, "on related character contrasts".[54] In his obedience and sobriety, Golding represents the idealized apprentice as a dutiful son. When Touchstone rewards him with the hand of his virtuous daughter, Mildred, and the freedom of the Company of Goldsmiths, Golding's gratitude reads like a prompt from a domestic guidebook: "Sir, as your son, I honour you; and as your servant, obey you" (88).

Reflecting the complex nature of apprenticeship and the ambiguity of adapting the father-son prodigal's narrative to the different social context of a labor relationship, Quicksilver rejects his master's upbraiding on the grounds of his own high social class. When Touchstone reprimands his flippant apprentice for mocking his speech mannerisms: "Dost thou jest at thy lawful master contrary to thy indentures?" Quicksilver responds that his wasteful, gallant-like finery and behavior do not contradict his status: "Why, 'sblood, sir, my mother's gentlewoman, and my father a justice of the peace and of quorum."[55] The prodigal apprentice is released from his indentures by

[54]A. Caputi, *John Marston, Satirist* (New York: Octagon, 1961), 224.

[55]"A justice of the peace could hear complaints; only the presence of a justice of quorum permitted a determination." Van Fossen, ed., *Eastward Ho*, 71, note 27.

Touchstone and falls in with a group of adventurers and specu-
lators, led by Sir Petronel Flash, a newly-created, penniless
knight and the husband of Touchstone's second, social-climb-
ing daughter.

Sir Petronel is at the center of the play's other subplot. He
surreptitiously seeks to invest his wife's dowry in a scheme of
gold prospecting in Virginia. Highlighting the satirical bent of
the play, the ship barely sails before it runs aground in the
Thames, cutting short the schemers' colonial careers and paro-
dying the motif of the voyage itself. Touchstone brings charges
against both his ex-apprentice and his son-in-law, who are
imprisoned for felony. The fortunes of Quicksilver fall to their
ebb when it turns out that Golding, who has risen to the post of
deputy aldermen, is his judge. Although he reprimands his wayward "brother": "thou hast prodigally consumed much of they
master's estate; and being by him gently admonished, hast
returned thyself haughty and rebellious in thine answers,"
Golding tricks his recalcitrant master into coming to prison
and witnessing the pitiful sight of Quicksilver's true repentance. The master's glad forgiveness of both "sons" ensures a
happy ending to the play.

In the play age functions both directly and symbolically.
When Touchstone eventually reclaims his prodigal apprentice,
he fulfills the duty of an elder to guide a young man, an obligation stressed by the domestic guidebooks. The authority of age
is also confirmed metaphorically: by limning the master as
father and the apprentices as children, the cultural labor relation of a specific era is disguised as a "natural" and timeless
family relation, and the father is endowed with an authority
that recalls Filmer's view. Quicksilver's eventual repentance and
submission uphold the moral message of the prodigal story. Yet
the prodigal's risible but daring adventure and his master's col-
loquial idiom and robust humor are more memorable than
Golding's pompous speech, insipid attachment to Mildred, and
pretentious self-deprecation. In fact, the latter's insufferable

perfection, modern critics argue, is evidence that the play satirizes him as well as Quicksilver and Touchstone; that the message of the play is not simply the triumph of virtue over vice, vindicating "the morals of the City against the attacks of the new comedy."[56]

It is not only our age that finds "family values" less interesting than rebelliousness. Reflecting this bias in his "Prodigal Son," Laurence Sterne connects the "fatal passion" that drives the prodigal to leave his father's house and "The love of variety, or curiosity of seeing new things . . . [that] seems wove into the frame of every son and daughter of Adam."[57] The disobedience and repentance of the prodigal prove more tantalizing both to the author of the biblical parable—whereas thirteen verses in Luke narrate the prodigal's tribulations, only eight relate the elder son's angry reaction—and to *Eastward Ho*'s three authors. Often narratives adapting the prodigal's theme omitted the elder brother's part altogether and concentrated on the waywardness and contrition of a young man. Leaving home in itself came to emblematize rebellion. As Hunter puts it, Puritan youth guides "often evince a particular concern about youths who manifest their rebellion by running off to a far country, like the prodigal son, or to sea."[58] Timothy Cruso, as we saw above, allegorically refers to "Wicked" youth as "Mad Prodigals," who have to be "fetch[ed] home."

The Great Chain of Being dictated not only a fixed station but also a circumscribed geographical location. "Movement elevated anxieties," Griffiths observes, positing a "politics of 'place,'" in which "every young person was in theory the property and subject of an adult householder."[59] If paintings and print narratives of the prodigal theme set the scene of the

[56]Van Fossen, ed., Intro. to *Eastward Ho*, 22.

[57]Laurence Sterne, *The Sermons of Mr. Yorick* (London: Dodsley, 1766), v. 3, 329.

[58]Hunter, 40.

[59]Griffiths, 71.

prodigal's "riotous living" in brothels, the nadir of his degradation stressed his solitude amongst the swine. The vast expanse of the social world is denied the prodigal, as his hunger forces him into a smaller space than he has left. Solitude almost reduces the prodigal to bestiality, not only threatening his very survival but also undermining the political order. The prodigal's return to the society of his father and elder brother (the absence of the mother is noteworthy) both redeems him and confirms the rules of the house.

The Rules of Misrule

By contrast with the prodigal's dangerous isolation, it is not solitude but rather grouping that seems to threaten the social order in another fascinating historical and literary representation of youth. A 1632 Stuart Chapbook, *The Pinder of Wakefield*, recounts the exploits of George a Greene, "a lusty Pinder," who organizes his friends into a formal group, appointing a drummer, lieutenant, colour bearer and sergeants."[60] The first part of the book shows the group challenging the servants of two wealthy clothiers from other towns "to make a token submission," and then bloodily beating them in a fight when they refuse. But the most remarkable anecdotes show the group engaged in meting out punishment to various inhabitants of the town. George, for example, "plays a trick on a jealous husband, needlessly suspicious of his wife's virtue, by terrifying him in the guise of a spirit." The group of young men also come to the aid of a long-suffering man tormented by "a rank scold" who "after hunny moone was past began to call him Rogue and Rascal instead of Lord and Master" and later "took the ladle and broke his pate." The group organizes a charivari in which they

[60]Bernard Capp, "English Youth Groups and *The Pinder of Wakefield*," in *Past & Present*, 76 (1977), 129–30.

> got a boy drest in womens apparel like the woman, and a man like her husband, and put them both on a horse: All the town and all the Countries thereabouts having notice of this new iest, came to see it. Thorow the town thus they rid, the woman beating the man, and scolding at him terribly, the poor man wringing his hands spinning with a distaffe, *Tom* the Taberer with his Taber and Pipe playing before them, others playing on Gridirons, Tongs, bagpipes . . . and all the people running and hooting after them (131).

Although their actions are violent and seem on the surface to be subversive, the group led by the Pinder buttresses the existing social order. In forcing the surrender of the youth from the surrounding towns, George a Greene and his friends defend the honor of Wakefield. The group, furthermore, discourages socially unacceptable behavior by humiliating henpecking wives and weakling husbands, thus upholding the town's moral code. It also targets other breakers of order: the youth trick a usurer, outmaneuver "a troublesome Knaue," and foil "a gang of housebreakers who are known to be planning to rob a gentleman's house." Although "the group exists in large part for the pleasure of its members," Bernard Capp concludes, "the protection of the values, interests and prestige of the community is an essential part of its function, and secure it a respected position within the town" (131-2).

The preceding analysis of *The Pinder of Wakefield* was reported in a short communication in *Past and Present*, and is the only instance thus far of an English formal youth group that closely resembles what the historian Natalie Zemon Davis described earlier, in a ground breaking article, as a widespread practice in the villages of medieval and early modern France and Continental Europe. Davis calls these formal groups, the "Abbeys of Misrule." In a 1566 festival in Lyon, for instance, rural formal youth groups took part in a charivari where seven floats in which husbands beaten by their wives were identified by street and occupation and "beaten variously with tripe, wooden sticks, knives, forks, spoons, frying pans, trenchers, and water pots."[61] The youth groups did not single out the husbands, "widows or widowers remarrying were vulnerable, as were husbands deceived by their wives and husbands who beat their wives during the month of May (a special month for women)."

The Abbeys of Misrule "were organizations of unmarried men in peasant communities, who did not marry till their early or middle twenties ... their period of *Jeunesse* lasted a long time and the number of bachelors relative to the total number of men in the village was quite high ... Each year before Lent, after Christmas, or at some other time, they elected a King or Abbot from among their midst" (104). The Abbeys had an important social function: the charivaris that denounced the second marriages of widowers, for example, "placated" the dead spouses, who were sometimes represented as an effigy; they publicized the plight of the children from the first marriage. They also aired the resentment of the young when an older widow or widower married a younger person, reducing the marriage possibilities of the young.

Misrule, Davis uncovered, "provided a rule that the youth had over others and perhaps too a brotherhood existing among themselves ... But license was not rebellious." It prepared the young men of the village for their future roles as "married men and fathers, helping to maintain proper order within marriage and to sustain the biological continuity of the village ... The activities functioned rather like *rites de passage*, here spaced over a number of years, in communities where the older generation's

---

[61]Natalie Zemon Davis, "The Reasons of Misrule," reprinted in *Society and Culture in Early Modern France* (Stanford: Stanford University Press, 1975 (1971)), 100.

expectations from the young and the younger generation expectations for themselves did not differ very much" (107). Davis's fascinating article provides a glimpse of a distant but familiar aspect of youth. Although they engaged in what is by any standards quite mischievous—at times downright dangerous—behavior, the young men contributed to the continuity of village life, not its change. Extending Davis's analysis to early modern youth culture in southern Germany, Norbert Schindler notes that charivaris had their "origins in the patriarchal surveillance exercised by young bachelors."[62] Young men took it on themselves to enforce codes of "the morality and honor of a village's unmarried daughters."

As young men and women flocked into French cities, however, the disruption of the old rural continuities altered the character of these organizations. The new economic and social life of the city "made it likely that male adolescents would be organized into groups either with adults or more directly dominated by adults than were the village Abbeys . . . [In the city] the *rite de passage* led to an economic status, not a new stage for life." Not so in England, it seems. Although, as mentioned above, historical examples of formal groups of misrule remain elusive, young people, particularly apprentices, continued to play a distinctive role in the cities, especially London. Apprentices led the unruly activities of Shrovetide Tuesday, in which they routinely insulted foreigners and sacked the capital's brothels.[63] They also held a prominent part in celebrating the parliament's deliverance from Guy Fawkes's Catholic Gunpowder Plot, "lending a distinctively

[62]Norbert Schindler, "Guardians of Disorder: Rituals of Youthful Culture at the Dawn of the Modern Age," in *A History of Young People in the West*, v. 1, ed. Giovanni Levi and Jean-Claude Schmitt, trans. Camile Naish (Cambridge: Harvard University Press, 1997), 249.

[63]In 1621, the Spanish ambassador avoided London on Shrovetide Tuesday, for he was "not ignorant of the yll affection generally borne him" which could flare up "on this 'furious' day." See Griffiths, 151.

national and Protestant flavour to the festive year."[64] Whether or not the London youth had a separate subculture, it is probable that the apprentice groups did not lose their youthful character thanks to the extraordinarily late age of marriage in the capital. As Margaret Spufford puts it in her study of seventeenth-century chapbooks and their readership, the "combination of late marriage and a high proportion of single people is so unusual for a pre-industrial society that it has been described as 'unique or almost unique in the world.'"[65]

Although both prodigal sons and youth groups appear subversive—the prodigal in his solitude and the groups in their rowdiness—their narratives confirm the given social world. While many moralists, whether religious writers of Puritan guidebooks and sermons or more secular writers of domestic conduct books, equated leaving home with rebellion, most of the apprentices who flooded London were driven by economic need. Their dependence on their masters is, however, often at odds with their energies and desires. Apprentices, therefore, constitute an important historical group where the dialectics of dependence and freedom, obedience and initiative, rule and misrule can be observed. That their dependence on their masters is imaged as a father/son relationship provides a striking resemblance to the dependence of the hero of the eighteenth-century novel. Apprentices furnish a historical glimpse of young people reacting to authority envisaged as fatherhood, the analogue of a dominant national political fiction.

Entering a crowded discursive field in which childhood figured practically and symbolically, Filmer and Locke battled over the proper English national narrative. Will the nation assume the shape of an absolutist monarchy, as in the French

[64]Griffiths, 144

[65]Margaret Spufford, *Small Books and Pleasant Histories: Popular Fiction and its Readership in Seventeenth-Century England* (London: Methuen, 1981), 157.

example, or will it develop into a parliamentary state more attractive to the rising Whig commercial classes? The triumph of Locke's views was as much the result of William and Mary's successful invasion and James's spinelessness, as it was a consequence of Locke's political argument. Yet, Locke's consensual story in the *Second Treatise* expresses, more than any other political formulation, the British national conviction that was to endure and to come into conflict with other European views of the nation, then and now. I will return in chapter four to the implications of the Lockean civic narrative to the rising novel. For now, we note in closing that the child assumes a great symbolic value in both national narratives, despite their glaring differences: in Locke's, signifying the exception (he/she is merely a subject but not a consenting "individual"); in Filmer's, allegorizing the universal state of subjection (all the king's subjects are children).

THREE

ROUSSEAU AND
THE NATIONAL CHILD

> Gradually we realized the political implications and
> understood that we were in the presence of a national ideal.
> The beach, in fact, was alive with patriotic children—
> a phenomenon as unnatural as it was depressing. Children
> are a human species and a society apart, a nation of their
> own, so to speak.
>
> Thomas Mann, *Mario and the Magician*

> Save that we do not die when a knife pierces the tongue.
> To that degree, we may say the tongue belongs to the world
> of play, whereas the heart belongs to the earnest.
>
> J. M. Coetzee, *Foe*

This chapter will explore the roots of the idealization of childhood, and the creation of the national child. We saw above how Locke's political view of children not only was jaundiced—since they lack the rationality and the freedom of the adult—but also contradicted his more "realistic" characterization of children in his educational treatise. By contrast, nationalism, in its self-portrayal as *the* natural form of human association, has always viewed children as its natural seed, so to speak. This is not simply to dismiss this type as the "racialist" as opposed to the cultural type of nationalism. On the contrary, children seem curiously to unite these two types of nationalist feeling. In *The Idea of Nationalism*, Hans Kohn asserts that "Nationality has been raised to an absolute by two fictitious concepts which have been accepted as having real substance. One holds that blood or race is the basis of nationality, and that it exists eternally and carries with it an unchangeable inheritance; the other sees the *Volkgeist* as an ever-welling source of nationality."[1]

For racial nationalism, children act as the emblem of the purity and vitality of "genetic" or racial continuity. The *Nazi Primer*, for example, teaches the Hitler Youth that "One could also say . . . that living beings without the same heredity are recognizable by the fact that their descendants are unlike the parents,"[2] thus suggesting a type of victimology of the race through bastardy inflicted on it by foreigners who abuse its "hospitality." Children also represent the "material" of the future, a protection against the exhaustion of the population. Witness the type of adulation accorded to women by the French revolutionaries, Nazi Germany or Fascist Italy for performing their incubative "function."[3] In a study of Italian cinema under Fascism, Marcia Landy relates how "On Christmas Day 1933, in Palazzo Venezia, Mussolini celebrated the first "Mother and Child Day" . . . [where] he publicly honored ninety-three women, one from each province in Italy, for their reproductive fecundity."[4]

Concern with the dwindling population of the nation has been a stock obsession of nationalist regimes. Nazi propaganda not only taught "scientific" racial biology as proving the superiority of the "Nordic" race to the other races but also emphasized that lack of vigilance on the part of "Nordics" led to a crossbreeding that was "polluting" the "Nordic race."[5] The solution was to prevent this dangerous crossbreeding, and to

[1] Hans Kohn, *The Idea of Nationalism* (New York: Macmillan, 1944), 13.

[2] *The Nazi Primer: Official Handbook for Schooling the Hitler Youth*, trans. Harwood L. Childs (New York: Harper, 1938), 36.

[3] See, for example, Claudia Koonz, *Mothers in the Fatherland: Women, the Family, and Nazi Politics* (New York: St. Martin's Press, 1987)

[4] Marcia Landy, *Fascism in Film: The Italian Commercial Cinema, 1931–1943* (Princeton: Princeton University Press, 1986), 72.

[5] *The Nazi Primer*, 16 & ff.

ensure national survival through "necessary" population growth. "The essential and insoluble link between blood and soil was a recurrent theme. The acquisition of more territory in which the *Volk* could sink its roots was viewed as essential for the preservation of the race."[6]

On the other hand, confirming Kohn's second "fictitious concept," children, "free" from the corruption of foreigners and foreign ideas, from the impurities of cosmopolitanism, present fertile ground for a constellation of ideas and beliefs— "culture"—that the nation can teach: ideas and beliefs, one must remember, that might not be those of the parents. Hence, the poignant pitting of child against parents in many novelistic portrayals of nationalist dystopias, such as *1984*. Or, more disturbingly, the total separation of the children from their parents to become pure wards of the state in *Brave New World*. To speak of the linkage between dystopia and nationalism is simply to consider nationalism on its own terms, or, more precisely, on the opposite of its declared terms, for the link between nationalism and utopian thought is well known.

Related to this view of the national child is the cluster of nationalist institutions that center on children, such as the Hitler Youth, Stalin's Pioneers, or Mao's Cultural Red Guards,[7] which exploit and revel in the energy and irrationality of children and seek to appropriate them for the nation. If the summons to the October 1913 meeting of the Youth Movement in Germany proclaimed that German youth did not intend to remain "a dependency of the older generation, excluded from public life and relegated to a passive role," Hitler's later incorporation of the youth Bünde within other National Socialist organizations

[6]Norbert A. Huebsch, "The "Wolf Cubs" of the New Order: The Indoctrination and Training of the Hitler Youth," in *Nazism and the Common Man: Essays in German History (1929–1939)*, ed. Otis C. Mitchell (Washington, D.C.: University Press of America, 1981), 104.

[7]The nationalist aspect of many communist regimes and states has been pointed out by Benedict Anderson in *Imagined Communities*.

vitiated the threat of independent youthful rebellion. Although it "became part of the mythology of the regime that the Nazi leadership represented the essence of youth . . . Hitler assured the older generation that under a National Socialist regime young people would be taught to venerate their parents, tradition, and above all the army."[8]

German youth, who sought autonomy from their elders, were subordinated to the needs of the regime, which channeled their energy into nationalist streams. Hitler was unequivocal in his demands for his "brutal" youth:

> There must be no weakness or tenderness in it. I want to see once more in its eyes the gleam of pride and the independence of the beast of prey. Strong and handsome must my strong men be. I will have them fully trained in all physical exercises. I intend to have an athletic youth—that is the first and chief thing. In this way I shall eradicate the thousands of years of human domestication. Then I shall have in front of me the pure and noble natural material. With that I can create the new order.[9]

Norbert Huebsch stresses that "the belief in one's racial superiority [was] wedded ideologically to the need for physical conditioning and military training."[10] And indeed one can cite the numerous propagandistic nationalist posters—Nazi, Fascist, and Stalinist—that depict healthy-looking youths involved in athletic activities. It is as though the youthful bodies represent an offering to the Führer or Duce, the national father, a promise of devotion, fertility, and longevity.

[8]Robert Wohl, *The Generation of 1914* (Cambridge: Harvard University Press, 1979), 72.

[9]Herman Rauschning, *The Voice of Destruction* (New York: Harper & Row, 1949), 252.

[10]Huebsch, 106.

Many intellectuals during these turbulent European years remarked the propensity that children have for being seduced by such nationalist-totalitarian ideology. Paul Klee, for example, who was stripped of his position because of his non-conformist political views, in 1939 produced an abstract drawing entitled "Kinder spielen Tragödie," in which two comparatively huge children gesture grotesquely; the child on the right has a bestial-looking eye that contrasts with his upward gaze—a negative assessment of transcendalist idealization, perhaps—whereas the other gazes downwards on two smaller bodies—dead?—who seem to hurtle downwards under the children's feet. In another drawing called "Närrische Jugend Krieg" (1940), four children gesture wildly, and triumphantly trample on an adult corpse.[11]

Children, the Nazis believed, had in fact to be protected from the pernicious effect of such art. The historian Lynn Nicholas, in her fascinating detective-like study of the fate of European masterpieces—sold, transported, and lost—by the Third Reich during World War II, describes that most famous of art "exhibits," the "Degenerate Art" show ordered by Hitler, who "delivered the coup de grace" to his nation's modern collections." Nicholas reports that "Before it closed . . . more than two million people poured through this exhibition . . . The catalogue, a badly printed and confused booklet, was laced with the most vicious quotes from Hitler's art speeches. The walls were covered with mocking graffiti. To 'protect' them, children were not allowed in."[12]

[11]Paul Klee, Paul Klee-Stiftung, Kunstmuseem, Berne. Both drawings are in crayon on paper. Klee's drawings might refer to Arnolt Bronnen's play *Die Geburt der Jugend* (The Birth of the Youth), which "portrayed roving bands of boys and girls on horseback who galloped over the aged, trampled them to dust, and shouted that they themselves were God" Wohl, 44.

[12]Lynn H. Nicholas, *The Rape of Europa: The Fate of Europe's Treasures in the Third Reich and the Second World War* (New York: Vintage, 1994), 19–24.

A Child Shall Lead Them

The emphasis on children as national raw material, as it were, and the celebration of the irrationality of the child as "natural" is a striking departure from Locke's view. The creation of the national child was a concomitant of that of the Romantic child, the result of the development of a new literary climate that revolted against the mechanistic philosophy of the Enlightenment; the new sensibility lay "in the whole movement of the late eighteenth century from Reason to Feeling."[13] As Simon Schama summarizes: "In this new world, heart was to be preferred to head; emotion to reason; nature to culture; spontaneity to calculation; simplicity to the ornate; innocence to experience... It generated a new literary vocabulary, saturated with emotive associations that drowned out not only the light repartee of rococo wit, but even the hallowed sonorities of classicism."[14]

The age of sensibility, however, did not always produce fine sentiments; its tears were not always "delicious." In commenting on the humiliation of the French royal family during the October Days of 1789, Edmund Burke rued that "In the new age, all the pleasing illusions, which made power gentle... [and which] incorporated into politics the sentiments which beautify and soften the private society, are to be dissolved by this new conquering empire of light and reason."[15] Burke, in fact, did not appreciate the extent of the transformation of politics caused by the demand that it conform to the sentiments of private life. What later killed Louis XVI and, more strikingly, Marie-Antoinette, was not that they were seen as inefficient despots who obscured the light of reason, but that they were

[13]Peter Coveney, *The Image of Childhood* (Harmondsworth, England: Penguin, 1967), 37.

[14]Simon Schama, *Citizens: A Chronicle of the French Revolution* (New York: Knopf, 1989), 149.

[15]Edmund Burke, *Reflections on the Revolution in France* (New York: Penguin, 1973 (1790)), 89–91.

depicted as bad "parents" who did not reciprocate the filial sentiments of their subjects.

If Burke grieved for the queen's disgrace "in a nation of gallant men, in a nation of men of honor and of cavaliers . . . [where] I thought ten thousand swords must have leaped from their scabbards to avenge even a look that threatened her with insult," the new national narrative of the Revolution scorned the exquisite language of courtly chivalry in favor of the earnest words of domestic rectitude. Appealing to the queen for her aid in supporting "The Declaration of the Rights of Woman and the Female Citizen," the pioneering French feminist Olympe de Gouges wished Marie-Antoinette "a nobler function . . . [that] would excite your ambition"; and, eschewing "the adulation of courtiers," de Gouges admonished the queen to "bear in mind that you are mother and wife."[16]

Reversing Aristotle's valorization of the public realm of freedom over the private domain of privation and necessity, the French Revolution created the nation, a realm of association where domestic virtue and public glory intermesh, with a crucial stake for every citizen. The domestic sphere, the realm of tender sentiments, became the measure of patriotic goodness. Rousseau marvels at those who behave as though "the love of one's nearest were not the principle of the love one owes the state; as though it were not by means of the small fatherland which is the family that the heart attaches itself to the large one. . . ."[17] Authority in the state was explicitly modeled on authority in the family. If the king ruled as a *pater patriae*, the "divine" Father soon became a delinquent father. For the revolutionaries exalting domestic sentiments as the yardstick of goodness, attempted to replace the ties of absolutist obedience

[16]Olympe de Gouges, "The Rights of Woman," in *Women in Revolutionary Paris 1789–1795*, ed. and trans. D. G. Levy, H. B. Applewhite, and M.D. Johnson (Urbana: University of Illinois Press, 1979 (1791)), 87–8.

[17]Jean-Jacques Rousseau, *Emile*, trans. Allan Bloom (New York: Basic Books, 1979), 363.

with those of nationalist affection. The father/king, who stood at the top of the earthly part of the Chain of Being, commanded divine authority, and had a mystical body that never died, became a bad father whose decapitated body, along with the head, was buried and covered with quicklime, in a deep grave in the Madeleine Cemetery.[18]

Familial-modeled national politics endowed children and childhood with great symbolic significance. Now, a hallowed symbol of the natural sincerity and innocence of man betrayed by the false ideals of an artificial court culture, the child became a symbol of the new citizen. The citizen was to be a child of nature and a child of the state. Perhaps the most striking demonstration of this valence of children exploited by the French revolutionaries took place during the trial of Marie-Antoinette. Because of Salic law, queens could never rule in France. Although Marie-Antoinette thus did not have a "mystical bodypolitic" that had to be eliminated, her "corporeal body" nevertheless represented "the possible profanation of everything that the nation held sacred."[19] The most damaging charge brought against her was that she had committed incest with her son, "forgetting her quality of mother."[20]

Children also come to express the new *beginning* that is a centerpiece of the ideology of nationalist movements. Primarily for that reason, perhaps, the child became one of the most potent symbols of the French Revolution, which, observes Lynn Hunt, in her study of its ceremonies and rhetoric, "brought the process of symbol making into particularly sharp relief, because revolution-

[18]In his seminal *The King's Two Bodies: A Study in Medieval Political Theology* (Princeton: Princeton University Press, 1957), Ernst Kantorowicz analyzed "the mystic fiction of the 'King's Two Bodies.'" According to him, kings in England and France had both a mortal, corporeal body and an invisible "body politic" that never died.

[19]Lynn Hunt, *The Family Romance of the French Revolution* (Berkeley: University of California Press, 1992), 95.

[20]From the account of the trial given in the *Moniteur universel*, no. 25, 16 October 1793, quoted in Hunt, 93.

aries found themselves in the midst of revolution before they had the opportunity to reflect on their situation . . . They invented their symbols and rituals as they went along . . . National regeneration required nothing less than a new man and new habits. . . ."[21]

As the stained glass windows of Chartres and Rheims conveyed the symbols and narrative of faith to the illiterate multitude, so did the revolutionaries use the "symbols and ceremonies" of the revolution didactically. But whereas God's symbols—if not his stories—were uncontested, these new ones had first to defeat the symbols of the royal past. Hunt relates how "According to the Duke of Dorset [the British Ambassador], the first cockades were made of green ribbons, but these were rejected because green was the color of the livery of the Count Artois, the king's much-maligned younger brother." The revolutionaries felt and represented themselves as being always busy with and vigilant over the creation of a new man and citizen: "Revolutionaries could only hope to win their 'symbolic' battles if they succeeded in educating their public . . . As a consequence, the political practice of the republicans was fundamentally didactic; republicans had to teach the people how to read the new symbolic text of the revolution" (68).

Hence the crucial figurative and practical value of children: practical because education began with children, whence the lasting emphasis on national education. Since the nation's lessons were new, parents could not teach them; if anything, the family could only have a corrupting effect. The French revolutionaries were the first to instill the view—later a central nationalist belief—that the national essence which resides in the nation's children can be corrupted by the family. Robespierre makes the point unequivocally: "The country has the right to raise its children; it should not entrust this to the pride of families or the prejudices of particular individuals. . . ."[22]

[21]Lynn Hunt, *Politics, Culture, and Class in the French Revolution* (Berkeley: University of California Press, 1984), 54-6.

[22]Marcel Garaud and Romuald Szramkiewicz, *La Révolution française et la famille* (Paris, 1978), 142.

Childhood itself became a symbol of purity and sincerity: not only did the nation have to teach its new lessons to its children, the child became an ideal image of the new citizen. That development more than influenced the rearing of children in families; it is perhaps not an exaggeration to say that it reversed the order of hierarchy between childhood and adulthood. The citizen became to the nation what the child was to its pedagogues. Such a reversal was not only instrumental but also affective. As the nation's essence was imagined to reside in its children, the nation became an object of love for its children to replace their parents, and for its citizens to replace the *pater patriae*. It was not enough that the ideology of the Father/King be replaced by the enlightened bureaucracy of a state—the citizens had to love, and exhibit their love for, the nation. The new familial ideology burnt the king in his own fire: We have seen that absolutist kings used the ideology of being *pater patriae* to demand obedience from their subjects. Now, French nationalists executed the king and queen for being bad parents.

Not the least surprising among all these reversals is the fact that the father of the cult of the family and child was none other than the father who abandoned his five illegitimate children to the foundling hospital. By revising the nature of ties between the child and his parents, and reversing the order of family and society, Rousseau created the national child who does not naturally belong to his family.

The Unnatural Family

Well into his discussion of the causes of inequality among men, Rousseau undertakes a curious digression not much examined by his many commentators: he analyzes the origin of language: "Qu'il me soit permis de considerer un instant les embarras de l'origine des Langues."[23] Rousseau has divided the causes of inequality into two categories: the physical, related to differences in strength, age, health; and the moral or political differences which ensue as a result of societal convention. In analyzing the second category, social inequality, the philosopher, with his search for the most elemental, the originary in the relation between man and society, observes that the progression from the state of animal solitariness to that of social intercourse is predicated upon the discovery of social memory, so that knowledge may be passed from one to another and not "perish with the individual who would have invented it."[24]

Making the logical step next of connecting that required communication to the existence of language—language is the prerequisite for that communication—Rousseau attempts to prove the near impossibility of the socialization sequence (language, communication, social units) by demonstrating the hurdles opposing the invention of human language. Rousseau, a musician and linguist who was later to write an essay on the origin of language,[25] does not find much difficulty in convincing his readers of the enormous complications inherent in language

[23]Jean-Jacques Rousseau, *Discours sur l'origine et les fondements de l'inégalité*, edited and annotated by Jean Starobinski, in J. J. Rousseau, *Oeuvres complètes*, ed. Bernard Gagnebin and Marcel Raymond (Paris: Gallimard [Bibliothèque de la Pléiade], 1964 (1754)), vol. 3, 146. All following page references are to this edition. Also, henceforth I shall refer to this work as *l'inégalité*. I follow the standard Pléiade edition; some of the accents and orthography seem unusual.

[24]J. J. Rousseau, *Discourse on the Origin of Inequality*, in *Basic Political Writings of Jean-Jacques Rousseau*, trans. and ed. Donald A. Cress (Indianapolis: Hackett, 1987), 47. All following page references to the English translation are to this edition.

[25]See *On the Origin of Language*. Rousseau also discusses the origin of music in that essay.

formation: the initial difficulty of apprehending abstract notions must have created a great superfluity of words; and it would have been arduous to express ideas that could not be indicated by gesture or voice.

But before he analyzes the growth of linguistic complexity, Rousseau takes pains to refute the common opinion regarding the origin of languages: that they arose out of familial intercourse: "Je dirois bien, comme beaucoup d'autres, que les Langues sont nées dans le commerce domestiques des Peres, des Meres, et des Enfans . . . [mais] ce seroit commettre la faute de ceux qui raisonnant sur l'Etat de Nature, y transportent les idées prises dans la Société, voyant toujours la famille rassemblée dans une même habitation, et ses membres gardant entre eux une union aussi intime et aussi permanente que parmi nous . . . (146).[26] Rousseau's argument here directly contradicts Locke's second, anthropological story of the formation of the commonwealth. If we accept his premises, Rousseau accomplishes no less than the destruction of the widely accepted naturalness of the human family, and hence all paternal-patriarchal authority. His move potentially liberates not only children but all those dependent persons, like servants and apprentices, who were traditionally considered in the position of children.

As discussed in chapter two, Locke leaves a wide-open window for patriarchal authority by accepting the naturalness of the patriarch's authority over his sons.[27] Children, in their "natural"

[26]"I might well say, as do many others, that languages were born in the domestic intercourse among fathers, mothers and children . . . [but] this would make the mistake of those who, reasoning about the state of nature, intrude into it ideas taken from society. They always see the family gathered in one and the same dwelling, with its members always maintaining among themselves a union as intimate and permanent as exists among us" (48).

[27]Again, it is significant that the anthropological story is essentially of fathers and sons, whereas the "consent" story is one that includes mothers and daughters.

helplessness, necessitate Locke's second story of the growth of political tyranny from the children's "scarce avoidable" consent to the patriarch-cum-prince. What is divinely ordained for Filmer, and, embarrassingly, a biological given for Locke, is, however, rejected by Rousseau. Indeed, so crucial is this point to his argument, so pervasive was the belief that political authority was paternal, that Rousseau devotes a long footnote to attacking Locke's view of the naturalness of the human family. "Je trouve dans le Gouvernement Civil de Locke [*Second Treatise*]," insists Rousseau, "une objection qui me paroit trop spécieuse pour qu'il me soit permis de la dissimuler" (214).[28] He then quotes a lengthy section from a 1749 French translation of Locke's *Second Treatise*. In the original (Ch. VII, sec. 79–80) Locke argues: "For the end of *conjunction*, between *male and female*, is but the continuation of the species; this conjunction betwixt male and female ought to last, even after procreation, so long as it is necessary to the nourishment and support of the young ones. . . ."[29]

I do not quote here all the passage that Rousseau frowns on, but this fragment is enough to demonstrate the nature of his objection. Rousseau rejects Locke's view because, primarily, he replies, "J'observerai d'abord que les preuves morales n'ont pas une grande force en matiére de Physique et qu'elles servent plûtôt à rendre raisons des faits existans qu'à constater l'existence réelle des ces faits" (214–5).[30] A family is not natural,

---

[28]"I find in Locke's *Civil Government* an objection which seems to me too specious for me to be permitted to hide it" (101).

[29]John Locke, *Second Treatise*, 43. The translation that Rousseau cites reads: "La fin de la société entre le Mâle et la Femelle n'étant pas simplement de procréer, mais de continuer l'espéce; cette société doit durer, même après la procréation, du moins aussi longtems qu'il est nécessaire pour la nourriture et la conversation des procréées." Rousseau, *l'Inégalité*, 214.

[30]"I will observe first that moral proofs do not have great force in matters of physics, and that they serve more to explain existing facts than to establish the real existence of those facts" (102).

according to Rousseau, since a man and a woman who had just copulated did not stay together in the state of nature because they had no need for each other, the primary motive of later socialization: "Les mâles, et les femelles s'unissoient fortutitement selon la rencontre, l'occasion, et le desir, sans que la parole fût un interprête fort nécessaire des choses qu'ils avoient à se dire: Ils se quittoient avec la même facilité" (147).[31]

Modern biology, not surprisingly, seems to have proven Locke right. Species survive chiefly because "parents" have a built-in imperative to insure the survival of their species. Certainly, Rousseau would have been aware that animal males and females do stay with their young after their "société"; that, in certain species—notably birds—the males even help with feeding the young. Rousseau also rejects, or conveniently ignores, the views of his greatest contemporary natural historian, Buffon—whom he cites as an authority in other contexts in l'Inégalité—on childhood and growth.[32] In his magisterial work, Buffon observed in 1749 (five years before Rousseau wrote l'Inégalité) the striking weakness and dependence of human children: "Si quelque chose est capable de nous donner une idée de notre faiblesse, c'est l'état où nous nous trouvons immédiatement après la naissance; incapable de faire encore aucun usage de ses organes et de se servir de ses sens, l'enfant qui naît a besoin de secours de toute espèce . . . il est

[31]"Males and females came together fortuitously as a result of chance encounters, occasion, and desire, without there being any great need for words to express what they had to say to one another. They left one another with the same nonchalance" (48).

[32]To establish the natural abundance of life in the state of nature, Rousseau writes: "La Terre abandonnée à sa fertilité naturelle et couverte de forêts immenses que la Coignée ne mutila jamais, offre à chaque pas des Magazins et des retraites aux animaux de toute espèce" (135). In a footnote, he cites a long passage from Buffon's Histoire naturelle as an authority.

dans ce premiers temps plus faible qu'aucun des animaux, sa vie incertaine et chancelante paraît devoir finir à chaque instant."[33]

It is not difficult to see why Rousseau had to ignore Buffon's very relevant view: such a hopelessly dependent creature could not have done much to bolster Rousseau's theories of natural equality and independence before civilization destroyed it all. Rousseau *does* cite Buffon in discussing childhood. But instead of citing Buffon's opinions in *Histoire naturelle de l'homme*, he cites a passage from the natural historian's observation on horses in order to mitigate the detrimental effect of children's helplessness on his argument. Trying to establish the natural vigor of man—which, of course, will be weakened in civilized life—Rousseau observes that "D'autres ennemis plus redoutables [than wild animals], et dont l'homme n'a pas les mêmes moyens de se défendre, sont les infirmités naturelles, l'enfance, la vieillesse et les maladies de toute espéce [sic] . . . et si l'Enfance est plus longue parmi nous, la vie étant plus longue aussi, tout est encore à peu près égal en ce point . . ." (137).[34] At this point, Rousseau cites Buffon in a footnote: "<<La durée de la vie des Chevaux>>, dit Mr. de Buffon, <<est comme dans toutes les autres espéces d'animaux proportionnée à la durée du tems

---

[33]Buffon, *Histoire naturelle* (Paris: Gallimard [folio], 1984), 63. My translation follows: "If one thing can give us an idea of our weakness, it would be the state in which we find ourselves immediately after birth. Incapable yet of using his organs or of benefiting from his senses, the newborn infant needs every kind of help. Uncertain and faltering, his life seems about to end at every instant."

[34]"There are other, more formidable enemies, against which man does not have the same means of self-defense: natural infirmities, childhood, old age, and illnesses of all kinds . . . And although childhood is longer among us, our lifespan is also longer; thus things are more or less equal in this respect . . ." (42).

de leur accroissement ... >>" (201).[35] That is to say, it does not matter that human childhood is longer than that of other animals since humans live longer.

It is quite entertaining to observe to what length Rousseau is willing to bend the rules of logic in order to protect the child and hence the species from natural dependence. For the proportion of man's life compared to, say, a horse, is utterly irrelevant if the child dies because childhood is too long for his "parents" to remember him and to care for him. Zero (death) multiplied by any other number is still zero (death). In order for a human being to survive the "enemy" of childhood, someone must take care of him/her while he/she is helpless for the long duration of human childhood. But Rousseau's own reasoning on parents' lack of recognition of their children—before the creation of families—contradicts this condition.

In this back and forth of citing of authority, on the one hand, and ingenious "interpreting" away of it, it is Buffon who perhaps should get the last word. In 1758, three years after the publication of *l'Inégalité*, Buffon responded directly to Rousseau's views on man and child in the state of nature. In a section on "L'état de nature," Buffon elaborates his disagreement with "un Philosophe, l'un des plus fiers censeurs de notre humanité":

> il n'est pas possible de soutenir que l'homme ait jamais existé sans former de familles, puisque les enfants périraient s'ils n'étaient secourus et soignés pendant plusieurs années; au lieu que les animaux nouveau-nés n'ont besoin de leur mère que pendant quelques mois. Cette nécessité physique suffit donc seule pour démontrer que l'espèce humaine n'a pu

---

[35] "'The lifespan of horses,' says M. de Buffon, 'is, as in all other species of animals, proportionate to the length of their growth period'" (88).

> durer et se multiplier qu'à la faveur de la société; que
> l'union des pères et mères aux enfants est naturelle,
> pisqu'elle est nècessaire. Or cette union ne peut
> manquer de produire un attachement respectif et
> durable entre les parents et l'enfant. . . .[36]

> It is not possible to maintain that man ever existed
> without forming families, for infants would perish if
> they were not aided and cared for during many
> years, whereas animal newborns need their mother
> for only a few months. This physical necessity is suf-
> ficient in itself to demonstrate that the human
> species could only endure and multiply because of
> the existence of society; that the union of fathers
> and mothers is natural, because it is necessary. Now,
> this union cannot fail to result in a durable attach-
> ment between the parents and the child.[37]

One does not need to be the greatest natural historian of the
eighteenth century to reach this conclusion. But one cannot be
invested in the redefinition of the relation between child and
family and accept the child's helplessness and dependence.

Language, according to Rousseau, develops later, *after* need
brought people together and families were created; it is not the
agent that motivates the creation of civil society. That is why
Rousseau's digression on language is important to his central
argument and why Paul de Man's assessment that "the section
on the origin of language is clearly a polemical digression *without* [my emphasis] organic links to the main argument . . ." is
mistaken.[38] Mutual need and interdependence necessitated a

---

[36]Buffon, 154–5.

[37]My translation of Buffon.

[38]Paul de Man, *Allegories of Reading: Figural Language in Rousseau,
Nietzsche, Rilke, and Proust* (New Haven: Yale University Press, 1979), 135.

common dwelling, creating the family, love, and language. Before that process, Rousseau sums up:

> Concluons qu'errant dans les forêts sans industrie, sans parole, sans domicile, sans guerre, et sans liaisons ... [l'homme sauvage] Si par hazard il faisoit quelque découverte, il pouvoit d'autant moins la communiquer qu'il ne reconoissoient pas même ses Enfans. L'art périssoit avec l'inventeur ... et chacune partant toujours du même point, les Siécles s'écouloient dans toute la grossiéreté des premiers âges, l'espéce étoit déjà vieille, et l'homme restoit toujours enfant (159–60).

> Let us conclude that, wandering in the forests, without industry, without speech, without dwelling, without war, without relationships ... [Savage man] If by chance he made some discovery, he was all the less able to communicate it to others because he did not even know his own children. Art perished with its inventor ... Since each one always began from the same point, centuries went by with all the crudeness of the first ages; the species was already old, and man remained ever a child (57).

If man remained ever a child, then there had never been, nor are there, any natural fathers/patriarchs. By making the family an artificial, cultural construct, Rousseau can powerfully attack the Filmerian position to which, as we saw, Locke's anthropological story was quite vulnerable. Rousseau concludes: "Au lieu de dire que la Société civile dérive du pouvoir Paternel, il falloit dire au contraire que c'est d'elle que ce pouvoir tire sa principale force: un individu ne fut reconnu par le Pere de plusieurs que quand ils restérent assemblés autour de lui ..." (182).[39] Not only does he

[39]"Instead of saying that civil society derives from paternal power, on the contrary it must be said that it is from civil society that this power draws its principal force. An individual was not recognized as the father of several children until the children remained gathered about him" (73).

negate the natural primacy of the father, but Rousseau establishes, I think, a much more radical premise regarding the child: his errant nature. The child "naturally" does not belong to a family but is essentially homeless. This homeless child is the philosophical counterpart to the child heroines and heroes of the eighteenth-century realist novel.

Rousseau: Childhood as Suffering

Rousseau's reversal of the order of family and society, rejecting both the animal analogy and Buffon's authority, is his most brilliant outrage—not a mean distinction in his oeuvre. It is stunning not only in its sheer rhetorical brilliance but, of course, in its utter disregard for common sense. Through this reversal he negates any natural power that is the patriarch's due. And natural here is both normative as in what the king should have by right—Filmer's position—and the norm in nature, in the state of nature, before civilization and the invention of the institutions of politics and government; that is, in the anthropological sense of Locke's patriarch.

Locke's consensual story is vulnerable to the enduring vestiges of patriarchal power; his strategy, however, is to separate the public and the private spheres. Even if a father should still rule his family with an iron fist, the monarch has no license for tyranny. A commonwealth is founded on the consent of its members, separate individuals who contracted to form a beneficent society that would serve their interests. Early feminists in Britain argued against male tyranny using Locke's writings. But Locke himself, at least in the political treatises, is more concerned with the political than the domestic sphere. He does not argue against the natural domestic power of the patriarch, though, as we saw, he tones that power down by making it the result of the care the father is obliged to provide for the child. By refusing the ancient identification of the Prince with the father, Locke was attempting to vitiate the ancient patriarchal theory of political rule given fresh justification by Filmer.

Rousseau transforms the type of analogy between family and state; first, he discredits the natural supremacy of the father/king; second, he valorizes the family in the Golden Age as the sole realm of open souls and authenticity; finally, he rails against the modern family, corrupted, as we will see, by the mother. Patriarchal power is not natural: the family, Rousseau radically opines, is a result of free choice. By discrediting the natural dominion of the patriarch, Rousseau overturns one of the most enduring of political myths: that the Prince's power is analogical to the father's. Paradoxically, however, Rousseau's ultimate intention is not at all to separate the home and the polity. It is rather to establish the virtuous household as the only remedy for the corruption of human nature wrought by civilization, and therefore, as the perfect germ and model for the nation. More than any other political philosopher before him, Rousseau promotes love as the proper political emotion; familial love becomes the model of the relation between citizen and nation. By praising an idealized family, however, Rousseau sets the stage for his disappointment with the modern family, whose corruption loosens the ties between child and home.

This brief account will be unpacked below. It gives the outline, however, of a new French national narrative in which the child's suffering acquired political signification. The pity the child elicited epitomized Rousseau's politicization of suffering. "Rousseau's teaching on compassion," argues Allan Bloom, "fostered a revolution in democratic politics, one with which we live today. Compassion is on the lips of every statesman . . . Rousseau singlehandedly invented the category of the disadvantaged. Prior to Rousseau, men believed that their claim on civil society has to be founded on an accounting of what they contribute to it. After Rousseau, a claim predicated not on a positive quality but on a lack became legitimate for the first time."[40] Losing his consanguinary home, the child was homeless. The stage was now set for the identification of nationalism and the care of the suffering child. The nation defended the child, ameliorated his anguish, and provided him with a home. In this role—as home—the state intrudes itself into the private sphere. During the decade of the 1790s, notes Marc Shell, "the idea of national regeneration through common lactation, already a theme in American politics, was literalized at national milk-drinking rituals . . . The revolution also realized a French national siblinghood by means of the Terror. A latter day rite of profession in the secular sphere, the Terror transformed hundreds of children into orphans by executing their parents and then ritualistically adopting them as members of the new nation of Frenchmen."[41]

The Revolution's redemption of the suffering child allegorized the revolutionaries' view of history: "The past was the ancien régime, the epoch of man corrupted by society, and in destroying it the Revolution opened up the way to regeneration."[42] Ironically, as François Furet concludes, "It is by virtue of the project of regeneration that the Revolution belongs to Rousseau," for Rousseau himself regarded regeneration with great pessimism. Judith Shklar emphasizes that although "Emile is brought up *not* to repeat the errors of the species . . ." and although "Each new-born child is a new opportunity and a new hope . . . [being] naturally at birth in a state of pure potentiality . . ." nevertheless, "The tragic tone of the early pages of *Emile* arises from the knowledge that the promise will not be fulfilled and that the swaddling clothes will inevitably strangle

[40]Allan Bloom, intro. to *Emile*, 18.

[41]Marc Shell, *Children of the Earth: Literature, Politics, and Nationhood* (Oxford: Oxford University Press, 1993), 143–4.

[42]François Furet, "Rousseau and the French Revolution," in *The Legacy of Rousseau*, ed. Clifford Orwin and Nathan Tarcov (Chicago: University of Chicago Press, 1997), 179.

each new child's intelligence and goodness."[43] Rousseau's pessimism did not, however, prevent the French revolutionaries, like Robespierre, from adopting his language of fiery rebellion against the corruption of morals and the family caused by the *ancien régime* while they ignored his ever-present denunciation of the present, almost hopeless, state of bourgeois man.

Amour-Propre, Inequality, and the Fall of Child and Man

In Locke's consensual story, children represent a kind of a philosophical nuisance: because they lack reason, they cannot consent. Hence, the original commonwealth could not have been formed through the mutual consent of *all* of its members. Furthermore, it is far from sure, because children have different inborn characteristics, that all children, when they reach adulthood, will consent to and preserve the commonwealth. The problem which Locke does not address in what I termed his national narrative (the *Second Treatise*) is a contingency his educational manual allows: What if "the Characters of [the child's] Mind . . . as he grows up, [and] the plot thickens" are not consistent with consent to civil society; what if "his *Predominant Passions*" are "fierce" and "cruel"?[44] Instead of the consensual adult that will perpetuate it, civil society might get a tyrant who will destroy it. That omission, as discussed above, is a fundamental error of Locke's narrative of the consensual commonwealth.

---

[43]Judith Shklar, *Men and Citizens: A Study of Rousseau's Social Theory* (Cambridge: Cambridge University Press, 1969), 36.

[44]See John Locke, *Some Thoughts Concerning Education*, in *The Educational Writings of John Locke*, ed. James Axtell (Cambridge: Cambridge University Press, 1968), 206–7.

There is a leap of faith in Locke's argument that Rousseau entirely rejects. Indeed children, even infants, are capable of tyranny and oppression when they learn how to impose their will on adults. Such an understanding of Rousseau's views militates against the facile and false "educational" interpretations of *Emile* as part of the Sixties philosophies of "anything goes." Rousseau does not glorify the actual child but rather idealizes childhood for its potential and rues its loss.

In *Emile*, Rousseau develops the theme of how the child initially uses his tears as his natural manner of pleading for help. Soon realizing that his tears serve to make the world servile to his wishes, the child begins to cry not for real needs but to gratify the desire to impose his will on adults. Rousseau's concern here, however, is deeper than that of a "how to" manual on raising one's child, for he uses the example of the child's tears to develop the crucial idea of how, even in an infant, *amour de soi* becomes *amour-propre*. This latter binary is a fundamental theme in both *Emile* and *l'Inégalité*. It is the germ of the fall from the happiness of equality and independence.

The child cries first to satisfy his natural self-love and desire for self-preservation (*amour de soi*). "L'enfant sent ses besoins et ne les peut satisfaire, il implore les secours d'autrui par des cris."[45] Only conscious of a single type of a "sensation de doleur," the child in the beginning stops crying when his needs are satisfied, the physical pain quenched. Realizing however that things that until then did not respond to him, now obey him through the intervention of

[45]Jean-Jacques Rousseau, *Emile ou De l'Éducation*, edited and annotated by Charles Wirz et Pierre Burgelin, in J. J. Rousseau, *Oeuvres complètes*, ed. Bernard Gagnebin and Marcel Raymond (Paris: Gallimard [Bibliothèque de la Pléiade], 1969 (1762)), vol. 4, 287. All following page references are to this edition. The English translation follows: "The child feels his needs and cannot satisfy them. He implores another's help by screams" (65).

adults, the child begins to crave this domination. His natural self-love soon turns into a desire to dominate others—things and persons confused—in order to satisfy his nascent vanity, his *amour-propre.* "Les prémiéres pleurs des enfans sont des priéres: si on n'y prend garde elles deviennent bientôt des ordres . . . Ainsi de leur foiblesse d'où vient d'abord le sentiment de leur dépendance, nait ensuite l'idée de l'empire et de la domination . . ." (287).[46] The child is separated from nature and "quickly learns that, for his life, control over men is more useful than adaptation to things. Therefore, the disposition of adults towards him replaces his bodily needs as his primary concern."[47] If he cannot master others, he will likely enslave himself to them to procure his needs. The master-slave dialectic is born.

Inequality thus comes into being when the child becomes dependent on others; that dependence is subtle, nefarious and inevitable. *Amour-propre* threatens the growth of every child, since once it takes hold "tout est perdu" (291). The Tutor will attempt to ensure that Everychild, Emile, will escape this corruption of his psyche. Ultimately, however, he will fail; "Emile brought up so carefully to be a man, leaves his rural abode, and he and his wife destroy their marriage in Paris,"[48] as Rousseau relates in *Emile et Sophie.* Emile's fall to the empire of opinion and inauthenticity repeats that of mankind whose fall from the state of nature into the slavery of civilization, vividly imagined by Rousseau in *l'Inégalité,* follows exactly the dynamic of the child's fall. The similarities between the two works have been observed by commentators. As Shklar puts it, "The *Discourse on Inequality* being the biography of 'man in general' and *Emile* that

---

[46]"The first tears of children are prayers. If one is not careful, they soon become orders . . . Thus, from their own weakness, which is in the first place the source of the feeling of their dependence, is subsequently born the idea of empire and domination" (66).

[47]Allan Bloom, intro. to *Emile*, 11.

[48]Shklar, 22.

of an imaginary child have the same structure, both are individual life stories."[49]

In *l'Inégalité*, probably his most eloquent composition, Rousseau offers a radical analysis of the degradation of man's nature as the result of inequality, the inevitable result of "uncontrolled" socialization. In the state of nature, man was solitary; hence, even if one man was stronger than another, the inequality lasted for as long as the weaker had to remain in the physical proximity of the stronger.[50] When people stayed together, however, as the result of their nascent interdependence once their needs exceeded what nature could provide, the new society was organized and based on unequal relations.[51] The natural inequality of intelligence and force, first limited, was magnified manyfold by the invention of agriculture and metallurgy and the ensuing division of labor.

Land was divided and property created. Slavery followed and wars erupted and societies were formed, not through consent, but deception: the rich convinced the poor to accept the fetters of law to create peace, turning theft into right: "Telle fut, ou dut être l'origine de la Société et des Loix, qui donnérent de nouvelles entraves au foible et de nouvelles forces au riche, détruisirent sans retour la liberté naturelle, fixérent pour jamais la Loi de la Propriété et de l'inégalité, d'une adroite usurpation firent un droit irrévocable, et pour le profit de quelques

[49]Shklar, 36.

[50]Cf. "Le plus fort n'est jamais assez fort pour être toujours le maitre, s'il ne transforme sa force en droit et l'obéïssance en devoir." Jean-Jacques Rousseau, *Du Contrat social*, edited and annotated by Robert Derathé, in J. J. Rousseau, *Oeuvres complètes*, ed. Bernard Gagnebin and Marcel Raymond (Paris: Gallimard [Bibliothèque de la Pléiade], 1964 (1762)), vol. 3, 354. All following page references are to this edition.

[51]For a precise explication of Rousseau's schema of man's fall from a first state of nature to a second and then to civil society, see J. Starobinski, intro. to *l'Inégalité*, LXII.

ambitieux assujétirent désormais tout le Genre-humain au tra-vail, à la servitude et à la misére."[52] I think that this reasoning explains why Rousseau was so fundamental not only to Kant's emphasis on the primacy of autonomy, but to Marx's later emphasis on the role of economic power as the agent of social domination. And one does not demean Foucault by emphasiz-ing that his magnificent, wide-ranging analyses of power rela-tions in society and his Enlightenment critique are but footnotes to Rousseau.

Rousseau's treatment of interdependence as the primary reason of inequality is deeper, however, than solely economic. Despite the well-known opening of the second part of the discourse ("Le premier qui ayant enclos un terrain, s'avisa de dire, *ceci est à moi*, et trouva des gens assés simple pour le croire, fut le vrai fondateur de la société civile"),[53] what forms civil society precedes and causes economic inequality. It is the birth of *amour-propre* that causes man to crave *préférences*, the preferential esteem that undermines equality. Rousseau links inequality essentially to the initial formation of intersubjective selfhood: that the other is part of the same. The self that has the other as an ele-ment—because of *amour-propre*—cannot, according to him, be authentic. It now wants "to seem" and not "to be." Human beings, once transparent to one another, now, through the developed faculties of memory and imagination, become obscured: "Etre et

---

[52]Rousseau, *l'Inégalité*, 178. "Such was, or should have been, the ori-gin of society and laws, which gave new fetters to the weak and new forces to the rich, irretrievably destroyed natural liberty, established for-ever the law of property and of inequality, changed adroit usurpation into an irrevocable right, and for the profit of a few ambitious men henceforth subjected the entire human race to labor, servitude and mis-ery." (70).

[53]"The first person who, having enclosed a plot of land, took it into his head to say *this is mine* and found people simple enough to believe him, was the true founder of civil society" (60).

paroître devinrent deux choses tout à fait différentes, et de cette distinction sortirent le faste imposant, la ruse trompeuse, et tous les vices qui en sont le cortége" (174).[54] Man is split: he becomes what cannot be divined. Obscured, insincere, he is also inauthentic.

The Lost Transparency

Transparency became an obsession of Rousseau; its loss, inseparable from the unhappy fall from the Golden Age of equality and independence. Simply put, transparency was that ability of men to read one another's heart before the corruption of civilization. Such loss of transparency forms the basis of his attack on the arts and sciences in his award-winning essay of 1750—showing Rousseau's utterly distinct mindset and presaging his break with the other *philosophes*:

> Avant que l'Art eut façonné nos maniéres et appris à nos passions à parler un langage apprêté, nos mœurs étoient rustiques, mais naturelles; et la différence des procédés annonçoit au premier coup d'œil celle des caracteres. La nature humaine, au fond, n'étoit pas meilleure; mais les hommes trouvoient leur sécurité dans la facilité de se pénétrer reciproquement, et cet avantage, dont nous ne sentons plus le prix, leur épargnoit bien des vices.[55]

[54]"Being something and appearing to be something became two completely different things; and from this distinction there arose grand ostentation, deceptive cunning, and all the vices that follow in their wake" (67).

[55]Jean-Jacques Rousseau, *Discours sur les sciences et les arts*, edited and annotated by François Bouchardy, in J. J. Rousseau, *Oeuvres complètes*, ed. Bernard Gagnebin and Marcel Raymond (Paris: Gallimard [Bibliothèque de la Pléiade], 1964 (1750)), vol. 3, 8. Henceforth, this work will be referred to as the *First Discourse*.

> Before art had fashioned our manners and taught
> our passions to speak an affected language, our
> mores were rustic but natural, and differences in
> behavior heralded, at first glance, differences of
> character. At base, human nature was no better, but
> men found their safety in the ease with which they
> saw through each other, and that advantage, which
> we no longer value, spared them many vices.[56]

Being and seeming were the same, not only rendering the individual authentic, but society more secure: Rousseau links trust to the ability of knowing the minds of others. The arts and sciences falsify language, reenacting the invasion of the one by the many, that obscured the transparency of the state of nature.

Rousseau was not the first to treat the theme of seeming and "masking." As Jean Starobinski sharply analyzes, "Le thème du mensonge de l'apparence n'a rien d'original en 1748. Au théâtre, à l'église, dans les romans, dans les journaux, chacun à sa manière dénonce des faux-semblants, des conventions, des hypocrisies, des masques."[57] Indeed, Fielding made the unmasking of hypocrisy and vanity the central province of his new "comic epic in prose," *Joseph Andrews*. The triumph of the pure Joseph over the machinations of Lady Booby; the farcical enactment of the uncovering of the hypocritical Parson Trulliber, who refuses to help the destitute with money but is generous with sanctimonious harangues—as well as the unmasking of the canting chaplain Thwackum and the

---

[56]J. J. Rousseau, *Discourse on the Sciences and the Arts*, in *Basic Political Writings of Jean-Jacques Rousseau*, trans. and ed. Donald A. Cress (Indianapolis: Hackett, 1987), 4. All following page references to the English translation are to this edition.

[57]Jean Starobinski, *Jean-Jacques Rousseau: La transparence et l'obstacle* (Paris: Gallimard, 1971), 14.

untruthful "philosopher" Square in *Tom Jones*—show that Fielding and others saw sham and pretense as vices characteristic of vulgar parvenus and hypocritical devouts. The virtuous are naturally virtuous; convention and masks are not an essential component of human nature. In the "age of reason," writes Alexander Welsh, "morals had been interpreted in terms of practice. In fiction, precepts were illustrated by example . . . [T]he reader [was invited] to "see" good or bad behavior and its consequences. . . ."[58]

There were, to be sure, others—notably Molière—who did not see masks as a failure of morality but as intrinsic to the human condition. Acting became a metaphor for life. Diderot, in his *Paradoxe sur le comedién,* gives one of the most influential accounts of this analogy. "The actor," writes Diderot, "has long listened to himself . . . [his] tears descend from his brain; those of the man of sensibility rise from his heart . . . [the actor] weeps like an unbelieving priest who preaches the Passion; like a seducer on his knees before a woman who he does not love."[59] With wonderful irony, Diderot illustrates the consummate actor's abilities, perfected after long practice, with actions that come naturally to many in real life. Diderot's linking of art and life, however, goes well beyond the actor's technical mastery of life's masks. The power and originality of Diderot's great *Le neveu de Rameau,* according to Lionel Trilling, lie in the nephew's performance of his own theory of man in society based on "his recognition of the systematic separation of the individual from his actual self."[60]

[58]Alexander Welsh, *The Hero of the Waverley Novels* (Princeton: Princeton University Press, 1992), 2.

[59]Denis Diderot, *Paradoxe sur le comedién,* in Diderot, *Oevres,* ed. André Billy (Paris: Gallimard [Bibliothéque de la Pléiade], 1951), 1010-11.

[60]Lionel Trilling, *Sincerity and Authenticity* (Cambridge: Harvard University Press, 1971), 31.

Diderot's narrative, which burst upon Goethe, when it was shown to him by Schiller, "like a bombshell," recounts a fictional encounter in a Parisian café between the narrator, the *Moi* of the narrative, and the younger Rameau, referred to as *Lui*. The astonishing section of the dialogue in which Rameau mimics an operatic scene, incarnating one actor then another with stunning facility, portrays not the immorality of a man betraying his true self but the aesthetic beauty of an artist who transcends having one self. "The entrancing power of *Rameau's Nephew*," comments Trilling, "is rather to be explained [by its suggestion] that moral judgment is not ultimate, that man's nature and destiny are not wholly comprehended within the narrow space between virtue and vice" (32). Although *Moi* is careful to condemn the Nephew for the lack of his moral commitment, "Diderot the author of the dialogue gives us full licence to take the Nephew to our hearts and minds . . . as the liberty that we wish to believe is inherent in the human spirit" (32).

Rousseau, however, sees this condition of masked man under the sign of tragedy. The actor "gives himself in representation" for money, his talent, according to Rousseau, is "the art of counterfeiting himself."[61] The mask is no less characteristic of man than it is in Diderot's view, but it is an attribute of civilized man; hence, a perversion. Trilling observes that Rousseau was pivotal not only in the triumph of a national cult of sincerity but also in the rise of the modern ideal of authenticity. What matters to Rousseau is not only that one proves virtuous in being sincere with others, but that one be true to his own authentic "being," which cannot survive man's desire to seem otherwise.

[61]J. J. Rousseau, *Lettre à d'Alembert sur les spectacles* (Paris, Garnier-Flammarion, 1967), 163. The original French reads: "se donne en représentation."

Rousseau's view of authenticity underlies much of the current belief in an authentic collective identity that demands the recognition of others.

The Two Utopias and Education

How can one heal the wounds of civilized man and restore transparency among individuals? The road back to nature is not open; man has been socialized. "The alternatives are therefore not nature or society," notes Shklar, "but domestic or civic education."[62] Rousseau offers two utterly irreconcilable routes. Let man live completely for others or completely for himself: "Donnez-le tout entier à l'etat ou laissez-le tout entier à lui-même, mais si vous partagez son cœur vous le déchirez."[63] The harmony of the two routes is impossible, since men who follow them obey different masters: nature or society. "Forcé de combattre la nature ou les institutions sociales, il faut opter entre faire un homme ou un citoyen; car on ne peut faire à la fois l'un et l'autre."[64] Bernard Yack summarizes: "Thus one must either try to protect the growth of natural inclinations from social influence or make dependence on others so complete that concern for the community will override the natural voice of self-love within the individual. The former is the goal of private education as outlined in *Emile*; the latter is the

[62]Shklar, 5.

[63]J. J. Rousseau, *Fragments Politiques VI*, in Jean-Jacques Rousseau, *Oeuvres complètes*, vol. 3, 510. My translation follows: "Give him entirely to the state or leave him entirely to himself, but if you divide his heart, you tear him apart."

[64]*Emile*, 248. "Forced to combat nature or the social institutions, one must choose between making a man or a citizen, for one cannot make both at the same time" (39).

goal of public education,"[65] the central subject of *Du contrat social*.[66]

Shklar, who emphasizes the striking novelty of Rousseau's insistence that we must choose between man and citizen, observes that, according to him, "All our self-created miseries stem from our mixed condition, our half-natural and half-social state" (5). To the injured soul of civilized bourgeois man, Rousseau offers a choice between two utopias: "a recreated Golden Age" or the model of a "Spartan Republic." Rousseau frequently expressed his intoxication with the civic virtue of the ancient Greeks and Romans, in terms of which modern man was entirely lacking: "Un Citoyen de Rome n'étoit ni Caius ni Lucius; c'étoit un Romain . . . Ces deux mots, patrie et citoyen, doivent être effacés des langues modernes."[67] Rousseau's infatuation with republican virtue was intensely personal: as he mentions in the *Confessions,* it began with his early readings of Plutarch and occupied the heroic daydreams he indulged in as an apprentice and later.

Rousseau's Spartan man is not an attractive humanistic construct. Man must be so thoroughly "denatured," insists Rousseau, in becoming part of the republican collectivity, that the most basic of nature's voices in man—pity, *amour de soi,* family love—are completely stilled. In the new Spartan Republic, whose recreation is the project of *Du contrat social,* divided man will be healed by becoming a part of society. Each man will totally alienate all of his rights to the community, thus creating

[65]Bernard Yack, *The Longing for Total Revolution* (Berkeley: University of California Press, 1992), 55.

[66]As well as of his incidental treatises: *Considérations sur le gouvernment de Pologne* and *Projet de Constitution pour la Corse.*

[67]Rousseau, *Emile,* 249. "A citizen of Rome was neither Caius nor Lucius; he was a Roman . . . These two words, *fatherland* and *citizen,* should be effaced from modern languages" (40).

a new collective; indeed, the very nature of man's life changes radically: "Sa vie n'est plus seulement un bienfait de la nature, mais un don conditionnel de l'Etat."[68]

In the Spartan Republic, a citizen is utterly transparent to his fellow citizens but not, surprisingly, because *amour-propre* has been destroyed. On the contrary, the citizen gratifies his desire for glory through self-exhibition in festivals and athletic competitions. Hence, paradoxically, *amour-propre,* acts as a glue, each citizen needing the others' recognition of his valor. The emphasis is on a relation of the one versus the "all others." Private interests must be scrupulously prevented; otherwise, the growth of factions will threaten the unity of the General Will. Taylor comments that Rousseau "is at the origin of a new discourse about honor and dignity." He rejects the two traditional manners of regarding honor: the Stoic-Christian view which enjoins man to overcome any concern for the good opinion of others; and the aristocratic ethic of inegalitarian *préférences.* In their place, he extols the Greek conception of honor: citizens vied for mutual honors that were reciprocal and egalitarian.[69] Recalling our discussion in chapter one, however, I find Rousseau less motivated by what Taylor calls the politics of "equal dignity," than by how *amour-propre* that normally hides the within becomes the guarantor of transparency.

[68]Rousseau, *Du Contrat social,* 376. "His life is no longer a bounty of nature but a gift he has received conditionally from the state," in Rousseau, *The Social Contract,* trans. Maurice Cranston (London: Penguin, 1968), 79.

[69]Charles Taylor, "The Politics of Recognition," in Amy Gutman, ed., *Multiculturalism: Examining the Politics of Recognition* (Princeton: Princeton University Press, 1994), 47.

The Transparent Family

Citizenship is a matter of self-repression; the family, however, is the realm of open souls. Like the Spartan Republic, the family is not proper to man's state of nature. If Aristotle believed man to be naturally a political animal, Rousseau sees him as naturally solitary. As we saw, only dependence brought human beings together, created property and fixed dwellings. That was a fateful step, for, according to him, space created time, and not time space. For Locke, the latter was certainly the case since the family was natural. Human beings always took cognizance of one another, first in the family, then in society. As they spent time together, they gradually became aware that a common space, a commonwealth was advantageous to their protection and prosperity. Rousseau reverses all that. When interdependence replaces natural solitariness, men are forced to share a common space; time then underlies their new shared recognition and social memory embodied in language.

Rousseau accomplishes something much more fundamental to his argument, I think, by rejecting the natural family: he establishes that institution as a beneficent product of civilization, of human work and man's act of freedom. The creation of the family is a free action; man chooses to stay with his children after he decides to recognize them because not only language but love result from "common habitation":

> Les premiers développemens du coeur furent l'effet d'une situation nouvelle qui réunissoient dans une habitation commune les maris et les Femmes, les Peres et les Enfans; l'habitude de vivre ensemble fit naître les plus doux sentimens qui soient connus des hommes, l'amour conjugal, et l'amour Paternel. Chaque famille devint une petite Société d'autant mieux unie que l'attachement réciproque et la liberté en étoient les seuls liens. . . .[70]

[70]Rousseau, *l'Inégalité*, 168.

> The first developments of the heart were the effect
> of a new situation that united the husbands and
> wives, fathers and children in one common habita-
> tion. The habit of living together gave rise to the
> sweetest sentiments known to men: conjugal love
> and paternal love. Each family became a small soci-
> ety all the better united because mutual attachment
> and liberty were its only bonds (62–63).

This is a key passage in *l'Inégalité* that explains why
Rousseau rejects the "natural" family. The love that is born
within the family—conjugal and paternal—is a very special
kind of love. It consecrates a small society of authenticity and
freedom; it is a sentiment mediated and anchored by the presence, actual or prospective, of children; it is very different from
the love between the sexes that is a "corruption" of sexual
desire.[71] In nature, man simply desires; in society, he loves.
"Commençons par distinguer le moral du Physique," dissects
Rousseau.[72] Moral love is natural; physical love is a perversion
engineered by women who seek to "rendre dominant le séxe qui
devroit obéir." Again this perversion is a direct result of *amour-
propre*, which teaches man to seek those "préférences" which he
ignored in the state of nature, women profiting from this vanity
by fixing man's naturally wandering temporary desire "on one
single object."[73]

Familial love, however, which ties the family once its
members stay in the same locale, ennobles this exclusive sexual love. Unlike sexual love which, because of the constraints
of *amour-propre*, is not free, the love in the family is freely
given and shared by all. Why is such an interpretation of the

[71]That sexual desire is related to a reproductive imperative is, of
course, ignored by Rousseau.

[72]Rousseau, *l'Inégalité*, 157–8. "Let us begin by distinguishing between
the moral and the physical aspects of the sentiment of love" (56).

[73]Rousseau, *Discourse on the Origin of Inequality*, 56.

human family so important to Rousseau? Like society, the family is an artifice, Rousseau argues. But, crucially unlike society, it is the sole realm of socialized man not corrupted by the intervention of *amour-propre*, that fatal passion born of inequality and *préférences*, and whose manifestation is the obstruction of truth, the creation of the difference between seeming and being, the inner and the outer. In the family, observes Shklar, "It is the *absence* of strangers that allows one to say exactly what one thinks, to express all one's feelings in perfect confidence, and simply to be whatever one is . . . Self-sufficient and self-contained, [the family members] need no one but each other. Theirs is the only relationship free from *amour-propre*" (23). As with Montesquieu's idea of balancing the passions, Rousseau needed a new passion in the family to balance the destructive passion of *amour-propre:* that new passion, familial love, ensures authenticity of the self by preserving transparency.

Rousseau Accuses the (Bad) Mother

My use of the masculine pronoun to refer to the child in *Emile* is not accidental. Rousseau's educational theories are of course gender specific. Declaring that "Il n'est pas bon que l'homme soit seul. Emile est homme; nous lui avons promis une compagne, il faut la lui donner. Cette compagne est Sophie," Rousseau finally turns his attention to girls' education.[74] His views of girls and their education outraged Mary Wollstonecraft, who took him to task for thinking girls naturally weak, passive, and coquettish: "Why, then, does he say," demands Wollstonecraft, "that a girl should be educated for

---

[74]*Emile,* 692. "It is not good for man to be alone. Emile is a man. We have promised him a companion. She has to be given to him. That companion is Sophie" (357).

her husband with the same care as for an Eastern harem?"[75] Especially deploring Rousseau's demand that a wife be obedient to her husband even if he is wrong, Wollstonecraft condemns his emotionalism: "When he should have reasoned he became impassioned, and reflection inflamed his imagination instead of enlightening his understanding" (192). Yet, as Ruth Yeazell shows, even as British "writers of popular conduct books and philosophers alike long insisted on the importance of female modesty," that virtue that was supposed to confound Rousseau's erotic prescriptions, was itself "both highly eroticized and gendered."[76]

Wollstonecraft does not miss the mark in her assessment of Rousseau's lack of rationalism here; the opening syllogism quoted above is about the only logical proposition in Book V. Yet when Rousseau largely abandons logic, it is not quite because of his repressed lasciviousness as Wollstonecraft diagnoses. Public virtue, the formation of virtuous citizens is utterly inseparable in Rousseau's mind from the success of his blueprint for the family. One cannot be rational in constructing a sphere in which ties between the sexes, according to Rousseau, revolve around love and sex. After Emile and Sophie are married, for example, the grave tutor turns his attention to the couple's sexual life, advising Sophie, much to the chagrin of Emile, to withhold her favors from her husband so the flame of love will not be extinguished between them. What bathos! Can one imagine Socrates in Plato's *Republic* advising his interlocutors on their intimate lives? But perhaps it is in this part of *Emile* that one can best appreciate the sometimes unexpected consequences of the intertwining of the domestic and the political in nationalist thought.

[75]Mary Wollstonecraft, *A Vindication of the Rights of Woman* (New York: Penguin, 1992 (1792)), 191.

[76]Ruth Bernard Yeazell, *Fictions of Modesty: Women and Courtship in the English Novel* (Chicago: Chicago University Press, 1991), 5–8.

Rousseau's thoughts on girls' education in *Emile* are not enlightened, certainly not by Wollstonecraft's standards. However, he hardly deals women any new blows here. The idea that women are weak, coquettish, and should obey their husbands would not have raised eyebrows in mid eighteenth-century Europe, though that attitude was not held universally. It is not his attack on girls, but rather on mothers that will prove novel and devastating. In fact, it is Rousseau's charges against mothers that have not been much remarked on by feminist critics, beyond their interest in the consequences of Rousseau's advocacy of breast-feeding.

Rousseau accuses the modern mother of losing the family, that charmed space of love and transparency. As I pointed out above, Rousseau, in a very characteristic move, idealizes an ancient institution—in this case, the family in the Golden Age—in order to attack what he sees as a corrupt modern one. Before fully attending to his attack on the modern mother, however, I need to reexamine Rousseau's views regarding the situation of the child in the state of nature, before the family came together.

The child's situation is untenable: As we saw above in the section on the "Unnatural Family," Rousseau stresses that the males and females in "nature" did not stay together after their *société*, even for the benefit of what Locke called their "young ones." How is it that the infants will survive, then? When he confronts this question, Rousseau makes an uncharacteristically hasty, offhanded, almost shy remark that "La mere allaitoit d'abord ses Enfans pour son propre besoin; puis l'habitude les lui ayant rendus chers, elle les nourrissoit ensuite pour le leur."[77] What is this "besoin" that the mother first feels? Does she enjoy suckling her infants; is such an activity pleasurable to her; what is the nature of this pleasure? Rousseau does not elab-

[77]Rousseau, *l'Inégalité*, 147. "The mother at first nursed her children for her own need; then, with habit having endeared them to her, she later nourished them for their own need" (48).

orate. He will take up again the politics and erotics of the maternal breast in *Emile* eight years later, but his Oedipal longing for, and unfinished business, with his mother—who died in childbirth—is here perhaps at its most unconscious.

Be that as it may, such a need to nurse would detract from the initial absolute solitariness of the race crucial to his prelapsarian argument, and Rousseau ignores any implications of this "endearment." Reverting instead to his earlier main theme, he stresses the ephemeral nature of such an attachment between children and mother: "Sitôt qu'ils avoient la force de chercher leur pâture, ils ne tardoient pas à quitter la Mere elle même . . ." (147).[78] Rousseau is careful to avoid transforming this woman who suckles, fulfilling a biological function, into a mother. Despite the fact that he refers to her as "mère," it is clear that she only becomes a human mother, a moral mother, in the bosom of the family. Still, it does seem from his language above—her children becoming "dear" to her—that she develops feelings for her children before their male progenitor, and later, father.

Even so, these sentiments are inferior to the familial love that will be born later. In fact, the children's own attachment to the mother is solely alimentary: not only do they leave her as soon as they can obtain their own nourishment, soon they cannot even recognize her or one another, "Et comme il n'y avoit presque point d'autre moyen de se retrouver que de ne pas se perdre de vûe, ils en étoient bientôt au point de ne pas même se reconnoître les uns les autres" (147).[79] The choice of "pâture" emphasizes Rousseau's alacrity to immerse the children back in natural man's animal-like solitariness.

Rousseau does more than differentiate the physical mother from the moral one; he remarkably distinguishes, in our modern

[78]"Once they had the strength to look for their food, they did not hesitate to leave the mother herself" (48).

[79]"And since there was practically no other way of finding one another than not to lose sight of one another, they were soon at the point of not even recognizing one another" (48).

parlance, "sex" from "gender." After the family is formed, the father recognizing his children who now remain "autour de lui," each family becoming "une petite Société," a new division of labor ensues based on gender roles:

> Et ce fut alors que s'établit la premiére différence dans la maniére de vivre des deux Séxes, qui jusqu'ici n'en avoient qu'une. Les femmes devinrent plus sedentaires et s'accoutumérent à garder la Cabane et les Enfans, tandis que l'homme alloit chercher la subsistance commune (168).

> And it was then that the first difference was established in the lifestyle of the two sexes, which until then had had only one. Women became more sedentary and grew accustomed to watch over the hut and the children, while the man went to seek their common subsistence (63)

This new division of labor is not as evil as the later economic one. Still, both man and woman lose some of their original ferocity and vigor. Humanity is not such a loser, however. As we have seen above, man and woman have just created the only social milieu in which a human being is both spontaneous and free: "Une petite Société d'autant mieux unie que l'attachement réciproque et la liberté en étoient les seuls liens."[80] Familial love excludes any domination.

Emile offers the royal road to the recreation of that Golden Age of familial love: It describes how a child must be educated against society, in isolation from and rejection of all prevailing customs and opinions. Emile, after the successful conclusion of his education, reunited with Sophie, is ready to found a family whose members enjoy mutual complete self-expression mediated by familial love. But why is Rousseau's educational treatise

[80]Rousseau, *l'Inégalité*, 168.

needed at all; why does not this Golden Age utopia last; why must Emile be educated by a non-consanguineous tutor away from his own family?

It is because the mother abandons her crucial duty. In a manner of speaking, Rousseau saw the Golden Age utopia as a utopia of breast-feeding: the injury to the natural order that follows a mother's abdication of her responsibility is truly astounding:

> Tout vient successivement de cette prémiére déprivation; tout l'ordre moral s'altére, le naturel s'éteint dans tous les cœurs; l'intérieur des maisons prend un air moins vivant; le spectacle touchant d'une famille naissante n'attache plus les maris, n'impose plus d'égards aux étrangers... l'habitude ne renforce plus les liens du sang; il n'y a plus ni péres ni méres, ni enfans, ni fréres ni sœurs; tous se connoissent à peine, comment s'aimeroient-ils?[81]

> Everything follows successively from this first depravity. The whole moral order degenerates; naturalness is extinguished in all hearts; home life takes on a less lively aspect; the touching spectacle of a family aborning no longer attaches husbands, no longer imposes respect on strangers ... habit does not strengthen the blood ties. There are no longer fathers, mothers, brothers, or sisters. They all hardly know each other. How could they love each other?[82]

Rousseau's language here repeats the language of *l'Inégalité* describing the relation of mother and progeny in the state of nature before the family: by not breast-feeding, the mother causes, so to speak, the regression of the human race. Ties revert to being ephemeral. The family disintegrates. When domestic

---

[81]Rousseau, *Emile*, 257–8.
[82]Rousseau, *Emile*, trans. Allan Bloom, 46.

order is destroyed, natural order follows. Unable, because already socialized, to return to the state of nature, man is lost.

The breast is political because it is contested: men or children; strangers or family; libertines in the city or future citizens at home, the woman has to decide who enjoys it. Schama describes "the moral politics of the bosom," which contrasted a "view of the bosom as either a sensual enticement, half-exhibited in fashionable décolletage, or as a natural gift offered in candid abundance from mother to child." Clearly, husbands must have contributed to the decline in nursing. In her *Avis aux Mères qui veulent nourir* (1767), Marie-Angélique Rebours "blamed male resentment of the interruption of their sexual habits and criticized men who became violently jealous or incensed against the presence of crying babies."[83]

Rousseau, however, underplays the Oedipal jealousy, presenting fathers as both dupes and victims. Women manipulate fathers into "telling" them to abandon breast-feeding: "J'ai vû quelquefois le petit manége des jeunes femmes qui feignent de vouloir nourrir leurs enfans . . . Un mari qui oseroit consentir que sa femme nourrit son enfant seroit un homme perdu. L'on en feroit un assassin qui veut se deffaire d'elle. Maris prudens, il faut immoler à la paix l'amour paternel. Heureux qu'on trouve à la campagne des femmes plus continentes que les vôtres! Plus heureux si le tems que celles-ci gagnent n'est pas destiné pour d'autres que vous!"[84] Linking the mother's rejection of nursing and cuckoldry, Rousseau hammers in the theme of the hapless

---

[83]Simon Schama, 147.

[84]*Emile,* 256. "I have sometimes seen the little trick of young women who feign to want to nurse their children. . . . A husband who dared to consent to his wife's nursing her child would be a man lost. He would be made into a murderer who wants to get rid of her. Prudent husbands, paternal love must be immolated for the sake of peace; you are fortunate that women more continent than yours can be found in the country, more fortunate yet if the time your wives save is not destined for others than you!" (45)

husband also betrayed by that erotic force that destroys the domestic sphere.

Fathers abandon their paternal duties because denatured mothers kill the love in them when they destroy the hearth:

> Ne nous étonnons pas qu'un homme dont la femme a dédaigné de nourrir le fruit de leur union dédaigne de l'élever ... Les enfans éloignés ... porteront ailleurs l'amour de la maison paternelle, ou pour mieux dire, ils y rapporteront l'habitude de n'être attachés à rien. Les fréres et les sœurs se connoitront à peine. Quand tous seront rassemblés en cérémonies, il pourront être fort polis entre eux; ils se traitteront en étrangers (262).

> Let us not be surprised that a man whose wife did not deign to nurse the fruit of their union does not deign to raise him ... The children, sent away ... will take the love belonging to the paternal home elsewhere, or to put it better, they will bring back to the paternal home the habit of having no attachments. Brothers and sisters will hardly know one another. When all are gathered together for ceremonial occasions, they will be able to be quite polite with one another. They will treat one another as strangers (49).

Gone are the transparency and openness of souls. The danger is more than that brothers and sisters will not love one another; it is that they may love one another in the wrong way: incest, clearly probable in the state of nature, may recur when siblings cannot recognize one another. What calamities do not follow from the mother's depravity?

Woman is condemned twice by Rousseau: She creates herself the "seul objet" of man's desire, perverting natural man from his errance. The family, the social result of this perversion, is, however, a potential glory for her. The latter is a charmed circle, as we saw, in which the nefarious effects of *amour-propre* are excluded and transparency of hearts can reign. But seduced by society, the woman does not maintain her family principle. As a coquette in society, she incarnates the fatal preoccupation with appearing not what she really is; thus, she lays waste the only locale of authenticity and freedom. She, the linchpin of the family, betrays her most precious creation. This is why Emile—Everychild—has to be raised away from his family: the father may also be bad; indeed, most often he is. But he owes his degradation to his wife's vanity, artifice, and neglect.

Locke feared that civil consensual society would be corrupted by the bad father/patriarch. Rousseau, in *l'Inégalité*, constructed an argument that refuted any patriarchal claim. However, when he considers the corruption of the family in *Emile*; when he looks for what caused and continues to cause, the corruption of current French and European civilized society, Rousseau blames the bad mother. This is a stunning reversal which has not been remarked by feminist critics of *Emile*, who, following the example of Wollstonecraft in *A Vindication of the Rights of Woman*, continue to focus their attacks on Rousseau's differential education for Sophie as well as to stress the influence of Rousseau's theories about breast-feeding.[85]

There were, to be sure, valid reasons for decrying the decline in nursing. "In Paris the lieutenant of police, Lenoir," reports Schama, "thought that perhaps only one thirtieth of mothers of the twenty

---

[85]In *The Sexual Contract*, Carole Pateman emphasizes the wife's subversive sexual role in *Emile*, and the importance the Tutor attaches to Emile's learning to enforce his rule on Sophie. Nancy Armstrong, following Althusser, observes in *Desire and Domestic Fiction*, that the logic of Rousseau's *Social Contract* is to constitute the parties it is supposed to regulate. Similarly, she argues, the novel redefines the lives of its readers, mostly women. It influences what they see as being happy or free. Neither critic, however, examines Rousseau's condemnation of the political consequences of the mother's misdeed. Pateman particularly faults Rousseau for consigning woman solely to the private sphere.

thousand babies born each year nursed their own babies . . . Others who could afford it had wet nurses come to their homes or sent their infants to the *Faubourgs*. But the vast majority of modest and poor homes [relied on official] traveling agents—the *meneurs*—to find village wet nurses in the country-side . . . For every one in two babies sent away in this manner, village wet-nursing was a death warrant . . ." (145–6). And Rousseau was not the only popular writer to advocate breast feeding. Beaumarchais enlisted his Figaro as a *porte-parole* for the cause, proposing to donate the proceeds from *Le Mariage de Figaro* to the establishment of "An Institute of Maternal Welfare" that would provide subsidies to poor mothers so they may be able to nurse.

Nor was Rousseau the first to connect mothers' spurning of nursing and the threat of depopulation. Advocates of breast-feeding emphasized how "its reduction of infant deaths would enable France to escape the threat of depopulation (always on the official mind)."[86] Characteristically, however, Rousseau gives that stock nationalist concern a moralistic cast fusing the domestic and the national:

> Non contentes d'avoir cessé d'alaiter leurs enfans, les femmes cessent d'en vouloir faire . . . Cet usage ajoûté aux autres causes de dépopulation nous annonce le sort prochain de l'Europe. Les sciences, les arts, la philosophie et les mœurs qu'elle engendre, ne tarderont pas d'en faire un desert (256).

> Not satisfied with having given up nursing their children, women give up wanting to have them . . . This practice, added to the other causes of depopulation, presages the impending fate of Europe. The sciences, the arts, the philosophy, and the morals that this practice engenders will not be long in making a desert of it (44–5).

[86]Schama, 146.

Here the twain meet. The desolation of society through the arts and the sciences matches the corruption of the family caused by the mother who refuses to nurse. Rousseau identifies the mother as the fifth column that allows the intrusion of the civilized artificial into the domestic authentic. By allowing the erotic to triumph over the fecund, the mother reenacts what the sciences and the arts wreak: the destruction of transparency, of morality and of society.

Rousseau emphasizes children's suffering as a result of the family's failure. In *Emile*, mothers neglect their duty in order to indulge the pleasures of the city, forgetting the cruel treatment to which their children will be delivered:

> Ces douces méres qui débarrassées de leurs enfans se livrent gaiement aux amusement de la ville, savent-elles cependant quel traitement l'enfant dans son maillot reçoit au village? Au moindre tracas qui survient on le suspend à un clou comme un paquet de hardes, et tandis que sans se presser la nourrice vaque à ses affaires, le malheureux reste ainsi crucifié ... J'ignore combien d'heures un enfant peut rester en cet état sans perdre la vie, mais je doute que cela puisse aller fort loin. Voila, je pense, une des plus grande commodités du maillot (255).

> Do they know, these gentle mothers who, delivered from their children, devote themselves gaily to the entertainments of the city, what kind of treatment the swaddled child is getting in the meantime in the village? At the slightest trouble that arises he is hung from a nail like a sack of clothes, and while the nurse looks after her business without hurrying, the unfortunate atays thus crucified ... I do not know how many hours a child can remain in this condition without losing its life, but I doubt that this can go on very long. This is, I think one of the great advantages of swaddling (44).

A jeremiad and a requiem for the dead child, Rousseau's language is denunciatory, elegiac, sardonic. French revolutionary nationalists, when they accuse Marie-Antoinette of being a bad mother and wife will prove far less humorous.

Rousseau's analyses, both of the education of Emile and the fall of mankind into mastery and slavery, put the child at the center of the new national narratives of suffering and regeneration. But before the child was identified to be the solution to national decadence, he had to become the locus of *ancien régime* tyranny and moral corruption: it was Rousseau who discovered the suffering child, whose agony he defined under the sign of homelessness. With the father a cuckold, the mother a coquette, Rousseau brands the modern family as perverse, unpatriotic. By emphasizing the failure of the modern family to restore transparency and heal modern man, Rousseau establishes the need for a national father, the final step in his new correspondence between family and nation.

Restored Transparency, or, the Return of the (National) Father

At the height of his celebrity, after winning the Dijon Academy's prize, Rousseau composed an operetta in the style of Italian opera buffa which he admired. The operetta, *Le Devin du village*, was performed twice in front of the king and queen at Fontainebleau.[87] In this enormously successful work, Rousseau dramatizes a theme which, more than any other, unites all of his disparate, and often contradictory, works: the longing for

[87]On 18 & 24 October 1752. Louis XV, who claimed that he didn't like the music, continued to sing the operetta's arias all day long "avec la voix la plus fausse de son royaume." The king's influential mistress, Mme. de Pompadour, even played the role of Colin (!) in one of the performances at Bellevue.

transparency. The shepherdess Colette, upset because her lover, Colin, has left her, complains:

> J'ai perdu tout mon bonheur;
> J'ai perdu mon Serviteur;
> Colin me délaisse.[88] (1099)

No need to worry; the "serviteur" will not tarry in begging her forgiveness.

Wondering why Colin runs away from her now even as he used to pursue her "tant autrefois," Colette seeks the help of the village soothsayer, or *Devin* who, she says, "sait tout/ Il saura le sort de mon amour" (1100). The *Devin* assures her that even though Colin has been unfaithful, "Pourtant il vous aime toujours." The *Devin* knows this, and is able eventually to unite the lovers, because, as he tells Colette, "Je lis dans votre cœur, et j'ai lu dans le sien" (1100). At the end of the operetta, the entire village celebrates the happy return of Colin to Colette, and the defeat of the "riche Demoiselle" who has seduced him for a while with her expensive gifts. Without the *Devin*, Colette would have been deceived by appearances—that Colin is courting the "riche Demoiselle"—into concluding falsely that he loves the Demoiselle. She would have missed the inner truth of Colin's heart. The *Devin* is one of a recurring type in Rousseau: all male, all older. Endowed with the ability to read the hearts of others, they use this preternatural power to repair tarnished social relations; for the loss of transparency is at the heart of social disintegration, at home or in the republic.

---

[88]Jean-Jacques Rousseau, *Le Devin du village*, edited and annotated by Jacques Scherer, in J. J. Rousseau, *Oeuvres complètes*, ed. Bernard Gagnebin and Marcel Raymond (Paris: Gallimard [Bibliothèque de la Pléiade], 1961 (1752)), vol. 2, 1099.

Rousseau cast the loss of transparency as the crucial moment of the loss of both his own childhood and the happy child-like Golden Age of humanity. Not surprisingly, transparency is child-like in Jean-Jacques's autobiography. In the *Confessions*, Rousseau relates how M. and Mme. Lambercier, his guardians at Bossey, unjustly punish him because they mistakenly believe he had broken Mme. Lambercier's comb. Appearances, however, are squarely against the young Rousseau. And it is this separation of the reality he knows and feels, and the appearances that speak against him to the usually "gentle" and "highly reasonable" guardians that come to have the power of an original sin to Rousseau. "Le maléfice de l'apparence," writes Starobinski, "la rupture entre les consciences mettent fin à l'unité heureuse du monde enfantin."[89] This outrage, Rousseau laments, marks the point where "memory of childhood's delights stop short . . . we [he and his cousin] no longer looked on them [the Lamberciers] as gods who read our hearts . . . we began to be secretive, to rebel, and to lie."[90] Echoing Augustine, Rousseau links transparency and virtuous community; the child Jean-Jacques and the citizen Rousseau suffer the same fall. For all of his life, Rousseau will give no quarter to modern society which, he believed, corrupted the sincerity and authenticity of its citizens, driving a wedge between seeming and being.

Just as the fall of the child to the empire of opinion, dependence, and *amour-propre* repeats that of man, so are they both to be cured by similar father figures. Lycurgus, by "denaturing" his fellow Spartans, overcame the first fall into *amour-propre* and inequality in society that destroyed the state of nature.

---

[89]Starobinski, 20.

[90]Jean-Jacques Rousseau, *The Confessions*, trans. J. M. Cohen (London: Penguin, 1953 (1781)), 30–1.

Restoring transparency, the Lawgiver transformed bad vanity into civic honor. The impossible difficulty of finding a Lawgiver who has Rousseau's qualifications in *Du contrat social* is matched by that of finding a suitable Tutor in *Emile*. That is not surprising: the Tutor in *Emile* repeats in the education of the individual what the Lawgiver accomplishes for the State; he restores the transparency and authenticity that the modern family could not.[91] Both figures are omniscient men who, replacing patriarchs, excluding mothers, and infantilizing men, are national fathers who *create* the virtuous nation by restoring transparency among individuals. The lost transparency of the childhood of man, of the nation, and of Rousseau himself—has been restored. Never was there a personal loss that created a more lasting political myth.

[91]Another such father figure in Rousseau's oeuvre is M. de Wolmar in *La nouvelle Héloïse*.

FOUR

THE CHILD'S STORY
AND THE RISE OF THE NOVEL

Did you not name a tempest / A birth, and death?

Shakespeare, *Pericles*

An offence against the Determination Regulations Page
Four, paragraph I c, viz.: 'Any thing or person seen to diverge
significantly from its or his own known identity is
committing an offence and may be apprehended and tested.'

Angela Carter,
The Infernal Desire Machines of Doctor Hoffman

The eighteenth-century novel narrates not the lives of the middle class, but of its suddenly independent, and troubled, homeless children. Richardson's Pamela is fifteen when her charitable employer Lady B. dies, forcing her to come into contact with her new "master." Writing "Dear Father and Mother, I have great trouble, and some comfort, to acquaint you with," Pamela begins her prodigious epistolary feat. Fielding privileges Tom Jones's story over Squire Allworthy's—and Sophia Western's over Squire Western's. Defoe narrates the lives of children who leave home, such as Robinson Crusoe, or children who have no homes, such as the bastard Colonel Jacque, the kidnapped Captain Singleton, or the abandoned Moll Flanders. Sterne's narrator opens his story with a querulous assessment of his own conception. While it is true that *Tristram Shandy* does not relate the life of the child Tristram, it self-consciously parodies the major story of eighteenth-century novels: it sets the dawn of the child Shandy's experience long before any plausible Lockean consciousness.

The sad experience of children is central to the rise of the novel. In a well-known letter to his Dutch admirer Johannes Stinstra, Richardson professed that *Pamela* developed from the model of his *Familiar Letters on Important Occasions*, a letter manual collecting various letters that "might be of Use to those Country Readers who were unable to indite for themselves."[1] Most of these letters deal with the hardships that children undergo as they leave their fathers' houses, and hence their original state of dependence. In choosing to compose *Pamela* in the form of letters written and received by a child who leaves her family, Richardson, I want to stress, makes a specific choice. He does not, for example, elaborate in a novel the story of letter LXXVI: "A humorous epistle of neighborly Occurrences and News, to a Bottle-Companion Abroad."[2] In his novels Richardson never narrates the experience of a *paterfamilias*, as Naguib Mahfouz, a seminal novelist to the rise of the Arabic novel, does in *Palace Walk*, the first volume of his Cairo Trilogy.[3] Al-Sayid Ahmad Abd al-Jawad is the pivot of his house and the center of this novel. He is at once a voluptuary and a stern father who enforces the strictest rules on his wife and children, trampling their lives: "He did not drink without getting drunk." Set in the historical period of Egypt's struggle for independence from Britain, the trilogy narrates his passions, his long shadow on the lives of his children, who inherit many of his characteristics, making his story fundamental to their own. Clarissa's father also blights her life, but we see him only as an obstruction to her life story, and not as a character in his own right.[4]

[1]*The Richardson-Stinstra Correspondence*, ed. William Child Slattery (Carbondale: Southern Illinois University Press, 1969), 28. This letter is dated June 2, 1753.

[2]Samuel Richardson, *Familiar Letters on Important Occasions* (London: Routledge, 1928 (1741)). Letter XXVIII, "From a Maid-Servant in Town, acquainting her Father and Mother in the Country with a Proposal of Marriage, and asking their Consents," for example, describes a Pamela-like experience.

[3]Naguib Mahfouz, *Palace Walk*, trans. Peter Theroux (Garden City, N.Y.: Doubleday, 1991).

[4]Indeed, Richardson's letter CLXXI, "To a Father, on the Loss of his Son, who died under Age," echoes a major plot element of Mahfouz's novel, the death of Fahmi, al-Jawad's middle son.

That is not to say that alternative stories to the child's leaving the father's house did not exist in eighteenth-century British society. Considering the enormous number of women who died in childbirth, for instance, one must wonder why the eighteenth-century novel shuns pregnant women almost entirely.[5] Conversely, as I argued in my reference to Mahfouz, the British novel does not tell the stories of the more independent patriarchs. So many novels relate the stories of younger persons that it is easy to forget that the power and freedom of fathers should arguably have made them more interesting heroes of novels. Odysseus, after all, and Launcelot were fathers. That the child is a privileged subject of the novel seems evident. Far from natural, however, is this fact; and one must ask, why did reality yield to the imagination, content to form, precisely under this story and no other? Why was the rise of the novel intertwined with the child's story?[6]

∾   ∾   ∾

[5]By contrast, Shakespeare treats the theme of a woman's pregnancy beautifully in, for example, *Pericles, Measure for Measure,* and *The Winter's Tale*. In the latter, Leontes's injustice is underscored by his ordering his wife, Hermione, to stand trial before her lying-in period has passed.

[6]Both Lennard Davis and J. Paul Hunter demonstrate the predominance of the wonderful in pre-novelistic discourse. Davis's originary "undifferentiated matrix of news/novel discourse" comprises sixteenth- and seventeenth-century news ballads that narrate recent events, albeit with a clear preference for the wonderful, the monstrous and the bloody; criminal biographical ballads that purport to relate the lives and last words of condemned criminals; as well as Boccacio-like bawdy intrigues (see Lennard Davis, *Factual Fictions: The Origins of the English Novel* (New York: Columbia University Press, 1983), Ch. 3). Surveying the cultural contexts that conditioned the reader of the early novel, Hunter observes the preponderance of the extraordinary in both journalism and other writing modes like the literature of Wonder published by men like Nathaniel Crouch and Nathaniel Wanley (see J. Paul Hunter, *Before Novels: The Cultural Contexts of Eighteenth-Century English Fiction* (New York: Norton, 1990)) (*Continued on next page.*)

Richardson narrates the lives of children; and *Pamela* and *Clarissa* each opens with a fearful child. The reader may object, however, that is it a stretch to call Pamela, Clarissa, and especially Robinson Crusoe "children." Before proceeding further in my analysis, it is important to define what I mean by "children" in this discussion. The task is difficult: how possible is it to define appropriate boundaries between childhood and adulthood? What are the boundaries related to: size? age? sexual maturity? involvement in labor?

I think that Locke's association of childhood with dependence is justified, even though he over-emphasizes financial dependence. Before the eighteenth century, the child was defined not in terms of its age, but in terms of its inferior social status. "The long duration of childhood," argues Philippe Ariès in *Centuries of Childhood*,

> as it appeared in the common idiom was due to the indifference with which strictly biological phenomena were regarded at the time: nobody would have thought of seeing the end of childhood in puberty.

---

[6](*Continued from previous page.*)
Yet, if the nascent novel retains a good deal of the prodigious and the wonderful—Crusoe's "Print of a Man's naked Foot on the Shore," Roxana's "unaccountable Surprize" when she runs into the daughter she wants to escape on board the trading ship upon which she had, quite by chance, been invited to dine (323), the episode of the Old man of the Hill in *Tom Jones*, what Pamela calls "witchcraft in the house . . . that horrid bull, staring me full in the face, with fiery saucer eyes . . . I believe, in my heart, Mrs. Jewkes has got this bull on her side" (157)—"wonder" has receded to the background and is no longer the hero. Although, for instance, the story of Mary Toft "giving birth" to seventeen rabbits in 1726 captivated London and sparked medical and literary controversy, such tales did not form the kernels of novels. The novel's central story is not "Of Pygmes and Dwarfs," nor "Of such Persons as have changed their Sex," still not "Of the Dead Bodies of some Great Persons, which not without difficulty found their Graves," it is rather the child's narrative. (For a lively account of Toft's episode, see Dennis Todd, *Imagining Monsters: Miscreations of the Self in Eighteenth-Century England* (Chicago: Chicago University Press, 1995).

The idea of childhood was bound up with the idea of dependence: the words "sons," "varlets" and "boys" were also words in the vocabulary of feudal subordination. One could leave childhood only by leaving the state of dependence.[7]

Like Locke, Ariès stresses the child's dependence, but he extends Locke's equation of dependence and childhood. Ariès's observations uncover childhood's metaphorical signification; before the eighteenth century, Ariès contends, childhood stood for a wide range of relations of subordination: that of servant to master, of wife to husband, of man to king, among others.[8] Chapter two investigated how master-apprentice relationships, crucial to the social cohesion of seventeenth-century London, were imaged as father-son kinships.

We, however, tend to think of childhood in terms of age and the stages of education. Pointing out the emphasis on education in the romantic *Bildungsroman*, Alan Richardson recently dismissed the importance of childhood in the "earlier novel [that] tended to dispose of childhood expeditiously (Tom Jones grows

[7]Philippe Ariès, *Centuries of Childhood: A Social History of Family Life*, trans. Robert Baldick (New York: Vintage, 1962), 26. Ariès's seminal views have come under recent attacks, most notably in Linda A. Pollock, Forgotten Children: Parent-Child Relations from 1500 to 1900 (Cambridge University Press, 1983). See especially her chapters 1 & 2 on Ariès's thesis.

[8]Scholars who follow Ariès disagree with some of his ideas; most notably, Linda Pollock gives evidence that even before the seventeenth century—the putative period where, according to Ariès, childhood emerges and the child is discovered in his "particularité enfantine"—parents were aware of their children as organisms different from adults. Yet, Ariès never argues that parents before the transformation did not recognize their children as different: as helpless creatures, as organisms that, in Pollock's words, "indulge in play," and "need care and protection . . . and guidance." His powerful thesis is that their childhood was not regarded as a period unique in their development, related to age and education and not to their dependence and inferiority.

from two to fourteen in two paragraphs)."[9] The lack of an interest in education in the early eighteenth century, he concludes, meant that childhood was short, since it was education that brought about "the modern conception of a unique, extended childhood." Richardson's view is, however, anachronistic; it applies our own persuasion of an age-defined childhood to a period during which childhood was defined in terms of a relation to the father, in terms of dependence and inferiority. That *Tom Jones* elides twelve years of Tom's childhood does not mean he is not a child at fourteen. It may rather signify the novel does not believe that something happens to the child—such as education—which changes his dependent status. To insist on this definition of childhood is not to quibble over semantics, for to divorce childhood from its older meaning, a meaning at the center of social relations in the Western world, is to assume a modern status for the child. As Schochet emphasizes, "The child-parent relationship was thus seen as standing for the relation between subjects and magistrates, servants and masters, students and teachers, laymen and clergy, wives and husbands, and *youths and elders* [my emphasis]" (73–4).

I underscore that last hierarchy to stress that, for my argument, I do not believe that it is helpful to make the distinction between a "child" and a "youth": as long as the age difference does not bring consent and freedom, I will continue to call him/her a child to emphasize that dependence; hence, coercibility. Furthermore, I avoid the term "adolescent" for two reasons: first, the association of childhood and asexual "innocence" is recent. Pamela is fifteen when she is wooed, threatened with rape, and then married. That we do not think of her as a sexually abused child—or a Lolita manqué if one subscribes to Fielding's

[9]Alan Richardson, *Literature, Education, and Romanticism: Reading as Social Practice 1780–1832* (Cambridge: Cambridge University Press, 1994), 7.

implicit view that it is she who slyly pursues Mr. B—does not mean she is not a child; it rather means that the novel seduces us into accepting her age's view that a child can be an object of sexual pursuit. Noting that the shock value of the recent Calvin Klein advertisements is due to the fact they suggest children are sexual, Walter Kendrick muses: "Our imaginary segregation of adolescents from children has led to the shunting of sex onto teenagers, who seem, in fiction anyway, to think about nothing else, except possibly drugs. In the process, we've drawn a line across childhood that's as rigid and false as the line the Victorians wanted to draw across every woman's wedding night: a babe in arms at sundown, a complete adult before sunrise."[10]

I also eschew the term "adolescent" because of its association with peer groups, which diminish the family's influence and "provide the primary context for adolescence," as John Neubauer persuasively argues.[11] These peer groups, which formed as "education shifted away from the home, and a growing proportion of adolescents came to spend ever longer years in school" (7), are not a feature of the period of the rise of the novel. The "psychosocial stage between childhood and adulthood" which Erik Erikson thought the secondary school allowed, was not granted to Clarissa, Moll, or Tom Jones.[12] In my sense of the term, then, "childhood" is longer since it merges with stages that today we would refer to under different terms.

Apprentices, as chapter two analyzed, did enjoy such a "psychosocial stage between childhood and adulthood." So did, according to Natalie Zemon Davis, the youthful members of

[10]Walter Kendrick, "From Huck Finn to Calvin Klein's Billboard Nymphets," *New York Times Magazine*, 8 October 1995, 86.

[11]John Neubauer, *The Fin-de-Siècle Culture of Adolescence* (New Haven: Yale University Press, 1992), 47.

[12]Erik Erikson, *Childhood and Society*, second ed. (New York: Norton, 1963), 262–3.

the Abbeys of Misrule, whose behavior, she contends, refutes "Aries's assertion that Europeans made no distinction between childhood and adolescence before the end of the eighteenth century."[13] If the good child of the guidebooks represents youth as a long childhood, the rebellious prodigal and Davis's youth groups (and Smith's London apprentices) show youth as a long adolescence. I emphasize, however, that the nascent novel treats solitary dependent "children," not boisterous groups of youth with a common "subculture."

Ariès argues that "the child" in its modern sense—as a distinct social and biological category—did not exist till the eighteenth century. Yet, in a curious twist, it seems it is not the child who was missing before then, but rather the adult. For the dependent subject, a child, is ubiquitous. The emergence of childhood as a separate stage of human development and a theme of narration is, I believe, inextricably intertwined with the modern citizen's desire to differentiate himself or herself from the dependent subject of absolutism, a subject long imaged as a child. If the bourgeois sought freedom, he also desired a discovery of the "real," age-defined child and a limited childhood. "In the course of the seventeenth century a change took place by which the old usage was maintained in the more dependent classes of society," writes Ariès, "while a different usage appeared in the middle class, where the word 'child' was restricted to its modern meaning."[14] In other words, the absence shifted from the adult to the child, or rather to the "child."

Drawing up a new consensual narrative of the nation, it is John Locke, who in his attempt to counter absolutist theories of political rule that figured the nation's subjects as subordinate children, gives the most salient formulation to the Enlightenment's evacuation of the child. The presence of children who could not have consented is a deficiency that Locke could not

[13]Natalie Zemon Davis, 107–8.
[14]Ariès, 26.

have neglected to address in his model of the state of nature; the dependence of childhood was and continues to be a justification for absolutist rule. Paradoxically, Locke's argument against political subjection in the *Second Treatise* is also an argument against childhood. His emphasis on growth and lack of reason underscores the negative value which children, or more precisely childhood, has for him. Similarly, Kendrick comments on the recent controversy surrounding the Calvin Klein billboards, arguing that it arose because the ads touched on our belief in the "cipher-child": an innocent, passive, vessel "waiting to be filled with adult corruption."[15] Our view of that emptiness is, however, positive since what is lacking is "adult" negative experience and not, as for Locke, positive reason. That childhood is an absence imagined and regulated, idealized and spoken for, is an enduring paradigm of Western representation.

It is precisely this Lockean absence, this legal and subjective gap, that the nascent novel makes its original subject. Fathers in the novel often want to impose their will on their children; and that absent figure resists. Clarissa's mother exhorts her that "It is owing to the good opinion, Clary, which your father has of you, and of your prudence, duty, and gratitude, that he engaged for your compliance, in your absence . . . and that he built and finished contracts upon it [the marriage to Solmes], which cannot be made void, or cancelled" (v. 1, letter 20). As Tony Tanner concludes, "in her father's eyes she is a veritable absence offering no impediments to any contracts he may choose to build and finish."[16] Reading Clarissa's absence in terms of the semiotics of the act of reading within the novel, Terry Castle argues that Clarissa's cipher is a space for her correspondents to decipher the "great 'Book of Nature' itself"—yet their inconclusive and interrupted

[15]Walter Kendrick, op. cit., 84–7. It is notable that corruption has replaced reason in this development.

[16]Tony Tanner, *Adultery in the Novel: Contract and Transgression* (Baltimore: Johns Hopkins University Press, 1979), 7.

readings, as well as ours, Castle insightfully observes, match the unruly form of the novel and the incomplete view of Clarissa's body in her coffin, with its "half-screwed down" lid.[17]

Narrating the Unspeakable: Escaping Subjects

The eighteenth-century novel relates the story of a child escaping the shackles of the patriarchal household; likewise, as I argued above, Locke's social contract grounds its consent in the rejection of the analogy between father and king, child and subject. The nascent novel and new theories of political rule based on rational social contracts—both products of the rising middle class—sought to redefine older views of human association. The enemy of both—the novel and contractual political theories—was patriarchalism, which "takes its bearings on human beings' original status as dependent children and so arrives at a government that treats grown men as children."[18] Drawing a parallel between paternal and political abuse of power in a comment on *Clarissa*, Samuel Johnson condemned heartless parental authority, which "may wanton in cruelty without control, and trample the bounds of right with innumerable transgressions."

For not only kings, but also fathers, of course, committed "abuses of that power" of rule, which Locke seeks to limit in the *Second Treatise*.[19] Yet if Locke attacks Stuart absolutism overtly, the eighteenth-century novel, by representing children escaping the father's house, performs a criticism of pre-capitalist political patriarchalism and enacts a conflict with the father that cannot be explicitly stated. As John Richetti states, "Crusoe's 'propension of

---

[17]Terry Castle, *Clarissa's Ciphers: Meaning & Disruption in Richardson's "Clarissa"* (Ithaca: Cornell University Press, 1982), 19.

[18]Nathan Tarcov, *Locke's Education for Liberty* (Chicago: University of Chicago Press, 1984), 7.

[19]Locke, 60.

nature' is the internalized ideology of capitalism . . . that dangerously dynamic aspect of capitalist ideology which must in the
context of the early eighteenth century be denied and sup-
pressed."[20] Leaving—usually escaping—the father's house is the
narrative device and structure that allegorizes the middle class's
desire for, and ambivalence towards, the destruction of the feudal
past and traditional values. The child's experience in the novel,
when he/she enters the world, whether to make money (Pamela,
Crusoe) or to escape tyranny and seek domestic happiness
(Clarissa, Tom Jones), fictionalizes the experience of the nascent
bourgeoisie: its need to enter into life economically and experien-
tially, to break received traditions and narratives.

Jürgen Habermas, in his investigation of the genesis of the
modern public sphere—the political realm of the modern
nation—comments on the intimate connection between the
rise of the epistolary novel and the bourgeoisie's political awak-
ening. Habermas links the development of the public sphere in
which bourgeois citizens relate to each other through the "free
exercise of reason" to that private sphere which is the matter of
the epistolary novel:

> The standards of reason and the forms of the "law"
> to which the public wanted to subject domination
> and thereby change it in substance reveal their socio-
> logical meaning only in an analysis of the bourgeois
> public sphere itself . . . The public's understanding of
> the public use of reason was guided specifically by
> such private experiences as grew out of the audience-
> oriented subjectivity of the conjugal family's inti-
> mate domain (*Intimsphäre*).[21]

[20]John Richetti, *Defoe's Narratives: Situations and Structures* (Oxford:
Oxford University Press, 1975), 25.

[21]Jürgen Habermas, *The Structural Transformation of the Public
Sphere: An Inquiry into the Category of Bourgeois Society*, trans. Thomas
Burger (Cambridge: MIT Press, 1989 (1962)), 28.

The progressive withdrawal of the family from society—as a result of the separation of the sphere of economic production, formerly fused to the family—contributed to the development of a new subjectivity. The family, Habermas argues, became idealized as the human realm "in which privatized individuals viewed themselves as independent even from the private sphere of their economic activity—as persons capable of entering into 'purely human' relations with one another. The literary form of these at the time was the letter." Yet, emphasizing the often illusory freedom the children, such as Clarissa, thought they had, Habermas affirms that, "the independence of the property owner in the market and in his own business was complemented by the dependence of the wife and children on the male head of the family" (47).

Ironically, the discourse at the heart of the bourgeoisie's public struggle for freedom is influenced by a literary form—Habermas emphasizes the epistolary novel—in which the public agents, the fathers, are tyrannical in the private sphere. Greeting Clarissa with "Undutiful and Perverse," her father informs her in a letter that she is to be removed to her uncle's moated house until after her marriage to Solmes. Such a "deserved confinement" is a fit punishment for "such a rebel as [Clarissa] has been of late." The language is overtly political, recalling Dr. Johnson's comment above. And the impending injustice echoes, say, the fate of Doctor Manette in *A Tale of Two Cities*: that arbitrary imprisonment inflicted on a middle-class man by a despotic aristocrat. Yet it is the children in the novel whose resistance in the domestic realm mirrors that of bourgeois men and fathers in the public political sphere.

That resistance is also a tacit national allegory. The suffering child entered the national calculus in Britain as he/she did in France: the eighteenth century saw an explicit attention to the national value of the homeless child, though less theoretically formulated perhaps than the French example. When the Seven Years War broke out in 1756, the philanthropist Jonas

Hanway rallied his merchant friends to found and endow the Marine Society, whose purpose was to round up vagrant and orphaned boys and send them into the Royal Navy. His success, as Linda Colley reports, "was stunning. By the end of the war, the society had well over 1,500 subscribers, and some 10,000 men and boys have been sent to sea."[22] More cognizant of the pragmatic potential of children than their symbolic signification, Hanway expressly linked the "education" of young homeless children and the national good:

> If we instruct these young persons in the fear of God, and at the same time teach their hands to war, and their fingers to fight in the cause of their country . . . we may hope such a conduct will draw down the mercies of heaven on this nation.[23]

I should like, however, to suggest that it is another kind of heavenly gift that underlies the intertwining of the child's novelistic privileging and the values the British nation saw as distinctly its own. God's gift to Britain was liberty. "The predominant view [in Britain]," contends Liah Greenfeld in her anatomy of five different types of European nationalism, "defined the nation in terms of the individual dignity, or liberties, of its members, and anything that inhibited the exercise of these liberties was antinational . . . Liberty became the distinguishing characteristic of Englishness."[24]

Thus, Lord Acton distinguishes coercive French nationalism from the English version, grounded in a "theory of liberty" which regards the nation as "the bulwark of self-government,"

[22]Linda Colley, *Britons: Forging the Nations 1707–1837* (New Haven: Yale University Press, 1992), 91.

[23]Jonas Hanway, *Letter to the Marine Society* (2nd ed., 1758), 4.

[24]Liah Greenfeld, *Nationalism: Five Roads to Modernity* (Cambridge: Harvard University Press, 1992), 74–7.

and not a "source of despotism and revolution."[25] Acton's version of a Whig national narrative, based on individual liberties and protective of "private rights," underlies the "public sphere" that Habermas associates with the "use of reason" within "a category of bourgeois society." That is, I propose that this rational freedom lies at the core of a national narrative whose potential universality occludes its British specificity. "English nationality," asserts Greenfeld, "was not defined in ethnic terms; it was defined in terms of religious and political values which converged on the rational—and therefore entitled to liberty and equality—individual" (65). As we saw in chapter one, Burke, for instance, grounds British liberty in an "*ancient* constitution of government." Nothing prevented other nations from aspiring to this model, granted, but England was "God's Firstborn."

Fielding's version of this political allegory is less than subtle. Informed that Sophie is locked up in her chamber by her father, Squire Western, in *Tom Jones,* Mrs. Western disdainfully cries that "*English* Women, Brother, I thank Heaven, are no Slaves. We are not to be locked up like the *Spanish* and *Italian* Wives. We have as Good a Right to Liberty as yourselves."[26] The squire angrily denounces all knowledge of the world acquired at Court, under the lordship of "a Parcel of Roundheads and Hanover Rats," the enemies of his Tory "Country Interest," only to have his sister admonish: "I wish . . . you would think a little of your Daughter's Interest: For believe me, she is in greater Danger than the Nation." Fielding's masterpiece is not only prescient in its historical consciousness, associating, albeit lightheartedly, the father's bumbling tyranny and his support of the failed Jacobite invasion of 1745, it also explicitly links Sophia's tribulations and Britain's.

[25]Lord Acton, "Nationality," in *Essays on Freedom and Power* (Boston: Beacon Press, 1948), 184.

[26]Henry Fielding, *Tom Jones* (New York: Norton, 1973 (1749)), 245–6.

Other novels, however, narrate a less transparent link between child and nation. I do not mean to suggest that the eighteenth-century novelists were somehow craftily promoting British supremacy; rather that the narrative kernel they unfolded, the child's story, advertised a yearning for freedom that was an essential element of a central British national narrative.

Just as individual capitalism underlies the idealism of Locke's individual liberty, I submit that the child's conflict with the father invokes a national unconscious, a view of the nation that equates "Englishness" with what on the surface appears to be a natural desire for liberty. The subject of the nascent novel, the child, acts out this double belonging, allegorizing both the struggle of the rising middle class and the ideal condition of British national subjecthood.

The individualism and subjectivity that underlie the novel are actuated in resistance to the father. Still, individualism, as Lawrence Stone cautions, "is a very slippery concept to handle. [In Locke's time] what is meant is two rather distinct things: firstly, a growing introspection and interest in the individual personality [what Stone calls "affective individualism"]; and secondly, a demand for personal autonomy and a corresponding respect for the individual's right to privacy, to self-expression and to the free exercise of his will within limits set by the need for social cohesion. . . ."[27] Stone's affective individualism—evidenced by "a series of almost wholly new genres of writing, the intimately self-revelatory diary, the autobiography and the love letter"—parallels Habermas's "saturated interiority" above.

What are the implications of the double meaning of individualism (introspection and autonomy) as it pertains to children?

[27]Stone, *The Family, Sex, and Marriage in England, 1500–1800*, 151.

Experience follows individualism in its double meaning; it has the attributes of introspection and cogitation—not only comprising what the senses receive, but how this sensory data is written in the individual narrative of the self. It also partakes of autonomy and ownership; the experience belongs to the person, who acquires it as an attribute of her individual, separate body and mind. Children encounter obstacles to their freedom and independence, obstacles that create necessary struggles, and hence, narratable stories. That is why the novel—*Pamela, Clarissa, Robinson Crusoe*—opens with the hero leaving his/her father's house, for in that house experience is circumscribed; the child can neither own nor interpret her own experiences.

Locke, whose "possessive individualism" is central to his mediation between self and society, individual and commonwealth, is attuned to the second type of individualism discussed by Stone. He seeks to limit the father's power over his children. In defending the child from the restraint imposed by financial bonds, it is this individualism that Locke upholds. Consonant with his well-known attention to the origin of property in the *Second Treatise*, Locke hastens to deny that financial dependence entails political subjection. He argues that although some have taken the father's power to control his children's inheritance as an indication of political dominion, the two are not related since the child when he/she comes of age is completely free to reject his father's power by refusing the patrimony. According to Locke, the father cannot even force his adult offspring to submit to the laws of the father's commonwealth since the adult can move to another commonwealth (Ch. VI, sec. 73).

Locke seems blind, however, to the psychological bondage that children might suffer. That subjection to the father, however, is foundational for the novel, which records the tension between the freedom that children desire, and the material and memorial enduring power of the father which is quite real, and which does not "drop off" with the "swaddling clothes."[28] In what follows, I look closely at *Robinson Crusoe* and *Clarissa* to explore the dialectics of subjectivity, experience, and guilt toward the father. It is no wonder that both novels unfold two themes: self-exploration and the fear of the father's anger. Both Crusoe's capitalist urgings and Clarissa's frustrated domestic happiness encounter the tyrannical power of the patriarch.

The Father's Tears

According to Ian Watt, Crusoe's "original sin" is "really the dynamic tendency of capitalism itself . . . Leaving home, improving on the lot one was born to, is a vital feature of the individualist pattern of life."[29] Still, perhaps we should look closely at Crusoe's own view that "my original sin" was "that of not being satisfy'd with the Station wherein God and Nature has placed [me] for not to look back upon my primitive Condition, and the excellent Advice of my Father." As Michael Seidel cautions, Crusoe's religious idiom of self-condemnation, as well as his attempts to reach a definitive rational description of his personal psychology, smacks of an after-the-fact attempt to bound his impulses and desires, most fundamentally his love of adventure and his "settlement anxiety," his congenital antipathy to settling in one place.[30] His self-reproof, however, should not

---

[28]Locke affirms that, "The bonds of this subjection [to the parents] are like the swaddling clothes they art wrapt up in, and supported by, in the weakness of their infancy: age and reason as they grow up, loosen them, till at length they drop quite off, and leave a man at his own free disposal." (31).

[29]Ian Watt, *The Rise of the Novel* (Berkeley: University of California Press, 1957), 65.

[30]Michael Seidel, *Robinson Crusoe: Island Myths and the Novel* (Boston: Twayne Publishers, 1991), 85.

blind us to Crusoe's most salient qualities: his wanderlust and his compulsive price-tagging of persons and things. Crusoe, famously Watt's "illustration of *homo economicus*," epitomizes the lust for both new experiences and for money. He goes back to sea, even after he suffers a storm and is taken a slave before escaping with Xury; and he cannot resist material accumulation—the scene in which he disapprovingly apostrophizes the money he finds on his island, "O Drug!" but then takes it anyway, strikingly represents the visceral attraction of capital to Crusoe.[31]

Crusoe seeks to define and censure his "propension[s] of nature" in the languages available to him, languages that are always profoundly historical, their metaphors and thematics explicating some but muddling many of his impulses and drives. The most recurring characterization of his "sins" is that of violating the father-son relationship. Such a transgression, both individual and societal, realist and allegorical, becomes the most encompassing frame of exploring his failures. Crusoe not only disobeys his father, he also abandons and rises above his economic station, rejecting a fundamental dictum of absolutist and patriarchal rule—that every creature has a God-given place in the Great Chain of Being. To disobey the father is indeed to unleash the multi-layered significance of this metaphor.

That he fails adequately to define his flaws, however, does not mean that Crusoe's feelings and self-condemnation are just cant. While it is certain he does not accept the nearly cosmic significance of violating a father's will that absolutist theology

---

[31]Leopold Damrosch insightfully comments on this scene that "[Crusoe's] personification of the coins as a "creature" ["whose life is not worth saving"] carries its traditional Puritan meaning: all earthly things are "creatures" which the saint is to restrain himself from loving too much. Only on Crusoe's island is it possible to despise money as a useless and indeed harmful drug." *God's Plot & Man's Stories* (Chicago: University of Chicago Press, 1985), 202.

and politics promoted, his guilt is difficult to dismiss. For before he gains experience and money, Crusoe must withstand the enormous pressure of his father's tears:

> [A]nd tho' he said he would not cease to pray for me, yet he would venture to say to me, that if I did take this foolish step, God would not bless me . . . I observed in this last Part of his Discourse, which was truly Prophetick, tho' I suppose my Father did not know it to be so himself; I say, I observed the Tears run down his face very plentifully . . . his Heart was so full he could say no more to me . . . I was sincerely affected with this discourse . . . and I resolv'd not to think of going abroad anymore, but to settle at home according to my father's desire. But alas![32]

Even Crusoe, who, with his "unconscious cruelty," is "the true prototype of the British colonist,"[33] feels a father's despondency. Still, as Richetti observes, "the destruction of the father implicit in [Crusoe's departure] seems to be what lies behind Crusoe's desire to go to sea, that is, to become rich above his father's station. To surpass him economically is in a real sense to destroy him" (26-7). The new experience and the death of the father go together.

Crusoe is a son willing to withstand the horror of a father's anger in his desire for the new, for subjectivity and ownership. Although he gains, eventually, by leaving his family, his case represents the powerful psychological bond the father exerts. During the first storm he experiences, Crusoe speculates that it is a punishment for his transgression: "I began now seriously to reflect upon what I had done, and how justly I was overtaken by the

[32]Daniel Defoe, *Robinson Crusoe* (New York: Norton, 1975 (1719–1720)), 7. All subsequent references are to this edition.

[33]James Joyce, a lecture in Italian delivered at the Università Popolare Triestina in 1912, from *Buffalo Studies*, I/1, v. 7, 1964, 11–13. Quoted in Defoe, *Robinson Crusoe*, 356.

Judgment of Heaven for my wicked leaving my Father's House . . . my Father's Tears and my Mother's Entreaties came now fresh into my Mind . . . and my Conscience . . . reproached me with the Contempt of Advice, and the Breach of my Duty to God and my Father" (8-9). The reprise of the theme of his father's tears, now a memory, strikingly illustrates the point I made regarding Locke's blindness: the abiding psychological power inherent in the father's position. Crusoe's action, however—leaving his family for a place in the world—is foundational for the eighteenth-century novel. What is a central theme is that the child leaves but remembers. In that he/she is different from the picaro.

For, if, as Watt observes, "Crusoe is not a mere footloose adventurer, and his travels, like his freedom from social ties are merely somewhat extreme cases of tendencies that are normal in modern society as a whole," (67) it is also true that Crusoe's constant memory of his father, taken up at numerous instances in the text, belies Watt's view that "Not too much importance can be attached" to the absence of "conventional social ties" for Defoe's heroes. Crusoe's obsessive memory of his father's advice and tears, a crucial theme of this novel, points to a collective guilt of the rising middle class toward the destruction of the close filial ties of earlier times, even as his transgression signifies a rejection of the strictures of the static Great Chain of Being and the patriarch's power. Christopher Flint appreciates that lack and insignificance are not synonymous when he notes that, "the visible absence of the family is a constituting element in Defoe's narrative strategy."[34]

Crusoe's disobeying his father's advice and coming out on top is not the only narrative device undercutting the patriarch. Defoe subtly undermines the father's manner of life; when the elder Crusoe calls his son "one Morning into his Chamber," to

[34]Christopher Flint, *Family Fictions: Narrative and Domestic Relations in Britain, 1688–1798* (Stanford: Stanford University Press, 1998), 119.

warn Crusoe against leaving the "middle Station of Life" the family enjoys, he is "confined by the gout" (5). As Seidel insightfully points out, "a gout-ridden father sitting in front of Crusoe in many ways cancels the appeal of the advice" (86). Yet despite the fact that, as Leo Damrosch notes, "Defoe's story curiously fails to sustain the motif of the prodigal," the narrative transmutes the father-son relation, adapting its metaphorical signification to Crusoe's new condition as an imperial exile.[35] Crusoe himself becomes a colonial Father, transmogrifying the figure of the child into that of the slave. The latter analogy is at the heart of the master-slave relation. It must be remembered that, as Ira Berlin puts it in *Many Thousands Gone*, "White supremacy demoted people of color not only to the base of civilization as savages but also to the base of the life cycle as children."[36] It is not surprising that slaves, with what Du Bois calls "the double consciousness of the Black person in a predominantly White society," accepted the father-son metaphor for slavery. Even the freed Olaudah Equiano, whose *Interesting Narrative* is set largely aboard mercantile and military vessels, writes of one of his masters, "[H]e was like a father to me; and some even used to call me after his name . . . Indeed I almost loved him with the affection of a son."[37]

Crusoe almost dreams his son/slave into existence, vividly displaying how supply he can move up the domination chain of the father-son metaphor. Agitated and exhausted with thoughts of escape to the mainland that set his "very Blood into a Ferment," Crusoe falls asleep and dreams that he

---

[35]Damrosch, 188.

[36]Ira Berlin, *Many Thousands Gone: The First Two Centuries of Slavery in North America* (Cambridge: Harvard University Press, 1998), 99.

[37]Olaudah Equiano, *The Interesting Narrative of the Life of Olaudah Equiano, or Gustavus Vassa, the African, Written by Himself*, ed. Vincent Caretta (New York: Penguin, 1995 (1789)), 92.

> Saw upon the Shore, two *Canoes*, and eleven Savages
> coming to Land, and that they brought with them
> another Savage, who they were going to kill, in
> Order to eat him; when on a sudden [he] . . . ran for
> his Life; and I thought in my Sleep, that he came
> running into my little thick Grove, before my Forti-
> fication, to hide himself; and that I seeing him . . .
> show'd my self to him, and smiling upon him,
> encourag'd him; that he kneel'd down to me, seem-
> ing to pray me to assist him; upon which I shew'd
> my Ladder, made him go up, and carry'd him into
> my Cave, and he became my Servant . . . (155).

If *Robinson Crusoe* is the first novel, it is so more because of
Defoe's unmatchable mastery of detail and characterization
than any overall coherent philosophical or religious system the
novel expounds. When Crusoe reports that he "show'd" himself,
"smiling upon" the proleptic Friday, he employs an idiom of
divine or royal display of favor. Crusoe here catapults himself to
the top of the hierarchical Chain of Being. In his dream Crusoe
fantasizes Friday as a servant, not as a son. Later, when Crusoe
rescues the flesh-and-blood Friday, the latter kneels down before
Crusoe and "set[s] my Foot upon his Head; this it seems was in
token of swearing to be my Slave for ever" (159). It is only after
he ascertains Friday's total "Subjection, Servitude, and Submission," that Crusoe remarks Friday's filial feelings, observing that
his precautions against his manservant's feared betrayal had
been groundless, "for never Man had a more faithful, loving, sincere Servant, than Friday was to me . . . his very Affections were
ty'd to me, like those of a Child to a Father" (163).

Crusoe "adopts" Friday after he enslaves him, displaying
how mastery is the first element in any social interaction that
Crusoe undertakes. This fact, as well as Crusoe's self-deification
and his frequent references to his absolute dominion over the
island, its animals, and any newcomers, suggests a subtle cor-

rection to Flint's claim that "When Crusoe saves Friday, the latter is made at once an obliging servant and son by the laws of gratitude."[38] It may be true that Friday feels this gratitude, but Crusoe, both during his dream and when he saves Friday, is at pains to assure the latter's total submission. It is the metaphorical signification of the father-son relation, however, that allows Crusoe's initial domination to be read as prefiguring his later "fatherhood," and not as contradicting it.

In Defoe's writings, the father-son metaphor operates in terms of an attempt at mastery often displayed through a didactic relation between the "father" and the "son," an attempt that may succeed or fail. I would like to explore a recurring detail: three instances of a gesture in which a "father" points to an object in the world, interpreting it for a "son." At the beginning of *The Family Instructor*, a catechistic "religious play," written in 1715 (roughly coincident with *Robinson Crusoe*) in the form of edifying dialogues between a father and members of his family, Defoe sets the scene of the First Dialogue. "The father, walking in the field behind his garden, finds one of his children wandering out, all alone, under a row or walk of trees, sitting upon a little rising ground, by itself, looking about, and mighty busy, pointing this way and that way; sometimes up, and sometimes down, and sometimes to itself; so that the father . . . asks the child what he was doing; and so sits down by him; which question begins—

> I was looking up there, says the child, pointing up in the air.
> Fa. Well, and what did you point thither for, and then point to the ground, and then to yourself afterward, what was that about?
> Child. I was a wondering, father.
> Fa. At what, my dear?

[38]Flint, 137.

Child. I was a wondering what place that is.

Fa. That is the air, the sky.

Child. And what is beyond that, father?

Fa. Beyond, my dear! Why above it all there is heaven.

Child. Who lives there, father. My nurse talks of heaven sometimes, and says God is in heaven. Is that the place up there?

[...]

Fa. Yes, my dear; [God] made heaven and earth, and the sea, and all that in them is, as you read in your Commandments, child.

Child. And what a creature am I father? I an't like them [cows and horses, dogs and cats]; I can speak; they can't speak, father.

Fa. No, child, you are not like them; God has made you a rational creature, and given you a soul.

[...]

Child. I am glad I am made a better creature than they, I'd thank him for it if I knew how; should I not do so, father?

Fa. Indeed you should, child.

Child. But you never told me so before, father, as I remember.

Fa. Not so often as I should have done, child, but remember it now my dear. (*And Kisses him.*)[39]

Defoe paints a subtle conflict in which the child wins the day. Although the father answers rationally, attempting to interpret his son's pointing gesture, he is a big loser in this scene. In Defoe's words, "The father represented here, appears knowing

[39]Daniel Defoe, *The Family Instructor: In Three Parts, The Novels and Miscellaneous Works of Daniel De Foe*, ed. Sir Walter Scott (Oxford, 1841), 5–8. The three parts are "Relating to Fathers and Children," "To Masters and Servants," and "To Husbands and Wives."

enough, but seems to be one of those professing Christians who, acknowledging God in their mouths, yet take no effectual care to honour him with their practice" (3). The child has received his religious instruction from his mother and his nurse, not from his father, who has neglected his didactic duty. The scene ends with the child dreading God's anger because the father has not taught him to thank God properly for making him a boy and not an animal without a soul. Defoe delivers the coup de grâce with the following "stage instructions," "Here the child cries, the father blushes, or at least ought to have done so" (8).

"Who" is this child, "wandering out, all alone . . . sitting upon a little rising ground, by itself, looking about, and mighty busy, pointing this way and that way"? Who else but Robinson Crusoe? The manner in which the child undermines his father's position even as the father appears to be the master echoes Crusoe's early encounter with his bedridden father. Both instances point to Defoe's undercutting of the father's prerogative to guide his son. Having abandoned his father, Crusoe resolves the struggle between the individual and the family because son or father, alone or with others, he is the master.

Before he dominates others, however, Crusoe must master his own desperate self. A second instance of "pointing" and struggle stages Crusoe's inner striving. Shortly after being cast on the Island of Despair, the shipwrecked Crusoe appraises his "dismal Prospect," with tears running

> Plentifully down my face when I made these reflections, and sometimes I would expostulate with myself, Why Providence should thus compleately ruine its Creatures . . . But something always return'd swift upon me to check these Thoughts, and to reprove me; and particularly one Day walking with my Gun in my Hand by the Sea-side, I was very pensive upon the Subject of my present Condition, when Reason as it were expostulated with me

> t'other Way, thus: Well, you are in a desolate Condi-
> tion 'tis true, but pray remember, Where are the rest
> of you? Did not you come Eleven of you into the
> Boat, where are the Ten? Why were not they sav'd
> and you lost? Why were you singled out? Is it better
> to be here or there? And then I *pointed* to the Sea
> [my emphasis] (51).

Crusoe teaches himself, mastering himself and his passions in
the process. Becoming his own "father," Crusoe here evinces the
double structure of his identity displayed in the many instances
in which he "call[s] a Council, that is to say, in my Thoughts"
(44). More than the tools he rescues from his sunken ship, it is
this doubling of the self—the stern master always correcting the
hasty judgments of the experience-driven pupil—that saves
Crusoe. Imagine an observer who has just landed on the island
beholding Crusoe's gesture. He/she would see a battered, solitary man pointing to what in the human imagination surely
stands for the absolute opposite of aloneness and helplessness.
Yet, privy to Crusoe's thoughts, the reader is struck with an
entirely different reading of this gesture—controlling his fears,
the castaway masters the sea and all those whom the sea brings
to his island.

Before Crusoe teaches Friday what a father teaches a son, he
teaches him what a master teaches a slave. Crusoe begins "really
to love the Creature," tutoring Friday in English and in religion,
but first he demonstrates to Friday the superiority of his own
power:

> I loaded my Gun again, and by and by I saw a great
> Fowl like a Hawk sit upon a tree within Shot; so to
> let *Friday* understand a little what I would do, I cal-
> l'd him to me again, pointed at the Fowl which was
> indeed a Parrot . . . I say pointing to the Parrot, and
> to my Gun, and to the Ground under the Parrot, to
> let him see I would make it fall . . . accordingly I fir'd

and bad him look, and immediately he saw the parrot fall, he stood like one frighted again, not withstanding all I had said to him; and I found he was
the more amaz'd, because he did not see me put any
Thing into the Gun; but thought there must be
some wonderful Fund of Death and Destruction in
that Thing . . . (165).

Perhaps no other moment in literature ever enacted with such
astounding clarity how guns cancel space, how they create such
a disparity between action and result, agent and effect. Crusoe's
pointing gesture to his slave/son instructs him on how to dominate nature, the finger metamorphosing into the gun, the parrot becoming one with the earth. Wielding his "wonderful Fund
of Death and Destruction," the stuff that colonial dreams are
made on, Crusoe survives his father's grief. Clarissa's fate, on
the other hand, proves very different indeed.

Clarissa's Two Fathers

You may well believe, after reading the first few pages of *Robinson Crusoe*, that its hero will come to no good, but you know his
life is going to be unusual, narratable; you would hardly think,
however, given *Clarissa*'s first letter, in which Anna Howe writes
to Clarissa, describing her as "so steady, so uniform in your conduct . . . sliding through life to the end of it unnoted," how
unpredictable the events of the novel will be; how remarkable
Clarissa's life and end will prove. Happiness is more noteworthy, as it turns out, in its frustration: the more Clarissa's will is
thwarted, the more deeply she opens her actions and motives to
interpretations; her identity to dialogism and, paradoxically,
uniqueness—departing more and more from Richardson's
moralistic view of her as "an Exemplar to her sex."[40]

[40]Richardson's Preface to *Clarissa*.

As with Crusoe, Clarissa's personhood—both her subjectivity and will—must reject the father's powerful chains on the soul. For if Crusoe needs adventure and is given to "rambling thoughts," Clarissa insists on her domestic happiness. Whether or not we agree with her mother that Clarissa rejects Solmes because her heart is not "free" from an attachment to Lovelace, Clarissa believes that "our sex . . . look[s] forward for happiness in marriage with the *man of their choice*," and observes to Anna Howe that "my mother loved my father." In a futile letter to Solmes, Clarissa blames him that "you addressed yourself to my friends . . . as if my choice and happiness were of the least signification" (52). Clarissa's (and Pamela's) struggle is, as Terry Eagleton invoking Gramsci puts it, an essential battle in "the practice of 'cultural revolution'—a fierce conflict over signs and meanings," that must accompany political change.[41]

Watt and Richetti both stress that Crusoe's repudiating his father's ways has a deeper meaning: capitalist energy; likewise, Clarissa's insistence on "happiness" is a demand which when conjoined to that of "life" and "liberty" composes a code. This code, deciphered, stands for Clarissa's domestic narrative and resonates with Thomas Jefferson's political "self-evident" truths, founding words of the nation whose own creation is symbolic of the triumph of the middle class.

Rejecting her father's will does not prove easy, however. It is both painful and shocking for the modern reader to trace Clarissa's breaking apart as a result of her father's cruel curse. Her sister, not ignoring the potential effect of her letter, writes that Clarissa's father "discovering your wicked, your shameful elopement, imprecated on his knees a fearful curse upon you." The malediction, at whose recital Clarissa is commanded to tremble, is "No less than you may meet your punishment, both

---

[41]Terry Eagleton, *The Rape of Clarissa: Writing, Sexuality and Class Struggle in Samuel Richardson* (Oxford: Blackwell, 1982), 2.

here and *hereafter*, by means of the very wretch in whom you have chosen to place your wicked confidence." Employing precisely the same language that she would use later to describe her affliction after the rape, Clarissa writes, "I think the contents of [the curse] have touched my head as well as my heart."[42] Lovelace reports to Belford that, upon his return, she was falling into fits, "and nobody expecting her life . . . [for] her filial piety gave her dreadful faith in a father's curses" (191). After the rape, still insisting, to Lovelace's surprise, "upon being a free agent," Clarissa leaves Lovelace's prison. Rejecting his pleas to marry him, she finally gives him false hope in the double-coded letter, in which she writes that "I am setting out with all diligence for my Father's House . . . You may possibly in time see me at my Father's."

Yet, if Lovelace is deceived by Clarissa's "allegories," the careful reader should not find it fanciful or peculiar that she confounds her father and the Christian Father. For part of the unspoken ideology of the novel is a close alliance between these two patriarchs. Although we, and Richardson, judging by the novel's subtitle, believe the father Harlowe in the wrong, his curse is fulfilled: Clarissa meets the most vicious of fates exactly at the hands of "the very wretch in whom [she has] chosen to place" her confidence. In extremis, and no wonder, Clarissa is obsessed with receiving her father's blessing and removing the second part of his curse, concerning the hereafter. In fact, when she orders her own headstone, Clarissa has the date she left her father's house engraved, since she cannot "tell what her *closing-day* would be" (450). Her father's curse has authored a day usually in the province of the Father.

[42]After the rape, Clarissa writes to Howe, "At present my head is much disordered. I have not indeed enjoyed it with any degree of clearness since the violence done to that, and to my heart too, by the wicked arts of the abandoned creatures I was cast among" (359).

Crusoe and Clarissa move in opposite directions, an almost chiastic couple. Although Crusoe is initially overwhelmed with guilt over leaving his father, the narrative later mostly drops this theme; there is no eventual reconciliation, and his father is long dead when Crusoe finally returns. Although Crusoe laboriously probes his experiences and beliefs, he does so alone: his language is utterly monological. When he hears another creature's voice for the first time since his marooning, it is his parrot repeating Crusoe's own "bemoaning Language," his self-pitying interjections, "Poor Robin Crusoe, Where are you? Where have you been?" Though he is "beside himself" when he sees the footprint in the sand, his subjectivity confronts and cannibalizes the "cannibals"; Crusoe co-opts but is unchanged by the ultimate other.

Clarissa, on the other hand, leaves her father's house without obsessing over his anticipated reaction, yet it is difficult to ascertain what eventually kills her—his curse or Lovelace's violation. In fact, so ardent is her belief in her father's imprecation that she dreads it will follow her to the grave; so overwhelming her guilt that she supplicates the patriarch who implored her ruin. Further, her identity, unlike Crusoe's, is formed dialogically: she is a person made of words—hers and her family's. In Habermas's view quoted above, her subjectivity is "audience-oriented," staged for her correspondents:

> From the beginning, the psychological interest increased in the dual relation to both one's self and the other: self-observation entered a union partly curious, partly sympathetic with the emotional stirrings of the other I. The diary became a letter addressed to the sender, and the first-person narrative became a conversation with one's self addressed to another person. These were experiments with the subjectivity discovered in the close relationships of the conjugal family . . . (48-9).

Habermas, however, is only partly right when he asserts that the epistolary novel developed out of "experiments with subjectivity discovered in the close relationships of the conjugal family." For distance was crucial too; and in this distance *Clarissa* and *Robinson Crusoe* resemble each other, and find their echo in nearly all eighteenth-century novels.

As I mentioned above, Pamela, although emotionally close to her parents, regales them with letters that narrate her new, and faraway, experiences in Mr. B's house. Clarissa, on the other hand, still resides in her father's house at the opening of the novel, but she writes to her friend, Anna Howe, relating her progressive alienation from her family, the result of her aversion to Solmes's suit. Robinson Crusoe opens his autobiographical narrative with his precise relation to his family, contained in his name and date of birth. Yet, his entire narrative follows from rejecting the ties that this relation entails.

Almost without exception, all of the novels associated with the "rise of the novel" in the eighteenth century narrate the life of a child leaving his/her family. That is the story of freedom. But there is a parallel narrative of capture. Nearly all of these escaping children are imprisoned or confined. Pamela, separated from her friends and confined for forty days in Mr. B's remote estate in Lincolnshire, is harassed by the violent Mrs. Jewkes and guarded by "the nasty grim bull" and the dark Monsieur Collbrand; Clarissa is aided then confined then violated by Lovelace and his underling procuress, Mrs. Sinclair. Robinson Crusoe, not heeding his father's warning, finds himself first a slave and then in a "second Captivity" on the "Island of Despair" for "eight and twenty Years, two Months, and 19 Days." Moll Flanders—though she doesn't leave her father's house, unless we consider Newgate prison to be that latter—is imprisoned and then transported to Virginia. Tom Jones departs only to be thrown in gaol.

The child leaves; in so doing, he/she enacts a new beginning. And the novel records his or her perilous freedom, evidencing, as Edward Said observes, "a desire to create a new or beginning fictional entity while accepting the consequences of that desire."[43] The hero of the eighteenth-century novel is solitary, paradoxically both to engage society and to withdraw from it. The novel alienates its child-hero from the world he or she is born into, a world that—according to the novel's unspoken ideology—should end. That the hero is homeless or imprisoned means the new world has not yet entirely come into being; that he is resisting older adversaries signifies his/her new world will triumph, bespeaking the novel's privileging of youth.

Comedic Struggles

That I postulate the child's story to be the kernel of the rising novel should not be taken to mean that generational struggle has not been foundational in other genres. In fact, this theme is as old as comedy itself. By way of contrast with Defoe and Richardson, Fielding's classical leanings and his conception of the novel as "the comic epic in prose" render his version of the father/child struggle in *Tom Jones* closer to its older comic treatment. Upon recovering Sophia from her trip in pursuit of Tom, Squire Western imprisons her yet again—this time, in her London room—after he finds out she still refuses to marry Allworthy's heir Blifil, preferring the affections of the bastard Tom. Salvation comes to the heroine inside her dinner. Black George, Squire Western's gamekeeper but also Tom's ally, brings a stuffed pullet for Sophia, and answers her protestations that he should take it back with a significant request for her to try "the Eggs of which it was full."[44] The pullet turns out to be worthy of the attentions of the miracle-hungry Royal Society, the wry narrator informs us, for Sophia discovers a "Letter in its Belly,"

---

[43]Edward W. Said, *Beginnings: Intention and Method* (New York: Columbia University Press, 1975), 82.

[44]Fielding, *Tom Jones*, 648.

which the grateful George has smuggled from Tom. The reader is told to consult his imagination as to "What Sophia said, or did, or thought upon this letter, how often she read it," as the narrator ironically defers Sophia's reply: "The Answer to it he may perhaps see hereafter; but not at present; for this Reason, among others, that she did not now write any, and that for several good Causes, one of which was this, she had no Paper, Pen, nor Ink." (650)

Although Fielding did not intend *Tom Jones* as a parody of *Clarissa*, the preceding chain of events bears a striking resemblance to *Clarissa*'s plot. A young woman faces the danger of being forced to marry an odious suitor, and is confined because of her refusal. But the scene of the miraculous letter inside the hen defuses the danger to the heroine and pokes fun at the central convention of Richardson's epistolary art: the claim that his characters always write "to the moment"; for only after her "liberty" is restored with the arrival of her firebrand aunt, does Sophia get access to the physical necessities of writing. Fielding's realism of things undercuts that of Richardsonian feelings. Even powerful emotions, Fielding seems to lightheartedly mock, need the presence of others to be recorded, if only to hand you the pen with which you might convert them into the stuff of novels.

For if the realist novel is a "full and authentic report of human experience,"[45] it is no less true that Clarissa's incessant scribbling, and Defoe's heroes' written self-justifications are fundamental in transmuting the elusive moments of life into individual "experience." But Crusoe runs out of the ink he has recovered from the ship's wreck and is forced to stop writing his "Journal."[46] Still, "his" narrative goes on and seamlessly elides the

[45]Watt, 32.

[46]"I began to keep my Journal, of which I shall here give you the Copy . . . as long as it lasted, for having no more Ink I was forc'd to leave it off." Defoe, *Robinson Crusoe*, 56.

necessary material interruption. More than a minor breach of formal realism, this continuity stages the essential isolation and self-sufficiency of the child-hero, exposing a vein of the nascent novel's ideology. Just as Rousseau attempts to dissociate the invention of language from the preexistence and permanence of the family, so the nascent novel divorces writing from sociability. While it is true that, as Charles Taylor emphasizes, "No one acquires the languages needed for self-definition on their own," the scene of writing in the novel is remarkably closeted. Especially, it bears emphasizing, when one considers the intense social involvement of both Richardson and Defoe. Shy and diffident as Richardson may have been, his writing involved a whirl of social dialogue with his many, mainly female, admirers, and Defoe's ubiquitous involvement in the political machinations of his day would humble the most engaged writer of any age.

But writing and its instruments in Fielding's world belong to a social universe in which the very act of writing, the adapting of the fleeting instant to novelistic discourse—and not just the exchange of letters or the later act of "editing" a first-person narrative—is profoundly social. Such a vision of the discursive universe is essentially comedic and undergirds a very different form of the conflict of generations. One fundamental difference between the comedic view and that of the novel, save Fielding's, is that the father's role in comedy is as significant as that of his son or daughter. Indeed, if the child's story is what holds the interest of the novel's reader, "of all the major characters [in Roman comedy]," contends George Duckworth, "the *adulescens . . .* is the least vivid and the least interesting."[47]

---

[47]George E. Duckworth, *The Nature of Roman Comedy: A Study in Popular Entertainment* (Princeton: Princeton University Press, 1952), 242. Such is not the case, it is worth emphasizing, in French and Restoration comedy, where the young characters are more witty and plucky that their older antagonists.

Another distinctive feature of the comedic representation of the generational conflict is that the father is not always right; and is often reproached, sometimes subtly and behind his back, occasionally loudly and to his face. In Molière's *L'Avare* (*The Miser*), a reworking of Plautus' *Aulularia*, Cléante, the youthful son, can only take so much abuse from his stingy and domineering father, Harpagon, the play's miser. Even though he admits to his sister that "I know that I am dependent on my father, whose wishes I am bound to respect," his piety has its limits, for as he concludes, "my love will brook no interference, and I beg you to spare me your remonstrances."[48] Later, when Harpagon discovers that it was his son who approached a usurer's agent for a loan, Cléante simultaneously finds out it was his father who was the usurer. The father and son engage in a delightful set of repartees, whose cadence of alternating give-and-take underscores the equality of the two parties. When Harpagon invokes the aura of his authority: "I wonder you dare to look at me in the face after this," Cléante retorts with an appeal to shame: "I wonder you dare to look the world in the face after this" (208).

Shame and the world go together. As with Fielding, the world is never far away, ever ready to rescue the child from tyrannical authority. Cléante finds out that his father is actually his rival in love; in one fell swoop, the old miser decides to wed his son's beloved, Mariane, to marry his son to an older widow, and to marry his daughter to an old wealthy man, whose sole attraction is that he is willing to take her "without a dowry." Élise, the daughter, objects to her father's choice of a "man, mature, wise and prudent, not much over fifty, and . . . extremely well-to-do," another Solmes-like horror. Yet, when her father submits her to the judgment of a neighbor, declaring that

[48]Molière, *The Miser*, trans. George Graveley and Ian Maclean (Oxford: Oxford University Press, 1998 (1668)), 188.

"The authority which Heaven gave me I resign to him," it turns out that her new stern judge is none other than her lover, Valère, who then tricks Harpagon. One recalls Clarissa's mounting isolation as she is handed from father to uncle. By contrast, in comedy the youthful hero is never quite alone.

These two differences—the interest the father's story holds and his frequent fallibility—are no doubt related. Locking horns, the father and his children negotiate roles within a received and accepted social world. One is reminded of Natalie Zemon Davis's discovery that the youthful members of the Abbeys of Misrule confirmed the given social rules even as they were being unruly. Remarkably, one of the actions most denounced by the charivaris was a prospective May-December marriage, which threatened the community's fertility. In *L'Avare*, Harpagon is admonished by Mariane's father that "you will easily understand that a girl would rather marry the son than the father" (256). The natural order of things in comedy is that fathers should not threaten what naturally belongs to the sons.

That the father is always right within the novel is a Pyrrhic victory, it turns out, however; for the novelistic attenuation of the father's presence is a consequence of his having become an emblematic fixity. The father stands for the old world, his role already shrunken to a symbolic ballast ready to be cast off. Although he forces the child-hero to leave home, the father is not part of the new world, the novel ending with all - passion spent, but no reconciliation and no continuity. Comedy, on the other hand, ends with a victory over the father (Molière and Plautus) or a reconciliation with him (Terence); but implicit in this reconciliation (or comic victory) is continuity, not only of the generations but also of the underlying social system. To put it more succinctly: the difference between comedy and the novel is between a social contest of generations which presumes and insures continuity and a solitary father/child conflict that symbolizes a breaking and an end.[49]

Comedic continuity is grounded in the usual happy ending of marriage: Cléante marries Mariane and Élise weds Valère. The younger generation's marriages ensure the fertility and continuity of the world, just as Tom Jones's and Sophia's wedding endows Paradise Hall with "two fine Children, a Boy and a Girl."[50] In fact, Roman comedy—less prudish regarding the "facts of life" and less delicate in its treatment of young women—portrays many of its youthful heroes as siring children even before they get their father's permission to get married. Their sexual conquests of the young women they pursue are somewhat accepted as part of the passion of youth. Micio, an old bachelor in Terence's *Adelphoe* (*The Brothers*), reprimands his adopted son, Aeschinus, for seducing a young woman, a fault "quite bad enough, though no more than human: honest men have done the same before you." His real fault, the father insists, is that he "delayed and did nothing while nine months went by."[51] Although young unmarried women do not appear on stage in Roman comedy, their pregnancy is often loudly proclaimed. While an old friend blames Demea, Micio's brother, because Demea's elder son has seduced Pamphila, the daughter of the friend's late army companion, the young woman, in the throes of labor, interrupts their conversation, screaming from inside her house: "Ah, the pain! Juno Lucina,

[49]Although Clarissa's father is clearly wrong, even according to Richardson's editorial commentary, paternal authority itself cannot be gainsaid.

[50]The comic conflict of generations could also be political. It played into class conflict often in surprising ways: Louis XIV enjoyed seeing the bourgeoisie burlesqued in Molière's comedies; the king thought paternal tyranny a central vice of that despised class.

[51]Terence, "The Brothers," in *The Comedies*, trans. Betty Radice (London: Penguin, 1976), 371.

help me, save me, save me!" (361) It is her only line in the play; still it is an utterance pregnant with the play's meaning.

By contrast with youth in comedy, not only is the child-hero of the novel a solitary figure, he/she either does not beget any children, or has them as an afterthought. Clarissa refuses Lovelace's offer and dies without issue; Crusoe spends more time narrating his and Friday's adventures against bears and wolves in the Pyrenees after they leave the island than in discussing his marriage in London, anemically informing the reader that "I marry'd, and that not either to my Disadvantage or Dissatisfaction, and had three children." As is usual for Defoe's protagonists, though, God turns out to be squarely on the side of profitable adventure. "But my Wife dying," Crusoe assures the reader, "and my Nephew coming Home with good Success from a Voyage to Spain, my Inclination to go Abroad, and his Importunity prevailed and engag'd me to go in his Ship" (236).

Marriage and fertility in the eighteenth-century novel are decidedly superseded by the hero's freedom. The case of the most prolific bearer of children in the nascent novel, Moll Flanders, is *the* case in point. One instance of her lack of maternal ties is particularly arresting. Confronted with a new pregnancy after she separates from her Lancashire husband, Moll is moved "to extreme perplexity" and grows "very melancholy," for, as she says, "I had Money, but no Friends, and was like now to have a child upon my Hands to keep, which was a difficulty I had never had upon me yet, as the Particulars of my Story hitherto makes appear."[52] As Michael Shinagel remarks: "Moll's candid remark about the uniqueness of her imminent motherhood, that she will this time have a child to care for, shows her fully aware of having systematically and successfully avoided the 'difficulty' of caring for any of her previous children."[53] Moll's children are either abandoned or forgotten. And, when she returns to Vir-

[52]Daniel Defoe, *Moll Flanders* (New York: Norton, 1973 (1722)), 126.

[53]Michael Shinagel, "The Maternal Paradox in *Moll Flanders*: Craft and Character," quoted in Defoe, *Moll Flanders*, 407.

ginia and meets the son she has left behind many years earlier, her resurgent maternal affection seems excited by her son's "flourishing circumstances."

Indeed having "Money" this time, as she puts it, Moll reduces her pregnancy to a financial transaction, the hallmark of Defoe's characters. She makes the acquaintance of a midwife, whom she informs that "I had Money sufficient, but not a great Quantity." A woman of business, the midwife presents Moll with a "Bill of Fare," offering her three options of cost for her birth and lying-in. Moll incorporates the three itemizations in her narrative and chooses the cheapest; after all she is paying out of her own pocket. Informed further that "If the Child should not live, or should be dead Born . . . then there's the Minister's Article saved," Moll smiles, reflecting that, "This was the most reasonable thing that I ever heard of." And, although she later delivers a moralizing tearjerker on the weakness of newborn children, asserting that "It is manifest to all that understand any thing of Children, that we are born into the World helpless . . . that these are partly the Reasons why Affection was plac'd by Nature in the Hearts of Mothers to their Children," Moll is prevailed upon to abandon her newborn, since it might endanger her new marriage prospect to a banker. The essential solitude of the novel's heroine supplants the "realism" of natural maternal affection and an older imperative of generational continuity. We are far away here not only from comedy, but also from the world of romance, with its cycles of the seasons and fertility—a world essentially collective if not always safe.

The Problem of Genealogy

I have argued that the homeless child's story underpins the rise of the novel in the eighteenth century. Rather than attempting to uncover an originary moment in previous genres, my study identifies a common masterplot, a metaphor whose shape structures the form of the novel. The story also emblematizes the meanings, political and national, explicit and unconscious, for which the nascent genre stands. Fundamentally as well, the child's story authorizes the manner in which the nascent novel adapts and pulls together a number of fictional and historical elements from several genres into a nationally-signifying narrative. We may benefit, before leaving this chapter, from interrogating how the child's story in the novel, while enabling these adaptations, remains new and distinct: How is the homelessness of the child-hero different from the picaro's; is the novel not simply a version of the prodigal's story; do not street ballads and chapbooks narrate similar stories of adventurous young persons? While the following treatment does not aim to be exhaustive, it attempts to seek these distinctions in the shape of the novelistic child's story itself, and not, say, in general paradigms of formal realism. Thus, for instance, the novel is different from the romance because of the distinct generational discontinuity of its child's story; and not only because, say, the romance tends to be episodic, to depict the lives of the aristocracy, and to be set in an idealized, distant past.

The novel's hero wanderings certainly recall the picaro's journeys. Two distinctions are crucial, however. First, an essential aspect of the novel's plot is the child's memory of the father's house, a continuing dialogue with the home he has left. Second, unlike the hero of the novel, the picaroon, to put it colloquially, has fun. Though the picaro does not fit easily in his world, he is of that world. The "servant of many masters" because as Robert Alter observes "he will not let the social system pin him down," the picaro nevertheless accepts his servitude. "His location . . . in the midst of the social system without being altogether part of it, is an invitation for him to turn satirist."[54] He may laugh at the world, but he is not out to change it.

---

[54]Robert Alter, *Rogue's Progress: Studies in the Picaresque Novel* (Cambridge: Harvard University Press, 1964), 15.

The hero of the novel, on the other hand, is his own master. His life story, an allegory of middle-class seriousness and purpose, sets him apart from the picaroon's lightness of being. Thus, for instance, although Moll's extreme lack of attachment to a stable location in society recalls the picaro's continuous movement, E. A. Baker asserts that Moll is not a picaroon because she is a rogue who does not rejoice "in her rogueries."[55] Emphasizing Moll's rigorous bookkeeping and her penchant for linguistic precision ("I understood what she meant by conscientious mothers, she would have said conscientious whores"), Alter stresses that even the heroes of Defoe, with their propensity for adventure, have a "leaden seriousness" when weighed against "the model of picaresque buoyancy."[56]

Novelistic formal realism, which Watt associated with the imperatives of Lockean experience, can in fact follow from one aspect of the new middle-class world: the desire for and insistence on the repeatability of outcome, on the effacement of luck and chance and the taming of Fortuna. Moll's and Crusoe's fascination with counting money and things is one manifestation of this insistence and desire. Bookkeeping is predicated on the removal of any consideration but repeatability from financial transactions. This repeatability also refers to the outcome of events: it manifests itself, for instance, in what scientists call the invariability of physical laws. The nascent realist novel's invariable law is the character of its child-hero, because he/she carries the seed of the passing of the old world and the birth of the new within that character. Thus, Crusoe's "propensity of nature," for example, means that he will not settle down to blissful matrimony when he returns to England, despite the fact that he now faces a wife not a father; Clarissa rejects Lovelace's offer of marriage after the rape

[55]E. A. Baker, *The History of the English Novel* (London: Witherly, 1929), v. III, 190.

[56]Alter, 47.

because her freedom would still be compromised. Because the novel's hero is in search of something definite, as it were, a new location, he/she remembers and regrets the father's house he has left.

The episodic nature of the picaresque, on the other hand, is possible because such a restriction on the outcome of its hero's luck does not hold. In other words, while it appears on the surface that formal realism obtains in the picaresque—the hero moves in and out of real places within defined particular times and so on—the outcomes of the hero's many adventures escape the rule of personality. The buoyancy Alter describes and the picaresque's lack of interest in personality are one and the same.

The prodigal theme's relevance to a genre centered around a child's leaving the father's house is as evident as the picaresque's. As with the novel's hero, the prodigal quickly loses his new freedom and is restricted to a small space. The novel's hero's confinement, however, is more than failure and punishment; it both emblematizes and enables his/her inwardness. Defoe's and Richardson's heroes are more psychologically developed than Fielding's precisely because of their solitariness and lack of sociability. Furthermore, the prodigal son, unlike the hero of the novel, is reunited with his father. The reclamation of the errant child into the father's house and social world is a central element in both the original biblical parable and the various plays, ballads, and spiritual autobiographies based on it.[57] The close association between the prodigal's sin, the father's forgiveness, and the moral lesson of the parable is underlined by the elder son's incredulity at the father's pardon. Even though the elder son is nonplused that the father wel-

---

[57]For treatments of the prodigal theme in medieval morality plays, ballads, prints, see above, chapter two, note 52. Examples of spiritual autobiographies modeled on the parable of the prodigal include John Bunyan, *Grace Abounding to the Chief of Sinners* and *The Journal of Richard Norwood.*

comes the prodigal back despite the fact that, as he says "he hath devoured thy living with harlots," the father assuages him with: "It was meet that we should make merry, and be glad: for this thy brother was dead, and is alive again; and was lost, and is found."

The prodigal's redemption fits within the comedic continuity analyzed above and is alien to the world of the novel. The father's role in prodigal adaptations varies with its new generic home. Not only are master and apprentice eventually reconciled in *Eastward Ho*, the Jacobean prodigal apprentice comedy discussed in chapter two, but the prominence of the father's part in the play echoes Terence and Plautus. That is not surprising, for besides "the native tradition of the morality play," the major dramatic influence behind *Eastward Ho* was sixteenth-century Continental adaptations of "the intrigues of Roman comedy to the Christian parable of the Prodigal Son."[58]

A new aspect related to the lives of London apprentices modifies the treatment of the prodigal's fate, however. When the master Goldsmith Touchstone is tricked into visiting Newgate, he is convinced of the true repentance of the wayward Quicksilver because he overhears him singing the "Repentance," an imitation, the repentant apprentice says, of a farewell ballad purported to be written by the famous highwayman Mannington just before he was hanged. That Quicksilver is both officially imprisoned and reprieved by mimicking the words of a condemned man highlight the intrusion of modern criminality into this particular version of the prodigal theme. Despite the novel's great differences from prodigal adaptations, it nevertheless incorporates a similar criminal aspect of the prodigal's play into its plot. Leaving the father's house partakes not only of the impiety of the parable but also of the criminality of its seventeenth-century London counterpart; and perhaps

[58]John Doebler, "Beaumont's *The Knight of the Burning Pestle* and the Prodigal Son Plays," S.E.L., 5 (1965), 333–4.

partly explains the novel's relation to criminal discourses.[59] John Bender has influentially argued that both the novel and new conceptions of the penitentiary eschew anarchic, random space and time in favor of an ordered reconstruction of the self.[60] One may theorize that criminal discourse, a ubiquitous theme in seventeenth-century broadside ballads, seeps through the boundary of the nascent novelistic discourse in the shape of a crime directed against the father.

The child's story's specificity is reflected not only in how it adapts narrative elements from other genres without mimicking them, but also in the fact that it eschews certain discourses altogether. Not all genres and life stories were of interest to the eighteenth-century novel; although Defoe and Richardson must have encountered apprentices everywhere they went in London, the novel's emphasis on the dependence of its child-hero explains the lack of interest in the unruly youth culture of apprentices, a culture that found copious expression in seventeenth-century chapbooks and broadside ballads. It is in this popular literature, as Ilana Ben-Amos argues, that we may "glimpse a set of images encapsulating the beauty, strength, vigour and wit of youth, rather than its follies and sins."[61] Some of these accounts, as well as earlier narratives, reflected the

---

[59]For an acute analysis of this connection, see Lennard Davis, *Factual Fictions: The Origins of the English Novel* (New York: Columbia University Press, 1983). Davis draws a connection between the novel and criminal ballads, "There seems to have been something novelistic about the criminal, or rather the form of the novel seems almost to demand a criminal content. Indeed without the appearance of the whore, the rogue, the cutpurse, the cheat, the thief, or the outsider it would be impossible to imagine the form of the novel" 125.

[60]See John Bender, *Imagining the Penitentiary: Fiction and the Architecture of Mind in Eighteenth-Century England* (Chicago: University of Chicago Press, 1987).

[61]Ben-Amos, *Adolesence and Youth in Early Modern England*, 23.

urban or trade interests and settings of its readers. Thomas Deloney's popular Elizabethan prose fictional accounts, for instance, exalted the clothiers' trade. His *Jack of Newbury*, so successful it was also adapted into shorter chapbook versions, narrates the exploits of an apprentice to a broadcloth weaver in Newbury. The story piques the reader with the tension, sexual and financial, between Jack and the widow of his master, who tricks him into marriage. Yet, the emphasis is on Jack's success which provides a showcase of the material successes possible in the trade.[62]

In another popular chapbook story, clearly a working-class transmutation of chivalric romances, Aurelius, the "Famous and Valiant London Prentice," performs miraculous valorous deeds, such as killing "Grodam, the son-in law of the Great Turk" and then the lions set upon him. But he gets to Turkey in the first place because his parents, fearing the revenge of the jilted Dorinda—but one of his many suitors—"sent him to London and bound him as apprentice to a Turkey merchant on London Bridge."[63] Naturally, he falls in love with his master's daughter. While clearly not realist—Aurelius's story rubs shoulders in the same chapbook with "Guy, Earl of Warwick" and "The Life and Death of St. George"—this and similar narratives also differ from the novelistic child's story in that they offer a view of young people as obstreperous adolescents, a view the nascent novel does not exploit, imaging its youth instead as dependent children. The apprentices' stories, however, provide interesting contrasts to the "lives" of the heroes of that new genre. The chapbooks, like Roman comedy, represent rebellion in terms of sexual license: the young men and women frequently have premarital sex, and agree to marriage themselves, with their fathers' consent no more than an afterthought.[64] Yet, unlike children in

[62]See Spufford, *Small Books*, 219–258.

[63]"The Valiant London Apprentice," in John Ashton, *Chapbooks of the Eighteenth-Century* (New York: Augustus Kelley, 1970 (1882)), 228.

the novel, the youth do not disrupt their given world. When they get married, they live next door.

Moll has the Last Word

Remarkably, the juxtaposition we saw above between Moll's abandoning her child and her pious discourse on the helplessness of children stages the debate regarding the belonging and homelessness of children discussed in chapter three between Rousseau and Buffon. Buffon, we recall, explicitly contradicted Rousseau, arguing that human "infants would perish if they were not aided and cared for during many years, whereas animal newborns need their mother for only a few months."[65] Although Moll gives lip service almost word-for-word to Buffon's view, her abandonment of her infant son acts out Rousseau's belief in the tenuous link between the newborn child and its mother—that maternal love is not natural but acquired within the society of the family. Were Rousseau's views influenced by Defoe's portrayal of the most unmaternal mother in fiction?

It seems to me immaterial here to speculate whether Rousseau read *Moll Flanders* or not, though it is probable he did. Rousseau's admiration for *Robinson Crusoe* is well-known: Emile's library, the reader is informed, will consist of only one book, that will "serve as our guide during our progress to a state of reason . . . You ask patiently, what is the title of this wonderful book?" The Tutor holds the reader in suspense, "Is it Aristotle, Pliny, or Buffon? No. It is Robinson Crusoe." Defoe's seduction of the most ardent defender of equality in the history of Western thought into adulating a slave-trader's narrative must stand as one of the marvels of rhetorical legerdemains. It is not merely Crusoe's self-sufficiency on the island, a model for Emile, that

[64]See Spufford, 161–3.
[65]See above, Chapter three, note 37.

attracts Rousseau. The castaway's leaving his father's house and his survival echo the philosopher's belief in a naturally homeless child, who rejects paternal rule. Further, his isolation and later supremacy on the island negate the odious other-dependence of civil society that Rousseau found to be at the root of inequality among men.

Rousseau no doubt would have condemned Moll; he blames contemporary French women for considerably less. Still, Defoe's two novels reveal a disturbing aspect of Rousseau's new mythical familial and national accounts. After all, Moll and Crusoe are alike, identical twins when it comes to lacking natural affective ties to others, family or not.[66] In fact, Rousseau's naturally homeless child appears to theorize not only Crusoe's narrative, but also Moll's treatment of her ever increasing brood of children. She, in other words, produces the naturally homeless children that Rousseau asserted the species to have been before society was formed. Defoe's egalitarian treatment of his two heroes exposes Rousseau's biased vision. That bias is, however, considerably more subtle than the charges critics have levied against Rousseau: that he relegates women to the family sphere as obedient helpmates of the public husbands.[67] For, as chapter three emphasized, Rousseau was at the heart of the national privileging of the domestic sphere as the measure of and the road to public virtue.

Rousseau's refutation of both the child's natural belonging and the primacy of the father's dominion, as well as his indignation against the modern mother, serve as elements in a new myth of the nation. His prescription for both civic reformation and domestic rehabilitation—the first necessitated by the fall of man into society and the tyranny of other-dependence; the second by the mother's dereliction in fulfilling her calling in the

[66]Moll does form romantic attachments; that they are always reducible to financial considerations is unarguable, however.

[67]See above, chapter three, note 84.

bosom of the family—is a mythical father that will reclaim the homeless child into a natural family man or into a citizen. But, whether the new national father is the Tutor of *Emile* or the Lawgiver of *Du contrat social*, Rousseau's two prescriptive narratives do not escape the supremacy of the father principle. His vision excludes mothers from both his reformed civic and domestic relations. Might a different shape of a foundational political myth, however, emerge if one does not omit the mother's "part" in the new mythic-political account, not merely restricting her role to the natural imperatives of fertility and reproduction?

Fifty years before Gulliver was awed by the splendid Houyhnhnms into recognizing that he and his "Family," "Friends," "Countrymen," and the "human Race in general" are no more than "Yahoos," another fictional mouthpiece in the service of his author's social critique conversed with the superior Australians and humbly learnt that human beings are no better than beasts. Sadeur, a freak among men because he is born a hermaphrodite, lands in the land of Australie, where, it turns out, he is the norm, for "Each Australian has both sexes, and if a child happens to be born with only one, they kill it as a monster."[68] Egged by the curious traveler to discuss reproduction, the Australians question whether the condition of human marriage between the two separate sexes would not lead to "great difficulties because the two wills could not easily be reconciled," and are horrified by Sadeur's sheepish assurance that "the mother and child [are] subject to the father" (54).

By mythologizing away the natural, Foigny's utopia avoids incorporating its imperatives in a new political narrative. His political myth vitiates the inevitable domination of the father, highlighting the bias of Rousseau's two accounts and the limitations of a domestic-based reformulation of public national

---

[68]Gabriel de Foigny, *La terre australe connue*, trans. David Fausett (Syracuse: Syracuse University Press, 1993 (1676)), 47.

roles. Moll's treatment of her children, though cruel, similarly militates against the conflation of the domestic and the national we saw in Rousseau. More generally, the eighteenth-century novel's homeless child does not fit easily into Rousseau's national narratives. Yet, his national father's omniscience closely resembles the national narrator's stance in Scott's historical novel.

FIVE

HISTORICITY, THE CHILD, & SCOTT'S HISTORICAL NOVEL

Whither is fled the visionary gleam?
Where is it now, the glory and the dream?

Wordsworth, "Ode,
Intimations of Immortality From
Recollections of Early Childhood"

The nineteenth century's discovery of History has been well noted by literary critics and historians. Hayden White's magisterial *Metahistory* examines the forms and rhetorical devices of nineteenth-century historical narratives and philosophies of history. Stephen Bann, in studying the "historical representation" of nineteenth-century Britain and France, speculates that the nineteenth-century desire for a historical re-creation, "the Utopia of life-like reproduction," was a result of a sense of loss and death.[1] Carolyn Steedman observes that "the nineteenth-century emergence of the modern discipline of history has been aligned with historical explanation in the life sciences. In their purposiveness, natural history and history both offered the comforts of narrative exegesis: the comforts of a story."[2] The story still has a child at its center.

---

[1] Stephen Bann, *The Clothing of Clio: A Study of the Representation of History in Nineteenth-Century Britain and France* (Cambridge: Cambridge University Press, 1984), 15.

[2] Carolyn Steedman, *Strange Dislocations: Childhood and the Idea of Human Interiority 1780–1930* (Cambridge: Harvard University Press, 1995), 78.

No nineteenth-century novelist assumed the mantle of historian like Walter Scott; indeed Scott's transformation of the novel's literary reputation from a low esteem when he published *Waverley* to its having "a place among the highest productions of human intellect," as the *Edinburgh Review* eulogized him in 1832, is in large measure due to history's authority. Scott's historical novel has been seen by critics as "masculinizing" the genre by spurning the domestic for the authority of the historical, public sphere. Ina Ferris connects Scott's enormous popularity to his perceived "manly intervention" in the novel, substituting both the "truth" and the energetic struggles of history for prim feminine domestic themes: "For these first male readers, Waverley reading offered a compelling alternative both to female reading and to feminine writing. In particular, in this period of conservative reaction, evangelical revival, and the domestic-didactic novel, *Waverley* and its successors licensed a nostalgic male-inflected romance of history."[3]

Yet, paradoxically, the narrative kernel of the Waverley Novels (*Waverley* and *Old Mortality*, for example) is the "education" of a motherless youth, who leaves his father's house and is entangled with Britain's formative wars. That formula, enacting a separation between the knowledge of an omniscient national father-narrator and that of the less-knowing young hero, novelizes a national education narrative (of *Emile*, for example) in which proper domestic education (by a father figure, the mother safely absent) of the child assures national virtue. Danton proclaimed the importance of national elementary schools, asserting that: "Children belong to society before they belong to their family."[4] Chil-

---

[3]Ina Ferris, *The Achievement of Literary Authority: Gender, History, and the Waverley Novels* (Ithaca, N.Y.: Cornell University Press, 1991, 91.

[4]Marcel Garaud and Romuald Szramkiewicz, *La Révolution française et la famille* (Paris, 1978), quoted in Lynn Hunt, *The Family Romance of the French Revolution* (Berkeley: University of California Press, 1992), 67.

dren come potently to express a new beginning that symbolizes national renewal: their young age displays the uncorrupted potential of the nation, and their education reflects national desires.

That appropriation of the child is a striking feature of romantic nationalist thought, as we saw in chapter three. By reversing the order of family and society in his *Discourse on the Origin of Inequality*, Rousseau refutes the natural prerogative of the father.[5] The family, Rousseau contradicts Locke, is not natural: its only legitimacy is that it fosters goodness. Railing against the modern family—corrupted, as he surprisingly determines, by the mother, who neglects her duty to breast-feed her children—Rousseau offers an educational utopia in *Emile*, in which the child's tutor replaces the family. Rousseau's thought experiment—strangely enough for he would not have approved—became the blueprint for the nation's adoption of the suffering child.

To be sure, Scott's novel is neither as stridently didactic nor as self-assuredly programmatic. Yet, in his "care" of the young hero, the narrator supplants both the family Robespierre and Danton decry and the new political regime they propose.[6] Rather than turning away from the domestic, the novel that Scott bequeaths to Balzac and the nineteenth century—both its plot and its formal illusion of omniscience—is dependent on a narrator, whose sympathetic omniscient narrative situates the young protagonist in the new nation, replacing the familial affection the homeless hero lacks. Such a stance, however,

[5]"Au lieu de dire que la Société civile dérive du pouvoir Paternel, il falloit dire au contraire que c'est d'elle que ce pouvoir tire sa principale force: un individu ne fut reconnu par le Pere de plusieurs que quand ils restérent assemblés autour de lui . . ." Jean-Jacques Rousseau, *Discours sur l'origine et les fondements de l'inégalité*, edited and annotated by Jean Starobinski, in J. J. Rousseau, *Oeuvres complètes*, ed. Bernard Gagnebin and Marcel Raymond (Paris: Gallimard [Bibliothèque de la Pléiade], 1964 (1754)), vol. 3, 182.

[6]See chapter three, note 22.

figures the hero/subject as a dependent child, matching the citizen's location in the nation's autobiography.

Although Scott's new form co-opts and supersedes an already existing "female genre," the national tale, it continues what that genre highlighted: the conflation of the domestic and the political spheres. Such a merging is itself political. In Charles Maturin's *The Milesian Chief*, for example, the love story between Armida, the Anglo-Italian aristocrat, and Connal, the tempestuous Irish feudal prince, casts the political conflicts in erotic terms: Connal's rival for Armida's affection is the overbearing and treacherous English lord, Wandesford. Armida, vaticinating the imminent demise of Connal (who is executed as a rebel by a British firing squad), rues her own impending death and erasure from memory: "He is gone to make a new era in the history of man, and who will pause in writing the story to tell that he left the woman that loved him to perish."[7]

But both the national tale and the historical novel remember Armida, though in different ways. Connal's love story is at the center of Maturin's narrative, and the novel's hero is a "world-historical" figure. Praising Scott's choice of a middling hero, Georg Lukács, however, deplores that type of "romantic hero-worship": Scott's virtue, according to Lukács, is that the Scottish novelist does not choose as protagonist a Byronic hero such as Connal. Thus the hero of Scott's *Waverley* is the mediocre Edward Waverley and not the novel's feudal antagonist of British rule, the Scottish Highlander lord, Fergus Vich Ian Vohr. Such a modulation, I believe, does not mean that Scott eschews the domestic, sentimental sphere. That Waverley replaces Connal in the love plot (with *Waverley*'s version of Armida, the passionate, harp-playing Highlander lady, Flora,

[7]Charles Maturin, *The Milesian Chief* (New York: Garland Publishing, 1979 (1812)), v. 2, 175. I have benefited from the detailed discussion of the national tale in Katie Trumpener, "National Character, Nationalist Plots: National Tale and the Historical Novel in the Age of Waverley, 1806–1830," *ELH* 60 (1993): 685–731.

Fergus's sister) shifts the love plot from the domain of political action to that of the *Bildung* of the child-hero.[8]

Lukács, one of whose earliest literary studies is a typology of the novel, curiously elides that educational aspect of Scott's novel in the *Historical Novel*. Lukács's lionization of Scott in that late study (1937) is well known, but why does the young Lukács dismiss Scott in *The Theory of the Novel* (1916) as a writer who produces novels whose "inner emptiness becomes apparent in the work's lack of idea"?[9] Because as a young Hegelian, Lukács favors those novelists who are able to dialectically rise above the loss of totality that follows the epic. In offering this dialectic of the death of an initial epic totality, followed by the fragmentary separation of the "problematic individual" from a world deprived of transcendental meaning, finally replaced with the new higher self-conscious totality of the hero of the "novel of Romantic disillusionment," who "now carries his value exclusively within himself" (117), Lukács presents a variation of the Romantic spiral I described in chapter one.

The initial epic totality was that of a homogeneous world endowed by gods with a transcendental meaning, wherein the meaning "closed within itself can be completed" (34). The hero, guided by the gods, has no "abyss" within himself; there is no separation between man and world. The integrated civilizations that produced the epics are, however, gone. Gone are the happy ages "whose paths are illuminated by the lights of the stars" (29). For us moderns, living in a fragmented civilization, "Kant's starry firmament now shines only in the dark night of pure cognition, it no longer lights any solitary wanderer's path (for to be a man in the new world is to be solitary)" (36).

[8]I refer to Edward Waverley as a "child" even though he is well past the age that term denotes today for reasons I will explicate a bit later in my essay.

[9]Georg Lukács, *The Theory of the Novel*, trans. Anna Bostock (Cambridge: The MIT Press, 1971), 115.

The genre that narrates the life of this homeless hero is, according to Lukács, the novel, "the epic of a world that has been abandoned by God" (88). But Lukács's view of the novel is limited by his "humanism." Susan Suleiman justly observes that "Lukács's blind spot" in *The Theory of the Novel*, "was that he considered all novels as variants of the *Bildungsroman*."[10] This is so because the young Lukács saw the novel as the medium which narrates the hero's search for a new totality. The emphasis is squarely on the hero, on his developing relation with the new world abandoned by gods. The novel narrates the hero's quest for a meaning that would transcend his separation from other men and from his world. What Lukács emphasizes in the novel, therefore, is precisely the hero's development, his *Bildung*. It is man, the hero, who is the active part of the pair—man and world—that in the epic knew no separation.

"Happy are those ages" indeed in which a young literary critic could offer a typology of the novel entitled "*The* Theory of the Novel." For Lukács does no less. He divides the novel into two types, based on the relation of the hero's soul to his world, now that the soul is decidedly incommensurable with the world. In the novel of "abstract idealism," whose greatest exemplar is *Don Quixote*, the hero's soul is "narrower" than the "outside world assigned to it as the arena" of its actions: such narrowness of the soul is brought about by the hero's "demonic obsession" with an "existing idea" of the world. The hero acts in a world that he perceives as narrower than it really is; therefore, his quest in the world falls short. By contrast, in the second type, the novel of "Romantic disillusionment," the soul of the hero is wider than "the destinies which life has to offer it."[11]

It is in this latter type of novel—and Lukács takes *L'Education sentimentale* as its perfect representative—that he considers

[10]Susan Rubin Suleiman, *Authoritarian Fictions: The Ideological Novel as a Literary Genre* (New York: Columbia University Press, 1983), 64.

[11]Lukács, *The Theory of the Novel*, 112.

that "The inner importance of the individual has reached its historical apogee." The hero of the novel "now carries his value exclusively within himself" (117). Refusing all engagement with the world, he considers all action to be "hopeless and merely humiliating." Like his counterpart in the novel of abstract idealism, though for very different reasons, the disillusioned hero's quest ends in failure. The only novel, according to Lukács, in which the hero achieves a synthesis between self and world, action and contemplation, is Goethe's *Wilhelm Meister*, which is the only novel Lukács explicitly classifies as a *Bildungsroman*.

This is an aporia in Lukács's text which Suleiman identifies: "After having defined the novel in terms that apply only to the *Bildungsroman* [the success or failure of the hero's quest in the world], Lukács constructs a typology of novelistic forms which leads to the conclusion that the veritable *Bildungsroman* has almost never existed [except for *Wilhelm Meister*]."[12] I think the reason for this confusion in Lukács's system is that he really offers two dialectics in *The Theory of the Novel*: The first, aesthetic, is predicated on the concept of recovered totality; the second, ethical, is based on the evaluation of the hero's quest in the world. It is this latter which finds its only example in Goethe's great novel.

Recall that in the epic, man both acted perfectly and existed perfectly. Since there was no separation between man and world, the hero was part of the whole, but also incorporated the whole. Aided by the gods, his quest was successful. Separated from his world, the modern hero of the novel searches for perfection in both his actions and his being. One dialectic—based on *Bildung*—sees the hero as going from perfect action (in the epic) to inefficacious action (in all novels save one) to perfect action in the world (in *Wilhelm Meister*). The second dialectic is less social and more ontological: It describes the attempt at a recovery of the totality of being. From this point of view, the

[12]Suleiman, 66.

novel of Romantic disillusionment seems to be higher than the novel of abstract idealism.

It is because the idealist hero cannot experience a totality, so pierced is he through and through with anachronistic "transcendent worlds." Quixote's "transcendent homeland" is the world of chivalry. Because the hero is demonically obsessed with this "existing idea" of the world, he succeeds neither in action nor in achieving an independence of being. The disillusioned hero, on the contrary, carries his own world within himself. His conflict with the world is "a struggle between two worlds, not a struggle between reality and a general *a priori* state" as in the novel of abstract idealism. Although, just like the Knight of the Mournful Countenance, Frédéric Moreau's action in the world is disastrous, the hero of *l'Education sentimentale* possesses "a life capable of producing all its content out of itself [that] can be rounded and perfect even if it never enters into contact with the alien reality outside" (112).

Such a victory in transcending the fragmentary reality of the world and achieving a totality is "rendered possible by time." It is here, in the recovery and containment of time, that the novel of Romantic disillusionment comes close to the stillness of the *Bildungsroman*. Time here, though, is not that of the ever perfect here and now of *Wilhelm Meister*. Rather, it is the quality of future time—hope—or past time—memory—incorporated into the novel, which recreates the totality of the epic that knew no time. No time, because although it passes in order for actions to unfold, time changes nothing in the epic: Agamemnon is still king; Odysseus is still resourceful; Achilles is still doomed. What the epic's heroes experience "has the blissful time-removed quality of the world of gods" (122). In that sense, time never threatens the totality of the epic's world.

In the novel, however, time becomes "constitutive": "the entire action of the novel is nothing but a struggle against the power of time." The passage of time is what initially destroys the naive (epic) totality of the novel's world. However, that loss can be recovered as memory. *L'Education sentimentale* "of all novels of the nineteenth century . . . in the unmitigated desolation of its matter, is the only novel that attains true epic objectivity," because although—in complete contradistinction to the epic— "the separate fragments of reality lie before us in all their hardness, brokenness, and isolation . . . the unrestricted, un-interrupted flow of time is the unifying principle of the homogeneity that rubs the sharp edges of each heterogeneous fragment" (124–5). Time is represented in the novel as memory; the latter "occur[s] as a creative force affecting the object and transforming it. The genuinely epic quality of such memory is the affirmative experience of the life process" (127). Memory, that is, cancels out the separation in the novel of the "temporal" from the "essential" which in the epic were fused. Triumphing against the passage of time, memory restores to the novel its epic quality: "The duality of interiority and the outside world can be abolished for the subject if he (the subject) glimpses the organic unity of his whole life through the process by which his living present has grown from the stream of his past life dammed up within his memory" (127).

Hence, the totality of our fallen world can be restored through the power of memory in the novel. I think, although Lukács himself does not emphasize this point, that such a restoration of totality is only possible within the type of novel in which the hero can incorporate totality within himself, I mean the novel of Romantic disillusionment. Although it is true that *Don Quixote*, the greatest novel of abstract idealism, "overlaps still more obviously into the epic in its formal and historico-philosophical foundations," "the events in *Don Quixote* are almost timeless, a motley series of isolated adventures complete in themselves" (129–30). The totality of time here is not self-consciously restored through the power of memory as in *L'Education sentimentale*, but is naively epic-like. That is why the novel of abstract idealism must be lower in Lukács's totality dialectic.

Suleiman is right in finding that Lukács, in the *Theory of the Novel*, defines "the novel in terms that apply only to the *Bildungsroman*."[13] What is important to the young Lukács is the emphasis that the *Bildungsroman* places on a final stillness of development. Lukács defines that quality as "totality"; Franco Moretti in terms of time stopping "at a privileged moment."[14] What both definitions imply is excluded from the *Bildungsroman* is precisely what cannot be stopped at a privileged moment in the interest of the hero: history. It is because Scott privileges history over contained time that he is dismissed by the young Lukács.

As historical explanation and narrativization become the dominant discourse in the nineteenth century, the individual Lockean experience—an experience at the heart of the eighteenth-century novel—loses its capacity to underpin the novel's mimetic project. For a fundamental conceit of the examination of one's experiences is that one can stop time and, as it were, examine the sum total of one's experiences. It also requires a knowledge of the agents that can effect change—characters and events. The Lockean self, as Charles Taylor charges, is a "punctual self": it presumes self-control, mastery over one's understanding of one's destiny—if not that destiny itself: "To take this stance is to identify oneself with the power to objectify and remake, and by this act to distance oneself from all the particular features which are objects of potential change . . . This is what the image of the point is meant to convey, drawing on the geometrical term: the real self is 'extensionless.'"[15]

[13]Suleiman, 66.

[14]Franco Moretti, *The Way of the World: The Bildungsroman in European Culture* (London: Verso, 1987), 26.

[15]Charles Taylor, *Sources of the Self: The Making of Modern Identity*, 171–2.

Involvement in history, being overtaken by history, is, on the other hand, diachronic, nebulous, and collective; rather than the controlling point, the romantic self is a depth seething with memories.

This is not to say that the content of the Lockean self is static. On the contrary, Locke stresses the receptive quality of the mind. With no innate ideas of its own, it constantly synthesizes the sensations it receives through the process of association of ideas. That process is nothing if not dynamic. However, the consciousness that examines the content, Taylor's punctual self, is presumed able to examine that tumultuous content, as it were, serene from the influence of change—that is, time. The ahistoricity of the eighteenth-century realist novel reaches an apex in the *Bildungsroman* of the early nineteenth century, whose greatest representatives such as Goethe's *Wilhelm Meister's Apprenticeship* and Jane Austen's *Pride and Prejudice* narrate an educational journey that reaches its end with the integration of the hero and society, usually through the perfect marital choice.

Moretti observes that the *Bildungsroman* sees youth as the "most meaningful part of life," but abstracts "from 'real' youth a 'symbolic' one epitomized ... in mobility and interiority" because "Europe has to attach a meaning not so much to youth, as to *modernity*."[16] Scott, in inventing a form that restores history to the novel, also takes a child-youth as his hero in many of the Waverley Novels. His novels, however, do not privilege the happy *Bildung* of his heroes; as much as a search for a perfect and static happiness is at the center of the *Bildungsroman*, the forces of national history almost always frustrate the hero of the historical novel. Scott's achievement lies not only in his masterful representation of historical events, of mass movements and

[16]Moretti, 5.

wars, but crucially in his invention of a form that could represent the hero's ineluctable historicity on the one hand and, ironically, on the other hand, his powerlessness in the face of— and his victimization by—history.

The historical narrative of one's own life, being the product of history, is the hostage of the actions of many; therefore it partakes of the inscrutability of history. For the historical novel it means that the experience of the hero is not enough; it cannot eventually, as in the *Bildungsroman*, encompass a final truth of life, permit a reconciliation between individual and society. Scott's historical novel enacts a separation between the narrator's knowledge and the hero's. No longer will the hero's experience, even enlarged by the journey, be equal to the narrator's, or surrogately, the reader's. That Scott came up with such a hero, the older Lukács celebrates in the *Historical Novel* as the basis of the nineteenth-century great realist novel. In his novels, Bakhtin applauds, Scott "overcomes the closed nature of the past and achieves the fullness of time necessary for the historical novel."[17]

Childhood, Narrativity, and Memory

Scott's new historical novel and national narratives, however, share more than just the meshing of domestic life and the public political sphere. They are both discourses that privilege the past, deeming the present moment the culminating point of a narrative. It is here that we can recognize another value of the child figure for both discourses: the concentration of memory. The child's life story allows the recuperation of past events; if character in the novel has a history, often that history is con-

---

[17]M. M. Bakhtin, "The *Bildungsroman* and its Significance in the History of Realism (Toward a Historical Typology of the Novel)," in *Speech Genres and Other Late Essays*, trans. Vern W. McGee, ed. Caryl Emerson and Michael Holquist (Austin: University of Texas Press, 1986), 53.

densed into the figure of the child or youth: the child is the nucleus the narrative unfolds. As Carolyn Steedman eloquently puts it, "In this kind of account, a self was formed by the laying down and accretion of bits and pieces of a personal history, and this detritus, these little portions of the past, most readily assumed the shape of a child when reverie and memory restored them to the adult."[18] Childhood comes to express the depths of historicity within individuals.

By turns vulnerable and vital, alternately representing extinction and survival, the child is at the center of nineteenth-century historical-national (and biological) narratives, and his education is increasingly seen as a cure for national sickness. In privileging the child as the carrier of history, the novel and national narratives betray their common romantic influence. The Romantics, contrary to their claims, did not discover history. The Enlightenment, Lukács argues, had without a doubt its great historians. But Lukács is decidedly wrong in deriding the Romantic historical achievement.[19] For what Romantic historians discovered—when they discovered the past—is that both human identity and history have the same form: that of narrative. Human identity could best be elaborated, according to them, not through a dissection of man's memory—Locke's great achievement—but through the excavation and narrativization of the "foreign country" that is the past. Childhood is idealized in part because it is an anterior—hence more authentic—stage of life: as history was idealized, so was childhood.

The Enlightenment historians and *philosophes* wrote histories for the benefit of the reader in the here and now. By criticizing the past through enlightened eyes, the errors of the superstitious medieval past or the excellences of the Classical could be avoided or emulated: the dominant intention was

[18]Steedman, 10.

[19]See Georg Lukács, *The Historical Novel*, trans. Hannah and Stanley Mitchell (Lincoln: University of Nebraska Press, 1962 (1937)), 20.

critical; the pervading tone, ironic. By contrast, the Romantics idealized the past. Ernst Cassirer observes, in appraising the great importance of myth for the Romantics, that "There is, however, one fundamental difference between the conception of history in the eighteenth and nineteenth centuries. The Romantics love the past for the past's sake. To them the past is not only a fact but also one of the highest ideals."[20] Romantic historiography narrated histories that sought to portray the genealogy and genesis of a particular people or event: the dominant form was narrative itself.

Narrative itself, whose meaning is precisely the illusion of resurrected time, sought to recover the lost depths of history. Paul Ricoeur, whose *Temps et récit* is qualified by Hayden White as "the most important synthesis of literary and historical theory produced in our century," saw "historical narrative as a kind of allegory of temporality, but an allegory of a special kind, namely, a true allegory."[21] If Scott was so successful in the creation of a new mode of historical writing that one of the greatest historians of the nineteenth century, Ranke, sought to compare his own method to Scott's, it was because Scott saw history under the sign of narrative, not irony. Narrating the history of the dead became an ethical endeavor. Jules Michelet apostrophizes the "great day" of the fall of the "cursed" Bastille. "Combien de temps nos pères vous ont attendu et rêvé," exults the son who saw the wish of his ancestors fulfilled, "L'espoir que leurs fils vous verraient enfin a pu seul les soutenir ... ô beau jour, premier jour de la délivrance ... J'ai vécu pour vous raconter!"[22] To narrate is to

[20]Ernst Cassirer, *The Myth of the State* (New Haven: Yale University Press, 1946), 181.

[21]Hayden White, "The Metaphysics of Narrativity: Time and Symbol in Ricoeur's Philosophy of History" in *The Content of the Form: Narrative Discourse and Historical Representation* (Baltimore: Johns Hopkins University Press, 1987), 171.

[22]Jules Michelet, *Histoire de la Révolution française*, ed. Gérard Walter (Paris: Gallimard, 1952 (1847)), v. 1, 203.

bear witness to the birth of the nation and to vindicate the suffering of the ancestors. The "aim of history . . . I have named it *resurrection*, and this name will remain," wrote Michelet.

If narrative is the literary form which allegorizes temporality, the child is the literary *content* which acts similarly. Herder emphasizes the role of childhood in the evolution of national specificity through education. "An intellectual genesis," writes Herder in "Ideas Toward a Philosophy of History," "that is, education, connects the whole formation of an individual's humanity to that individual's parents, teachers, and friends . . . consequently to that individual's people and their ancestors. . . ."[23] That is familiar enough: it is how theorists of cultural nationalism view Herder. But, in a manner that prefigures Freud, Herder goes farther in endowing the child with a determining effect on the narrative of the adult's life:

> In order to become fully aware of this [the essence of genuine human immortality], let us simply think about the most lively moments of our life, especially of our childhood and youth. Because we enjoyed these moments, did we not let go of ourselves and open ourselves to others? . . . We believe we exist in isolation from others, but this is never the case; we do not even exist in isolation when by ourselves, for we are affected by the spirits of the dead, of ancient deified heroes [*Dämonen*], or by the spirits of our teachers, friends foes, those who form us, those who deform us . . . We cannot avoid seeing their faces and hearing their voices; even the spasms of their deformed creations are passed on to us. Happy are those to whom fate allots an Elysium and not a Tartus as the Haven for their thoughts, as the realm of

[23]Johann Gottfried Herder, *Against Pure Reason: Writings on Religion, Language, and History*, trans. Marcia Bunge (Minneapolis, Minn.: Fortress Press, 1987), 50.

> their feelings, principles, and behavior; their souls
> are grounded in a happy immortality (59–60).

Because children are open to others, they enfold history within, as it were. Herder's words clearly find their echo not only in Freud's case studies—narratives of childhood— but also in Charles Taylor's discussion of the formative effect of our continuing dialogue with "our significant others."[24] Surprisingly, perhaps, to our modernist sensibilities, Herder discovered the tormented child to be at the root of national suffering before Freud discovered him in the depths of the tormented individual.

The Romance of the Child Hero

The eighteenth-century novel has as a central problematic the alienation of the child from his/her family and society: that novel seems to stipulate that the child must leave home to gain experience. Yet, in recompense, the hero/heroine is isolated from the forces of history, though not evil, or danger. In Scott, the opposite seems to be true. The hero's dangerous journey—both physical, through the nation's tumultuous terrain, and inner, his *Bildung*—reenacts the nation's historical evolution. But the child-hero survives his ordeal to become a citizen of the new state.

If the hero of the Waverley Novels is "passive," encumbered by the possession of property; if he is "always a more or less

[24]"We define [our identity] always in dialogue with, sometimes in struggle against, the identities our significant others want to recognize in us. And even when we outgrow some of the latter—our parents, for instance—and they disappear from our lives, the conversation with them continues within us as long as we live." Charles Taylor, "The Politics of Recognition," in Amy Gutman, ed., *Multiculturalism: Examining the Politics of Recognition* (Princeton: Princeton University Press, 1994), 32–3.

mediocre, average English gentleman,"[25] it is more because Scott sought to represent a post-revolutionary version of society that has come to be our own than because of Balzac's charge of "English Philistinism." As Alexander Welsh well puts it: "The war with revolutionary France and with Napoleon had more to do with the nature of fiction in this period than is implied by the small part it plays in the novels of Jane Austen or of Scott."[26] The hero of the Waverley Novels, as I will argue below, is a child who is allowed to experience passions that the structure of the victorious world, the emerging British nation, will exclude.

As opposed to the tumultuousness the characters experience in the novels of Stendhal, "in England the novel figured forth a vision of permanence and perpetuity, consigning the kinetic energies of life to a series of romantic episodes."[27] True enough. Yet, remarkably, in his passivity and fear of the authority of law, the hero—at the end of the novel, with all passion spent—stands in fact for the citizen, or the ideal citizen, the gentleman. Thus, as with the French revolutionaries—whose vision of society is the very opposite of Scott's conciliatory, middle-of-the-road views—the citizen is infantilized.

The intertwining of realism and romance in *Waverley* has been much commented upon. Welsh goes so far as to suggest that, because the Waverley Novels eschew altogether the critical view of society characteristic of the eighteenth-century novel, "in Scott's lifetime the novel reverted to the romance" (6). And, in comparing the "history effect" in *Waverley* and Sydney Morgan's national romance *The Wild Irish Girl*, Ferris observes that although Scott "may playfully recall Morgan's Glorvina in the introductory chapter of *Waverley* [in which Scott self-consciously explicates his choice of title] when he mocks literary heroines 'with a profusion

[25]Lukács, *The Historical Novel*, 33.

[26]Alexander Welsh, *The Hero of the Waverley Novels* (Princeton: Princeton University Press, 1963), 19.

[27]Welsh, 19.

of auburn hair' who manage to transport harps around inhospitable landscapes ... his harp-playing Flora and the journey structure of his novel have strong affinities with Morgan's popular tale."[28]

It is more accurate to say, however, that the romance belongs only to the youthful hero, and surrounds his *Bildung*. After the skirmish at Clifton, in which Waverley's friend, the Highlander feudal lord Fergus Vich Ian Vohr is taken prisoner, Waverley has time to reflect upon the many misfortunes of his friends: the supposed death of Fergus (yet to come), the desolate situation of both Flora, Fergus's sister, and Rose, the daughter of the Lowland Baron Bradwardine. The narrator observes that "he felt himself entitled to say firmly, though perhaps with a sigh, that the romance of his life was ended, and that its real history had now commenced."[29]

Generically speaking, the hero of the romance is not marked as a child; he is rather a mature man.[30] Waverley, however, escapes the dangerous consequences of his actions precisely because he is seen as a child. When he is taken prisoner on suspicion of Stuart loyalty and interrogated by the stern Major Melville, the evidence seems decidedly against Waverley. He has, apparently, ignored numerous summonses from his commanding officer to rejoin his regiment; he carries a poem, written by Flora eulogizing the exploits of one Wogan who fought for Scotland and the Stuarts, which to Melville seems a clear indication that "the writer seems to expect [Waverley] should imitate"; and he is carrying in his saddle some risible, long-winded manu-

---

[28]Ferris, 123.

[29]Walter Scott, *Waverley*, ed. Claire Lamont (Oxford: Oxford University Press, 1986 (1814)), 415. All following references are to this edition.

[30]Clearly some knights (Arthur, Launcelot) are older than others (Gawain, Galahad), but the hero is not given a special treatment like a child. Wagner's interpretation of the Parsifal's story, however, emphasizes the simplicity of the child Parsifal who redeems the injured king.

scripts written by his tutor which he has never read, and that Waverley carries only to oblige Mr. Pembroke, whom Melville, however, sees as "a non-juring clergyman, the author of two treasonable works" (245).

The chapter in which this scene unfolds is entitled "An Examination." In it Scott, the lawyer, constructs a trial scene in which Waverley's actions can be explained by one of two narratives, one of guilt, the other of innocence. When Melville informs him that he is accused "of high treason, and levying war against the king, the highest delinquency of which a subject can be guilty," and hands him the warrant to his arrest, Waverley is stunned: "The astonishment which Waverley expressed at this communication was imputed by Major Melville to conscious guilt, while Mr. Morton was rather disposed to construe it into the surprise of innocence unjustly suspected" (243). Waverley is clearly not innocent. At this point, he has not yet pledged his loyalty to the chevalier, but he has already proposed his love to Flora and his loyalty, though tepid as she protests, to her Stuart cause. His lack of guilt, however, is ascribed, by the defense, explicitly to his child-like state.

Mr. Morton, a mild-mannered clergyman, speaks for the defense. He responds to Melville's express summary of the guilty case (Ch. 32) by attempting to interpret the evidence in a different manner, telling Melville, for instance, that Waverley says that "he never read" the treasonous pamphlets. Later, after Melville permits him to visit Waverley, the latter recounts to Morton his adventures in the Highlands, especially his first visit to Donald Bean Lean, a scheming conspirator. "'I am glad,' responds Morton, "'you did not mention this circumstance to the Major. It is capable of great misconstruction on the part of those who do not consider the power of curiosity and the influence of romance as motives of youthful conduct'" (259).

Even more than displaying "youthful conduct," Waverley is referred to as a child numerous times in the novel; and romance is the genre through which Waverley lives his life, a life, however, completely enmeshed in historically-decisive events. The novel, furthermore, signals the transitions from his romance-like story to history by having Waverley "wake-up," thus realizing that this romantic episode or that was a "dream." After he is aided to escape the imprisonment ordered by Melville, Waverley is finally conducted by Fergus into the presence of the Stuart prince.[31] Here, Waverley explicitly embraces the Jacobite cause when, "kneeling to Charles Edward, [he] devoted his heart and sword to the vindication of his rights!" (295). "Rejected, slandered, and threatened" by the Hanoverian side, Waverley plights loyalty to "the Prince, whose form and manners, as well as the spirit which he displayed in this singular enterprise, answered his ideas of a hero of romance" (295).

Yet, Waverley awakes from this, and other, romantic episodes just in time to avoid any irreversible revolutionary involvement. In fact, it is important to stress—the narrator's observation that "the romance of [Waverley's] life was ended" above notwithstanding—that Waverley awakes from each episode separately. It is not the case that he lives a long romantic adventure, fighting and loving, to "learn" the error of his ways at the end. Every episode is a romance which passes like a dream from which he awakes at the end of that episode. Thus, after vowing his "sword" to the prince, Waverley finds himself, after the march south, in the midst of Fergus's Highlander clans facing the king's troops.

The soldiers approach so near that "Waverley could plainly recognise the standard of the troop he had formerly commanded . . . He could hear, too, the well-known word given in the English dialect, by the equally well-distinguished voice of the commanding officer, for whom he had once felt so much

[31]It is difficult, in describing the actions of the hero of the Waverley Novels, to avoid the usage of passive tenses. The hero, as Welsh argues, is so passive that he is mostly the recipient of the actions of others.

respect. It was at that instant, that, looking around him, he saw the wild dress and appearance of his Highlander associates, heard their whispers in an uncouth and unknown language, looked upon his own dress, so unlike that which he had worn from his infancy, and wished to awake from what seemed at the moment a dream, strange, horrible, and unnatural" (chapter 46, 333). Waking up, Waverley's breathless actions at Gladsmuir are exclusively in the defense of vanquished English soldiers, such as Talbot.

Another crucial romantic episode in *Waverley* is the hero's unsuccessful wooing of Flora, Fergus's superb sister, whose belief in the rights of the chevalier and the exiled Stuarts exceeds her brother's in both "fanaticism" and "purity." Waverley first meets Flora in the clan's Highland home. Mesmerized by the "land of romance" which the narrator describes with the obligatory rocks, desolation and waterfall, Waverley beholds "with a sensation of horror . . . Flora and her attendant appear, like inhabitants of another region . . ." (175). She salutes him. Dizzy, he is unable to return her greeting.[32] Mist invades not only the landscape but also Waverley's awareness. As he is falling in love, the hero yearns for solitude: "He would not for worlds have quitted his place by her side; yet he almost longed for solitude, that he might decipher and examine at leisure the complication of emotions which now agitated his bosom" (178). The hero's love of solitude: is it not an unconscious awareness that the rules of the romance apply only to himself; that, as soon as he allows others to enter, history will enter too, and the romance will end?

---

[32]It is here, perhaps, that Waverley appears, in the words of Judith Wilt, "feminized": "The author of the Waverley Novels has been unfixing the boundaries of male identity ever since Edward Waverley rode out from home to be kidnapped, 'educated,' seduced, and otherwise feminized." *Secret Leaves: The Novels of Walter Scott* (Chicago: University of Chicago Press, 1985), 117.

"Agitated by new and conflicting feelings . . . [Waverley] fell asleep and dreamed of Flora Mac-Ivor" (185). The next day, news arrives that impugns the honor of both Waverley and his father. Decided by both his humiliation and his hope for Flora, Waverley, though waveringly, joins the clan's cause. Yet, even before Flora rejects his suit, he, faced with the real possibility of historical involvement, wonders why he is joining "plans dark, deep, and dangerous" (212). Here again, as during the march, the hero dreams and awakens.

The hero dreams; therefore he is safe. The Waverley Novels seem to pardon the hero's infractions because figures of author-ity see him as an errant child. After his involvement in the ill-prepared and short-lived Jacobite Rebellion of 1745, he is pardoned by the Hanoverian king through the intercession of an English officer whose life Waverley had saved in the Battle of Gladsmuir. Colonel Talbot writes Waverley a letter in which he informs him that although "his Royal Highness [King George II] . . . was very angry," Talbot, by threatening to resign his com-mission, has managed to obtain a pardon for Waverley. "You are therefore once more a free man, and I have promised for you that you will be a good boy in future, and remember what you owe to the lenity of government" (456).

But the charmed circle of romance, while it does protect the child-hero—the "good boy"—himself from the vicissitudes of history, does not protect his friends. Dreams are solitary after all. Even as Talbot is engaging Waverley in some ill-timed badi-nage that "*my* prince [the king] can be as generous as *yours* [the chevalier Charles Edward Stuart]," boorishly declaring that "I do not pretend, indeed, that [the king] confers a favour with all the foreign graces and compliments of your chevalier errant; but he has a plain English manner," Fergus is about to face a most horrible death, and a way of life its extinction. When Waverley visits his friend in jail moments before his execution, "the unfortunate chieftain, strongly and heavily fettered," reminds Waverley, who objects to his cheerful manner, that "We have entered Carlisle with happier auspices ... when we marched in, side by side, and hoisted the white flag on these ancient towers. But I am *no boy* [my emphasis], to sit down and weep because the luck has gone against me" (471). Unlike Waverley, Fergus's narrative genre is not the romance; he pays the full price of "levying war against the king." Scott's juxtaposition of the contrasting fates of the two rebels is here clearly marked in terms of the puerility of the hero.

Although Fergus has ample reason to berate Waverley for his about-face, he forbears. He even spares Waverley the sight of his imminent torture and death. Nor will the fact of Waverley's betrayal of the prince's—and the clan's—cause he embraced mar his future reputation and status. This is not only to make an ethical point. Both Lukács and Welsh emphasize the class status of Waverley. The hero of the Waverley Novels is, Lukács argues, a "mediocre average English gentleman," who can "enter into human contact with both camps [of the historical conflict] ... [and] who sides passionately with neither."[33] Welsh stresses the importance of honor to the Waverley hero. Originally honor was "the code of behavior of the aristocracy ... By the time of the Waverley Novels, however, the aristocracy has been redefined as the gentlemen of England ... The class of gentlemen must ideally maintain a high sense of honor" (138).

But surely the most elementary of the duties of a gentleman is that he keep his word. Waverley breaks his vow to the prince, to Fergus and to the clan in which he has become an honorary brother. His passion for Flora eventually proves as limited as she suspected from the beginning. So why is he forgiven? In his "Introductory" chapter to *Waverley*, Scott engages the continuity of human passions through the ages, "which have alike agitated the human heart, whether it throbbed under the steel corslet of

[33]Lukács, *The Historical Novel*, 33–37.

the fifteenth century, the brocaded coat of the eighteenth, or the blue frock and white dimity waistcoat of the present day" (35). Passions, however, are colored by the times. Only by being a child can the hero of today engage the archaic violent passions of yore and be spared the punishment of his transgression; only by being a child can Waverley relive the national conflicts that preceded the establishment of the civil state, and still live to become a good citizen of it.

Like Don Quixote, Waverley is a romance hero outside the genre's proper time. Colonel Talbot explicitly connects Waverley to Quixote when, commenting on Waverley's narrative of his own actions, he upbraids the child-hero that he has "been trepanned into the service of this Italian knight-errant by a few civil speeches from him . . ." (359). Through this connection, childhood and madness are analogized. To Sancho Panza and others, Quixote tilting at the windmills is mad; to other characters, especially figures of authority in *Waverley*, Waverley joining a mutinous army in a civil war is a child seduced by romance. The new nation, the nation of civil law, can suppress madness— the mad are locked up—but children are still around; and it is to them that the forbidden passions are assigned. At least until the romance is over and real life begins.

Fathers and Sons

Like Locke, Scott explores the conflict between patriarchal authority and freedom and the yearning of the sons for individual liberty. As in the eighteenth-century novel, the child-hero becomes the center of the narrative when he leaves home. But in the Waverley Novels, not only does the hero become involved in national history, but he does so as a direct result of his father's national politics. This is more evident in *Old Mortality* than in *Waverley*, for if Waverley is marked as a child because he is protected from the consequences of his national involvement, Morton, the hero of *Old Mortality*, is a son never allowed to forget the exploits of his heroic father in the Civil War and later.[34] "Affected by the spirits of the dead," in Herder's words, the child unfolds the (national) story of his father. Morton's dilemma is to reconcile the politics of his father with that of the established government; to harmonize the public responsibility of defending his own freedom and civil liberties with his love for a Royalist young woman.

Old Mortality opens with a ceremony of authority and repression, enforced joy and smoldering rebellion. "Under the reign of the late Stewarts, there was an anxious wish on the part of the government to counteract . . . the strict or puritanical spirit which had been the chief characteristic of the republican government, and to revive those feudal institutions which united the vassal to the liege lord, and both to the crown."[35] The narrator disapprovingly describes the wappenschaw, a ceremonial display of fealty to the king, instituted by the restored Stuarts to enforce the absolutist ideas of hierarchy and obedience to authority. As David Brown avers,

> For its encapsulation of an entire period with all its leading features and contradictions in one descriptive scene, the occasion of the 'wappenschaw' which opens the novel proper was probably never surpassed by Scott . . . The wappenschaw is intended to manifest the feudal order of Scotland under the Stuarts; in theory, it is a gathering of the aristocratic hierarchy, supported by their retainers and vassals in the lower orders. Yet as the scene progresses it becomes clear that the assembly is actually a monumental façade, a ceremony reintroduced by the Stuart government long after any significance it has

[34]Although, of course, Waverley decides to join the rebels partly because of the government's humiliation of his father.

[35]Walter Scott, *Old Mortality*, ed. Angus Calder (London: Penguin, 1985 (1816)), 70. Following citations refer to this edition.

had as an actual expression of feudal relationships
has disappeared. . . .[36]

The wappenschaw not only makes clear the archaic nature of
Stuart absolutism, but perfectly contrasts the Royalists' obsession
with outward signs of obedience and loyalty (such as enforced
oaths of allegiance) to the Covenanters' emphasis on freedom—
often anarchic—of the inner conscience. The Royalists' penchant
for physical display of conformity to a well-ordered universe is
likened by the narrator to another, unambiguously evil, circus of
harmony:

> To compel men to dance and be merry by authority,
> has rarely succeeded even on board of slave-ships,
> where it was formerly sometimes attempted by way
> of inducing the wretched captives to agitate their
> limbs and restore the circulation, during the few
> minutes they were permitted to enjoy the fresh air
> upon deck. The rigour of the strict Calvinists
> increased, in proportion to the wishes of the gov-
> ernment that it should be relaxed (70–1).

The absolute (Stuart) father/king's authority is being ques-
tioned in *Old Mortality*, a novel in which religion and politics
intertwine. When Mause Headrigg, a strict Covenanter, pro-
hibits her son, Cuddie, from attending the wappenschaw
because she sees "nae warrant" to it, she affirms her own Calvinist principles, and, indeliberately, rejects her inferior position in
the feudal hierarchy. To Lady Margaret Bellenden, Mause's feudal mistress, the only "warrant" needed is her own will. Such
questioning of the king's authority coming from a lowly, humble woman, who insists on the freedom of her actions, contrasts

[36]David Brown, *Walter Scott and the Historical Imagination* (London:
Routledge, 1979), 70.

with Morton's inability to break from an ascriptive identity as his father's son.

We first meet Morton as he enters the shooting competition during the wappenschaw. After he wins the field—triumphing over Lord Evandale, his rival to Edith Bellenden's affections—Morton bows deeply to Edith Bellenden, Lady Margaret's niece, who blushes violently, revealing to the reader her affection for Morton. The aunt asks who the "young person" is, and a gentleman in the crowd responds "'The son of the late Colonel Morton of Milnwood, who commanded a regiment of horse with great courage at Dunbar and Inverkeithing" (81), mentioning two battles in which the elder Morton fought for the king, for Scotland, and for the Covenant before the schism between the restored monarch and the Covenanters.

Morton is thrust into decisive national politics moments after he wins the prize at the wappenschaw. Burley, a fanatical Covenanter, meets and recognizes Morton in the tavern where Morton is being feted. One of the assassins of the Archbishop of St. Andrews, whom the Covenanters accused of colluding with the "perjured Charles Stewart . . . even as he renounced the Covenant," Burley follows Morton and asks him for shelter from the pursuing Royalist forces. Suspecting the older man of involvement in bloody opposition to the government, Morton initially refuses him shelter at his uncle's estate.

Burley, however, prevails on Morton to hide him at Milnwood when he reveals that he is that John Balfour of Burley who, as Morton himself recalls, was the elder Morton's "ancient friend and comrade, who saved his life, with almost the loss of his own . . ." (97). Burley continues the child and son identifications of Morton. In a crisis of conscience, Burley, indirectly commenting on the Archbishop's assassination, rhetorically asks Morton: "Think you not it is a sore trial for flesh and blood, to be called upon to execute the righteous judgments of Heaven while we are yet in the body, and continue to retain that blinded sense and sympathy for carnal suffering, which makes our own flesh thrill when we strike a gash upon the body of another?"

Avoiding Burley's attempt to move him, Morton replies that he doubts "any inspiration which seemed to dictate a line of conduct contrary to those feelings of natural humanity." Burley parries the thrust by coolly pointing out that Morton ignores the truth because he has not yet outgrown his rational principles: "It is natural you should think so; you are yet in the dungeon-house of the law, a pit darker than that into which Jeremiah was plunged, even the dungeon of Malaciah the son of Hamelmelech . . . Yet is the seal of the covenant upon your forehead, and the son of the righteous, who resisted to blood where the banner was spread on the mountains, shall not utterly be lost, as one of the children of darkness" (chapter 6, 105). By linking the (symbolic) seal of the covenant and the hoped for influence of the older Morton, Burley's language suggests that the metaphorical marking is literalized through paternity, that Morton inherited a physical "seal" on his body which marked him as a dissenter—a seal of the Father and of the father.

The Omniscient Novel and History

Herodotus opens his *History* unforgettably:

> I, Herodotus of Halicarnassus, am here setting forth my history, that time may not draw the color from what man has brought into being, nor those great and wonderful deeds, manifested by both Greeks and barbarians, fail of their report, and, together with all this, the reason why they fought one another.[37]

[37]Herodotus, *The History*, trans. David Grene (Chicago: University of Chicago Press, 1987), 33.

The historian battles the ravages of time that it may not welt the glory of men as it welts, inevitably, men. As François Hartog observes, what is remarkable is the stance the historian-narrator assumes: "[T]he prologue to the *Histories* sets out both to invoke the epic tradition and to rival it. The *Iliad* and the *Odyssey* are certainly present, but the intention is at the same time to mark out a distinction from that tradition: here, it is not the goddess who sings of 'which of the gods it was that made the son of Atreus and the divine Achilles quarrel,' but Herodotus of Halicarnassus who tells 'the reason why the Greeks and Barbarians warred against each other'; it is not the Muse singing of 'the man who saw the cities of many peoples and learned their ways,' but Herodotus, who 'goes forward with his history and speaks of small and great cities alike.'"[38] The historian's authority lies in the narrative conceit of an omniscience in time and space.

In his study, Hartog identifies in Herodotus a topos of great importance to our inquiry of the new narrator's stance in the nineteenth-century historical novel: autopsy. In the famous story in which "Candaules, the king of Lydia, seeks to convince Gyges, his close friend, of the beauty of his wife" by having him see her naked, since "men trust their ears less than their eyes," Hartog sees a mise-en-abyme of the primacy of eyewitnessing for the narrator. Herodotus, unlike Thucydides who insisted that the only history he could write was contemporary history since the historian should only report what he saw, mixes both *opsis* and hearsay, sight and hearing, to attempt to determine the cause of the greatest war in Greek history which took place many years before his birth. The omniscient historian-narrator vastly expands the scope of the knowledge of the *histor*, whose original meaning, according to Emile Benveniste, is that of a "witness . . . first and foremost in that he has seen" (261). For

---

[38]François Hartog, *The Mirror of Herodotus*, trans. Janet Lloyd (Berkeley: University of California Press, 1988), 276.

Herodotus' effort to ascertain the truth of who was *aitios*, or juridically responsible, for the start of the war cannot be satisfied by the eye alone: "I have seen with my own eyes as far as the city of Elephantine, and beyond that I learned by question and hearsay," writes Herodotus (263).

Eminently pertinent to this chronological omniscience is of course the historian's geographical omnipresence. Herodotus has traveled widely, and the increased knowledge that has come from his travels will aid him in discovering and narrating the causes of the war, since these causes will turn out to be related to the current characteristics of the peoples involved. "The eye of the traveler," writes Hartog, "thus marks out the geographical space, dividing it into more or less well-known zones . . ." (263). What cannot be comprehended through *opsis* can be through hearing. The limits to eyewitnessing knowledge whether spatial, through distance—any knowledge after Elephantine—or temporal—what happened before the historian's arrival—can be remedied through *akoe*, "I have heard."

Related to the narrator's autopsy is his stance as a surveyor as well as a traveler. As Gregory Nagy observes: "The *histor*, whose authority is derived from Zeus as king, can be understood as thereby having the privileged vantage point of the gods themselves, who can see without being seen."[39] Nagy links his observation to Benveniste's explanation of how a "clandestine witness," an *arbiter* evolves into an arbitrator, a judge: "[The *arbiter*] judges by coming between the two parties from outside like someone who has been present at the affair without being seen, who can therefore give judgment on the facts freely and with authority, regardless of all precedent in the light of the circumstances" (261).

Hartog's observations about autopsy are germane to both narrator and hero of Scott's historical novel. An important *topos*

---

[39]Gregory Nagy, *Pindar's Homer: The Lyric Possession of an Ancient Past* (Baltimore: Johns Hopkins University Press, 1990), 261.

of the omniscient historical novel of the nineteenth century is the stance of the narrator as surveyor. The great historical novelists of the nineteenth century, beginning with Walter Scott, replace the Lockean experiential paradigm of knowledge of the realist narrators of the eighteenth century with a model that stresses the omniscience of the narrator as an interpreter, and arbiter, of the nation's history. In Scott particularly, this stance is clearest when his narrator describes the battles crucially formative in Britain's history.

In the instance of Drumclog, the enthusiastic forces of the Scottish Covenanters, led by the fanatical Burley, have prepared an ambush for the smaller army of loyalists commanded by John Graham of Claverhouse. Morton, the novel's "passive hero," has barely escaped execution by Claverhouse for giving shelter to Burley, his late father's friend. As a prisoner, Morton is marched by the Royalist troops—together with Mause Headrigg, the old Covenanter and her son Cuddie, both now homeless, and Gabriel Kettledrumle, a Covenant preacher—as they prepare to give Battle to the Covenanters. The prisoners find themselves, as Lukács observes, in the middle of action, and the middling hero pulled apart between two partly sympathetic camps.

The narrator does not establish the authenticity of his knowledge by motivating his experience as in the realist novel of the eighteenth century; rather, he surveys the field of the impending battle:

> They had now for more than a mile got free of the woodlands, whose broken glades, had for some time, accompanied them after they had left the woods of Tillietudlem . . . A few birches and oaks still feathered the narrow ravines . . . But these were gradually disappearing; and a wide and waste country lay before them, swelling into bare hills of dark heath, intersected by deep gullies; being the passages by which torrents forced their course in winter, and

> during summer the disproportioned channels for
> diminutive rivulets that winded their puny way
> among heaps of stone and gravel ... This desolate
> region seemed to extend farther than the eye can
> reach ... and thereby impressing irresistibly the
> mind of the spectator with a sense of the omnipo-
> tence of nature, and the comparative inefficacy of
> the boasted means of amelioration which man is
> capable of opposing to the disadvantages of climate
> and soil (208–9).

The narrator begins with a neutral description of the visual
field that Morton is gradually seeing: From the woodlands with
"broken glades" to the "birches and oaks." Then he adds a bit of
geological-climatological information, the differing terrain in
summer and winter—that Morton may or may not know—
ending with a panoramic view and two related philosophical
judgments which, considering Morton's current stupor—having barely escaped execution by firing squad; believing his lover,
Edith Bellinden, faithless; being led in chains—seem strictly to
be the narrator's alone. The latter grounds his epistemological
authority in this passage through surveying the terrain, seeing
and categorizing it.

   As the army advances, the eye of the narrator scans the terrain before any character in the army gets close enough to do it:
the narrator acts as focalizer first. The archetypal formation of
the armies before the engagement seems to favor this view; the
two armies ascend opposing hills to take panoramic views of
the valley in which the actual engagement will take place, with
the commanders having a bird's eye view of the action. The narrator, however, shifts freely from one camp to another without
necessarily focalizing through a combatant's eyes. Typically
Scott will shift focalization to get his hero's assessment of the
formation. His passive hero finds himself engaged in the battle
despite himself: here at Drumclog since he is a prisoner of the
royalists, and at Gladsmuir (in *Waverley*) because he was misled

by the Highlanders. Because of his divided loyalty, Scott's hero's assessment is always negative: whoever wins, the hero loses.

Not only does the narrator's omniscience imply the conceit of a spatial superiority, but it is predicated on chronological omniscience. In the example we have been describing above, after the narrator's survey, Morton espies the royalist army and perceives that "Their numbers, which appeared formidable when they crowded through narrow roads . . . were now apparently diminished by being exposed at once to view . . ." (209). Here, Morton is the focalizer, and the character, less so the reader if he/she is aware of the historical outcome of the battle, has acceded to a piece of historical knowledge—that the royalists will likely be defeated—that was the property of the narrator all along because, for him, it is a past event.

This historical omniscience of the narrator creates narrative tensions: Will the fact that Waverley has joined the army of the young Pretender (the chevalier de Saint-George, the son of the exiled Stuart king) help the Highlander cause? Will Burley and the other assassins of the primate be captured? Tensions whose solutions must, in the end, tally with the historical facts the reader may know. The narrative puzzles find their solution through the historical omniscience of the narrator. This ironic disjunction of knowledge between character and narrator is formative to the nineteenth-century realist omniscient novel and explains Barthes's observation in *S/Z* that the Balzacian narrative consists of a series of enigmas and secrets that the narrative later solves. "Thus, with its designating, silent movement," writes Barthes, "a pointing finger always accompanies the classic text: the truth is therefore long desired and avoided, kept in a kind of pregnancy whose end, both liberating and catastrophic, will bring about the utter end of the discourse; and the character, the very arena of these signifieds, is only the enigma's passage. . . ."[40]

---

[40]Roland Barthes, *S/Z*, trans. Richard Miller (New York: Farrar, Strauss and Giroux, 1974 (1970)), 62.

Barthes's "pointing finger" surely points out to the reader what the narrator's eye has seen. The extradiegetic narrator's eye assumes its most omniscient view in Scott's historical fiction and the ironic separation between Scott's narrator's omniscience and his hero's diegetic confusion underpins the historical novel of the nineteenth century.

Scott's superlative depiction of battles such as Drumclog in *Old Mortality* and Gladsmuir in *Waverley* operates as a narrative device which, through the mobility it fosters, juxtaposes the various competing communities of discourse within the borders of the state at the historical moment when the hegemony of the latter is about to engulf them. Ironically, the omniscient narrator of the historical realist novel must assume the distinctly unrealistic position of an eternal and ahistorical knower. Yet his position, like Athena's, parallels the religious significance with which the nation itself is endowed; and his knowledge and incorporation of all the languages of the various communities of discourse qualifies him as a creator of a national language and a "unified" realm.

The National Narrator and the Child Hero

If the child-hero is at the heart of the content of Scott's novel, he also underlays its narrative structure: he is key to the meaning of Scott's third-person omniscient narrative form. In analyzing the epistemology of historical narrative, and, more broadly, the connection between the nature of narrative and that of "humanity itself," Hayden White questions the significance of endowing a set of historical events with "the formal coherency of a story."[41] Citing Hegel's emphasis on the intimate connection between the state, and both the keeping of historical records and the produc-

[41]Hayden White, "The Value of Narrativity in the Representation of Reality," in *The Content of the Form: Narrative Discourse and Historical Representation* (Baltimore: Johns Hopkins University Press, 1987), 4.

tion of historical prose, White concludes that "we cannot but be struck by the frequency with which narrativity, whether of the fictional or the factual sort, presupposes the existence of a legal system against which or on behalf of which the typical agents of a narrative account militate" (13).

The desire for moral order creates a desire for narrative order implicit in a plot with a beginning, a middle, and an end. White, analyzing the analogy between historical narrative and the older chronicle form, searches for an overarching principle that rules this narrative ordering:

> Does it follow that in order for there to be a narrative, there must be some equivalent of the Lord, some sacral being endowed with the authority and power of the Lord, existing in time? If so, what could such an equivalent be? (16)

The "sacral being" in Scott's Waverley Novels, I propose, is the nation, whose story is told both through the experiences of the passive child-hero—who, as Lukács observes, acts as the still hub of the wheel of history around whom revolve the clashing nations of the British state—and through the formal feature of a third-person narrator whose very ability to narrate the life of the hero he "postdates" (by sixty years in *Waverley* and more than a century in *Old Mortality*) implies the survival of the language, the records, and the ordered world of the nation. The existence of the narrator allegorizes the survival of the nation. "I know its history, I can tell its story, it has outlived (the diegetic time of)*Waverley* and *Old Mortality* and will outlive you, reader" the narrator seems to say.

The omniscient narrator has the serenity of both belonging to and transcending the hero's time. Such a stance is not only an attribute of omniscient narrators, however, but also of Rousseau's mythical national father. "Pour découvrir les meilleures regles de société qui conviennet aux Nations, il faudroit une intelligence supérieure, qui vit toutes les passions des hommes et qui n'en éprouvât aucune, qui n'eut aucun rapport avec notre nature et qui la connût à fond . . . Il faudroit des Dieux pour donner des lois aux hommes."[42] Rousseau's Lawgiver's similarity to Scott's narrator is uncanny. Despite their great difference in character and political opinion, both writers reject the absolutist state but seek a new order under the laws of the nation. The omniscient national narrator, because of his study and national position, understands the passions that animate his characters, but the passage of time shields him from the feelings that may cloud his narrative judgment. Like *Emile*'s Tutor or *The Social Contract*'s Lawgiver, the omniscient narrator in the Waverley Novels acts as a guiding national father who both narrates the life of the protagonist (Waverley, Morton in *Old Mortality*) and provides a formulaic narrative prescription (or form) for the lives of other fellow citizens of the hero.

Scott's historical novel narrates the involvement of the child-hero in the nation's historicity through the superior vision of a "national" narrator.[43] This stance of the narrator is of fundamental importance to the form of the nineteenth-century novel: not only to the historical novel but also to the realist social novel—Stendhal, Balzac, and Tolstoy were all admirers of Scott. Remarkably, the nineteenth-century realist novel's form and content, its omniscience and epistemology, are closely related to

[42]*Du Contrat social*, edited and annotated by Robert Derathé, in Jean-Jacques Rousseau, *Oeuvres complètes*, ed. Bernard Gagnebin and Marcel Raymond (Paris: Gallimard [Bibliothèque de la Pléiade], 1964 (1762)), vol. 3, 381. "To discover the rules of society that are best suited to nations, there would need to exist a superior intelligence, who could understand the passions of men without feeling any of them, who had no affinity with our nature but knew it to the full . . . Gods would be needed to give men laws." *The Social Contract*, trans. Maurice Cranston (London: Penguin, 1968), 84.

[43]It is notable that the largest monument in Edinburgh is to Walter Scott, and not to any political, military, or religious national figure.

the interweaving of the fortunes of the nation and the child-hero.

Children, however, are not always good girls or boys, like Waverley. They can become wild cards in the game of political belonging. In a wry novella, André Gide rewrites the Biblical parable of the prodigal son. Returning to his family because of need but ultimately unrepentant, Gide's *enfant prodigue* encourages his younger brother to leave and to accomplish what he himself could not: forgetting home, "Laisse-moi! laisse-moi! je reste à consoler notre mère ... Il est temps à présent. Le ciel pâlit. Pars sans bruit. Allons! embrasse-moi, mon jeune frère: tu emportes tous mes espoirs. Soi fort; oublie-nous; oublie-moi."[44] Such a Nietzschean willed forgetting of the old would contradict not only the dependence of the child but also the allegorical belonging of the citizen.

[44]André Gide, *Le retour de l'enfant prodigue* (Paris: Folio, 1912), 182.

CONCLUSION

CHILDREN AND SURVIVAL

> "Till at last the child's mind *is* these suggestions, and the
> sum of the suggestions *is* the child's mind. And not the
> child's mind only. The adult's mind too—all his life long . . .
> But all these suggestions are *our* suggestions!" The Director
> almost shouted in his triumph.
>
> Aldous Huxley, *Brave New World*

> "He was all that one could wish England's noblest sons to be
> in days when no sacrifice but the most precious is
> acceptable, and the most precious is that which is most
> freely proffered."
>
> Winston Churchill,
> eulogizing Rubert Brooke, 1914

> The old Lie: Dulce et decorum est / Pro patria mori
>
> Wilfred Owen, "Dulce Et Decorum Est"

Like the two strands of a double helix, the novel and national narratives intertwine. Crossing and separating, they are closer at certain points than at others: Rousseau's *Emile* formally resembles a novel whereas Locke's *Second Treatise* does not; Scott's Waverley Novels stage their relation to national formation more explicitly than the eighteenth-century novel. Waverley's marriage to Rose Bradwardine, for example, figures national reconciliation and prospective unity as a romance plot that ensures continuity. Moll Flanders's squandering of children, an extreme case of the eighteenth-century novel's atomism, by contrast, does not rhyme with national prescriptions that stress the national duty of women to have and nurture children. Yet in both discourses—the novel and national narratives—a homeless child's story proves original, formally and thematically. The following should be regarded as footnotes to my earlier discussion of the two discourses and their overlaps. They are not intended to be definitive.

I. Of the Child's Story in Novels

Whereas Clarissa Harlowe's story is told in 1748, the other Clarissa, Mrs. Dalloway, will wait till 1925 for hers. The British novel's almost exclusive emphasis on having a child/youth as its hero continues well into the end of the nineteenth century. By contrast, because they often represent adulterous women, French and Russian novels do not fit this mold. Still, those Continental writers who portray men's stories (Balzac, Stendhal, Pushkin) do certainly privilege young age. Almost all of the novels that represent young people end with marriage, if a marriage is in the cards, for matrimony is the end of childhood. The orphan's story is, of course, central to the nineteenth-century British novel, but I believe it has its origins elsewhere. Incidentally, it is a great irony that, although as far as the development of the novel is concerned, *Tom Jones,* with its self-consciously comic narrator, is less relevant than, say, *Clarissa* or *Roxana;* Tom's fate anticipates that of the most important heroes and heroines of the novel of the following century. For, like the orphans of the nineteenth-century novel, Fielding's foundling's loose parentage allows him a freedom not granted the other child heroes.

Discussing the legacy of eighteenth-century novelistic masterplots, Nancy Armstrong has written that: "This was the difference between *Robinson Crusoe* and *Pamela,* then. Even Defoe could not write a successful sequel to his novel, and inasmuch as his masculine form of heroism could not be reproduced by other authors, we cannot say *Crusoe* inaugurated the tradition of the novel as we know it."[1] My own view of the novel's rise contradicts

[1] Nancy Armstrong, *Desire and Domestic Fiction,* 29.

this assertion; yet, it is her persuasion of the legacy of Crusoe's story that is worth disputing here. Defoe's novel strongly influenced popular novelists such as R. L. Stevenson (*Treasure Island*), Frederick Marryat (*Masterman Ready*), R. M. Ballantyne (*The Coral Island*) and, closer to our day, William Golding (*Lord of the Flies*), who all exploited the island plot in which adolescents have to survive through luck, pluck, and cruelty. That plot, with its potential as an imperial allegory, is also archetypal in nineteenth-century adolescent periodicals, such as *The Union Jack, Every Boy's Magazine, Young England,* and *The Boy's Own Paper.*

In one surprising reworking of the island plot, for example, an article in *The Boy's Own Paper,* "Robinson Crusoe's Island," criticizes Defoe for "writing fiction, not fact," preferring instead the "real" story of Alexander Selkirk's marooning on the island. And, unlike Stevenson's adolescent narrator in *Treasure Island,* who promises to tell all, "keeping nothing back but the bearings of the island," the article gives the longitude and latitude of "Robinson Crusoe's Island," going on to quote William Cowper's poem in honor of Selkirk: "I am monarch of all I survey/My right there is none to dispute." Rather than promoting a boyish longing for fantastical adventure in imitation of Crusoe, the article encourages its adolescent readers to link knowledge, conquest and purposeful travel, to recognize that much of the world awaits colonization. Yet, while it explicitly connects travel and Britain's colonial project and prefers "truth" over fiction, the article replays a fundamental feature of Defoe's novel: Crusoe's work ethic and his domination of the new territory in which he finds himself.[2]

To be sure, there was never a shortage of literary plots, of potential children's stories, to lure the young into the service of

[2]W. B. Keer, "Robinson Crusoe's Island," The Boy's Own Paper, 13 September 1879, 558. For this article, I am indebted to my student, Sarah C. Corbett, whose undergraduate thesis, "Sons Be Welded One and All": Interpretations of Patriotism and Empire in British Adolescent Literature (1998), I directed.

the nation. Owen's "children ardent for some desperate glory" learnt "the old lie," through which they lived their short lives from more elevated literary sources than adolescent popular magazines: Horace and Virgil, Arthurian romances, Tennyson, William Morris's *The Well at the World's End*.[3] Sir Henry Newbolt's allegorical poem "Vitai Lampada" memorably encapsulates the public schools' inculcation of patriotic honor through athletics and camaraderie among the boys:

> The river of death has brimmed his banks,
> And England's far, and Honour a name,
> But the voice of a schoolboy rallies the ranks:
> "Play up! play up! And play the game!"

II. Of the Child's Story in National Narratives

Underscoring the loss and suffering prevalent in national narratives, children become loci of vulnerable cultural memory, and, according to organic growth "theories," determinants of the future of the race and, hence, the nation. Children's stories continue to allegorize national victimization and "hope" well into our day. In April 1998, for example, a French couple in Vitrolles, a town with a council run by the racialist National Front, rejected an award aimed at encouraging "French" childbirth (immigrants were not eligible for the award), and said they "felt ashamed" they were the recipients. In a recent Russian film, *Burnt by the Sun*, Nadya, the young daughter of Kotov, a retired general and Hero of the Soviet Union, is infatuated with the Stalinist youth group, "the Pioneers." She salutes them as they pass her country home, a regiment of flute-playing and drumbeating adolescents. Later, Kotov explains to Nadya that Soviet

---

[3]For a brilliant treatment of the literary aspects of World War I, see Paul Fussell, *The Great War and Modern Memory* (Oxford: Oxford University Press, 1975)

successes will ensure that "roads will be nice and flat" and "socks will be soft," so "all the people can have feet as soft" as hers, which he lovingly caresses. "Respect your parents and cherish your Soviet motherland," he softly admonishes. Here, the citizen is to the nation as the child is to his parents. Later, Nadya's father, targeted by his wife's ex-lover, is put on trial, "confesses" to treason and is executed on orders of Stalin, the Pioneers' idol.

In *To Live*, a Chinese film portraying the life of a family following Mao's victory (dir. Zhang Yimou, 1994), young Red Guards at a maternity ward "overthrow" the old doctors during the Cultural Revolution, whom they accuse of reactionary beliefs. Worried, a young factory leader whose deaf wife is about to give birth, brings in the gynecology chief, ostensibly for "reeducation." When the youthful medical students (who later hysterically yell "we're only students," as the deaf woman bleeds to death after she delivers) protest, he replies: "Yes, this is the same Wang Bin who insulted me—a working-class man—and my wife, saying she wasn't fit to reproduce . . . We dragged him here today to educate him, to criticize him, and to let him witness her giving birth: To show him the heirs of this new, Red world." The film undercuts the notion that the child is the seed whose purity will restore the health of the nation corrupted by adults. Ironically, the factory leader's child, the heir of the "new, Red world," dies because medical expertise accrues with time and age, and does not automatically belong to the pure Red Guards.

Such narratives are not the preserve of totalitarian regimes, however. Most Americans would find Robespierre's claim that the child belongs to the nation radically intrusive. Yet, a new language, a familial model of politics, dominates American national politics today. Laura Berlant claims that the United States today has no public sphere. Instead, an "intimate public sphere" has superseded it since "during the rise of the Reaganite right, a familial politics of the national future came to define the urgencies of the present."[4] In an op-ed piece written during the last presidential campaign, the syndicated columnist Ellen Goodman wryly wondered whether Bill Clinton and Bob Dole were running for president or to "become father of their Country." "If he makes a ten-minute speech," Dole complained of his rival, "he'll mention children seventeen times. I've clocked him."[5] Goodman linked this fatherly one-upmanship to a national obsession with missing or deadbeat dads: that's a far cry indeed from Filmer's seventeenth-century argument in justification of the absolutist king as a *pater patriae*. Yet, what appears innocuous and wholesome is often related to other, less familiar and more disturbing, views of the link between child and nation, such as those dramatized in the two films or expressed in the National Front's racialist fertility award. This book presents the genealogy (non-American as it turns out) of such familial national politics.

I stressed earlier that I will not focus on racialist views of the child, whether in genetic formulations of nationalism (although they were briefly considered in chapter three) or in unsubtle, racialist literary treatments. Here, in conclusion, I would like to address some of the views propagated in late nineteenth- and early twentieth-century France and Britain in which the biological and the cultural are harder to separate.

The child incarnated national hope. In Zola's *Germinal*, Maheu, the levelheaded coal miner who is shot dead by the gendarmes during a strike, spends one Sunday fixing the bathtub and hanging a "portrait of the Prince Impérial that had been given to the children." Propagandists of the Second Empire in France attempted to combat the unpopularity of Louis Napoleon by encouraging a national cult of the child Napoleon Eugene, the Prince Impérial. Later, French advocates of organic

---

[4]Laura Berlant, *The Queen of America goes to Washington City*, 1–3.

[5]Ellen Goodman, "Searching for the First Father on the Campaign Trail," *TheBoston Globe*, 18 April 1996, p. 17.

populism and "rural democracy" also valorized young age. In his *Les Déracinés*, the once wildly popular novelist Maurice Barrès, prophet and darling of the French Right, narrates the tribulations of a number of adolescents who, seduced by their cosmopolitan rationalist lycée philosophy teacher, forget their attachment to their own soil. In this *roman à thèse*, the narrator (clearly standing at no distance from the author) deplores "Déraciner ces enfants, les détacher du sol et du groupe social où tout les relie, pour les placer hors de leur préjugés dans la raison abstraite. . . ."[6][My translation follows: "Uprooting these children, detaching them from the earth and the social milieu where everything connects them, in order to place them outside their predispositions and in abstract reason."] Because they may be led astray, the nation must protect its young people from negative adult influences and the loss of attachment to the soil, crucial to their well-being and the nation's. An admirer of Barrès and a fellow Lorraine native, the anthropologist and right-wing deputy Louis Marin, also rejected the "new Sorbonne," the veiled object of attack of Barrès's novel, which "rightist intellectuals . . . believed to be [an] overly theoretical, Germanized institution."[7] And, like his influential novelist friend, Marin linked childhood and national loss and recovery. Leaving politics behind, the old Marin turned to the study of "the role of fairy tales in keeping alive the old ways of his native Lorraine," searching for confirmation for the idea "that each nation had its special genius, a combination of the national psychology and historical circumstances."[8]

In Britain, Benjamin Disraeli, novelist and prime minister, explicitly saw children and youth as the solution to the national

---

[6]Maurice Barrès, *Les Déracinés* (Paris: Folio, 1988 (1897)), 85.

[7]Herman Lebovics, *True France: The Wars over Cultural Identity 1900–1945* (Ithaca: Cornell University Press, 1992), 19.

[8]Louis Marin, "La Naissance, la vie, la mort des traditions," *L'Ethnographie*, 44 (1946), quoted in Lebovics, 47.

decline formulated in the "Condition-of-England Question," as Thomas Carlyle termed it. Disaffected with the Whig liberal interpretation of British history and its hegemony after the Whig political triumph in 1832, Disraeli wanted to restore in his political program and his novels the importance of the ancient institutions of England: the Crown, the Church and the "People." In Disraeli's Young England Trilogy, so called after the youth-adulating politics he and his fiends espoused, as well as in his *Vindication of the English Constitution*, the fate of the youthful individual and the nation are intertwined. In *Coningsby*, for example, the education of the young eponymous hero at Eton, and the friendships he forms, are fundamental to his later rebellion against his own sinister grandfather, Lord Monmouth, a corrupt aristocrat. Contrasting patriarchal filiation and national affiliation, Disraeli unambiguously connects Coningsby's emancipation from the authoritarian Monmouth to future national regeneration. Further, Disraeli's nostalgia for his own days at Eton suffuses the novel: both Coningsby and his school friend Oswald are elected to Parliament, but "Men must have been at school together, to enjoy the real fun of meeting thus, and realising boyish dreams."[9]

Far more biological and racialist, however, were the persuasions of some of the later advocates of empire—some smacking of social Darwinism and racial superiority; others of outright population engineering. Toward the end of the nineteenth century, concern over the national implications of a declining birthrate superseded Malthusian fears of an overpopulation competing for meager resources. White British population was needed, imperialists argued, to fill the new spaces opened up by imperial pursuits. Acknowledging that his demands for "school canteens and free transport and baths for schoolchildren" may sound "terribly like rank Socialism," T. J. Macnamara, a Liberal MP, assures his reader that nevertheless "I'm not in the least dismayed. Because I know it also to be first-rate Imperialism.

[9]Benjamin Disraeli, *Coningsby* (London: Penguin, 1983 (1844)), 490.

Because I know Empire cannot be built on rickety and flat chested citizens."[10] Debate over empire, as Anna Davin reports, split the Socialist Fabian society, with most members including George Bernard Shaw and Sidney Webb, favoring "a lofty and public-spirited Imperialism." Webb wrote that the Empire must "breed and maintain in the truest and fullest sense of the word an Imperial race," stressing the need for education and sanitation since the Empire was "rooted in the home."[11]

Advocates of eugenics, on the other hand, preferred "quality" over quantity. National and imperial strength, they argued, lay in the strength of the race not its numbers: "A healthy people pruned of its decadents by a high mortality amongst its children is better than a degenerate race weakened by the survival of its progeny."[12] Such a position, a racist reincarnation of Malthusian anxieties, placed more emphasis on the training mothers needed to fulfill their roles in this national bioengineering. "Motherhood," Davin explains, "though a destined and national function, nevertheless needed to be taught; there were skills to be learnt so that the eugenically conceived baby would also be reared to its best advantage" (212–13). Not only children but also their mothers were in need of national attention and education. Women, however, had to be guarded against other types of education which might inhibit their fertility: one of the founders of eugenics, Karl Pearson, warned that "if child-bearing women must be intellectually handicapped, then the penalty to be paid for race dominance is the subjection of women."[13] Huxley's fictional

[10]T. J. Macnamara, "In corpore sano," *Contemporary Review*, Feb. 1905, 248. Quoted in Anna Davin, "Imperialism and Motherhood," in *Patriotism: The Making and Unmaking of British National Identity*, v. 1, ed. Raphael Samuel

[11]Sidney Webb, quoted in Davin, 210.

[12]William Butler, presidential address to Willesden and District Medical Society, reprinted in *Public Health*, 1899. Quoted in Davin.

[13]Karl Pearson, *The Scope and Importance to the State of the Science of National Eugenics*, a lecture given in 1907, quoted in Davin.

dystopia in *Brave New World* chillingly dramatizes these national eugenic aspirations.

Children and Cultural Survival

Such nationalist/imperialist ideas of the child are predicated on adult conceptions of the child as a potential victim. But, as Gide's novella shows, often that view is the result of adult desire. Nevertheless, the child's essential weakness and inborn dependence cannot be ignored. Even the rebellious German Youth were reincorporated by Hitler. One need not, however, turn to such extreme examples as Nazism to see how such dependence intersects with the value children are given in effecting national "survival." Consider as an example of this value and its ambiguities some of the issues raised by Quebecois nationalism in the debate that transpired between Charles Taylor and K. Anthony Appiah regarding the relevant questions of identity, recognition, and authenticity.[14] Taylor opens his essay—a wide-ranging discussion of the politics of recognition— by contrasting two versions of the modern politics of "equal dignity": the Kantian "politics of universalism" that emphasizes "the equalization of rights and entitlements," and, on the other hand, the Herderian "politics of difference," which is primarily the result of "the development of the modern notion of identity," an identity that is not defined by once socially given categories; hence, one that strongly needs recognition by others in a way the old socially derived identities did not (37–8).

These two views of "equal dignity" also differ in where they place the emphasis in terms of the individual versus the collective: the universalist view stresses individual rights and protections; the particularist, collective goals and values. In the latter, I

[14]See Charles Taylor, "The Politics of Recognition," and K. Anthony Appiah, "Identity, Authenticity, Survival: Multicultural Societies and Social Reproduction," in Amy Gutman, ed., *Multiculturalism: Examining the Politics of Recognition* (Princeton: Princeton University Press, 1994). All page numbers refer to this work.

demand recognition not as an autonomous Kantian subject—as in the universalist case—but as a member of a group with a distinct history, experience, culture. My authenticity depends on your recognizing and "respecting" that heritage. Hence, the paradox that Appiah points out early in his essay: "If what matters about me is my individual and authentic self, why is so much contemporary talk of identity about large categories—gender, ethnicity, nationality, "race," sexuality—that seem so far from individual?" Answering his puzzle, Appiah lucently disentangles two strands of our modern identity: "There is a collective dimension, the intersection of their collective identities, and there is a personal dimension, consisting of other socially or morally important features—intelligence, charm, wit, cupidity—that are not themselves the basis of forms of collective identity" (151).

Taylor, for his part, establishes his distinction between the two views in order to argue later—in discussing the Canadian Charter of Rights, and the Meech Lake accords—that the insistence on "procedural liberalism," which demands that the state not engage in protecting or promoting any substantive views about the ends of life, limiting itself to safeguarding the procedures through which the citizens may interact fairly and with "equal respect," may not always be adequate in respecting the identity essential differences between communities within a state. Appiah concurs that "there is not much to be said for the view that liberalism should be procedural . . . There can be legitimate collective goals whose pursuit will require giving up pure proceduralism" (156-7).

The two philosophers differ, however, in their stated goal of departing from procedural liberalism. In adducing the Quebec example to support his objection to procedural liberalism, Taylor states: "It is axiomatic for Quebec governments that the survival and flourishing of French culture in Quebec is a good. Political society is not neutral between those who value remaining true to the culture of our ancestors and those who might want to cut loose in the name of some individual goal of self-development"

(58). Taylor's use of indirect narrative discourse here belies his eventual, I would add circuitous, endorsement of the Quebec government's view as one of two "incompatible views of liberal society" (60). Therefore, it seems, he is in favor of the Meech Lake compromise, an amendment to the basic charter, whose "Law 101 forbid[s] (roughly speaking) francophones and immigrants to send their children to English language schools, but allows Canadian anglophones to do so" (55).

Appiah, however, objects that "one very strong demand [in Taylor's argument for collective goals], for which the state may need to accede, may be the survival of certain 'societies,' by which [Taylor] means groups whose continuities through time consists in the transmission through the generations of a certain culture . . ." (157). Taylor, for his part, states, it seems without disapprobation, that "Politics aimed at survival actively seeks to *create* members of the community, for instance, in their assuring that future generations continue to identify as French-speakers" (58–9). This is the part of the debate I would like to examine more closely, for it is evident that the goal of "*survivance*" is fundamentally achieved by adults acting on children. This action is accomplished through (depending on one's point of view) indoctrination that limits the child's horizons in order to fit into the desired group, or education that helps the child discover that his or her ancestral group is a major constituent of his/her self-making, from which one should not, as Taylor puts it, "cut loose." Children are again seen as instrumental to the continuity of the nation.

For, the fact is, children require not only food and material nurture for survival, but also linguistic nurture that is identity forming; the reason that the parents will cause to take the place—in Locke's words—of their children's "ignorant nonage" is crucially linguistic. Language is taught to children by adults—there is no other source for that process. Language, however, is not a neutral instrument that one imparts to one's children for their "use." In an earlier essay investigating the development of theories of language, Taylor sketches the decline of such a designative view of language, paramount in seventeenth-century empirical thought: Words mean because they designate something preexistent; learning language means acquiring the knowledge of words and putting them together—only thus can one avoid being enslaved by received ideas transmitted by unexamined language.

By contrast, the Romantics led by Herder, Taylor argues, reject this designative stance in favor of an expressivist view in which the very activity of language makes the human: "A pattern of activity, by which we express/realize a certain way of being in the world, that of reflective awareness. . . ."[15] And if this view seems somewhat elusive, it is no accident, for "expressive theories maintain some of the mystery surrounding language. Expressive meaning cannot be fully separated from the medium, because it is only manifest in it" (221).

Such an expressive view of language is not separable from the speaking subject; whence, Taylor elaborates, the Romantic rejection of art as *mimesis* in favor of seeing the artist as a creator god. This view feeds a too facile "Romantik" of our modern private sense of self: that I become myself in "being myself," in plumbing the depth of my own feelings and emotions.[16] Taylor rues that such a view of the private self— together with the crass scientism (objectivism) of public policy—"leave[s] out the really fruitful line of enquiry, a contemporary expressivism which tries to go beyond subjectivism in discovering and articulating what is expressed" (247). The "contemporary expressivism" which Taylor advocates would take note of the ever present interaction between the speaker and his/her language community, of Humboldt's view of language as

[15]Charles Taylor, *Human Agency and Language: Philosophical Papers,* v. 1 (Cambridge: Cambridge University Press, 1985), 232

[16]"Just be yourself!" is surely the motto of all talk shows, a mode of discourse that one cannot ignore in analyzing modern identity—at least in the U.S.

energeia, not *ergon*: "Language is shaped by speech, and so can only grow up in a speech community" (234).

Similarly in his later discussion of multiculturalism, Taylor rejects the "monological" concept of self formation, arguing that our identity is essentially dialogical:

> We become full human agents, capable of under-standing ourselves, and hence of defining our iden-tity, through our acquisition of rich human languages of expression. For my purposes here, I want to take *language* in a broad sense, covering not only the words we speak, but also other modes of expression whereby we define ourselves, including the "languages" of art, of gesture, of love, and the like. But we are inducted into these in exchange with others ... We define [our identity] always in dia-logue with, sometimes in struggle against, the iden-tities our significant others want to recognize in us. And even when we outgrow some of the latter—our parents, for instance—and they disappear from our lives, the conversation with them continues within us as long as we live.[17]

The essential difference here from his earlier discussion of language and agency is Taylor's emphasis on childhood as the orig-inary moment of language acquisition, and hence, community formation. Such an emphasis is subtle but unmistakable in his reference to the continuing dialogue with one's parents. I find Taylor's eloquence compelling. Appiah also approvingly cites the same passage on language in "the broad sense" in endorsing the dialogical formation of identity. He does not address, how-ever, how related Taylor's dialogical-linguistic view is to his communitarian, hence familial, emphasis on the identity for-mation of the child. In other words, Appiah accepts Taylor's

[17]Taylor, *Multiculturalism*, 32–3.

extension of dialogic language acquisition—necessarily community-dependent—to identity formation, an extension which implies, I think, a necessary limitation on the nascent autonomy of the child.

In elucidating how the seventeenth-century designative view developed, Taylor emphasizes how the great empirical philosophers—Hobbes, Descartes, Locke—came to realize that language is an instrument of *control* (Taylor's emphasis), that the older "cosmos of meaningful order," that of "correspondences" in which words participated in eternal essences, confined men in a prison of preconceived ideas that was fundamentally a prison made of language.[18]

Today, Taylor argues, both these older views of meaning: the ontic meaningful universe, and the designative seventeenth-century view are discredited, and he favors what he refers to as "contemporary expressivism," in which the self is embedded in a Humboldtian web of language that it modifies as that web constitutes it. Certainly one can make the argument here that the older divine chains of correspondences that Locke and Descartes broke have been replaced by the more subtle but no less binding webs of language in the "broad sense." Rousseau, who Taylor cites as one of the sources of the "politics of equal dignity," would, I believe, have screamed against such other-dependence. But Taylor and Appiah, in accepting the collective dimension of identity, overlook Rousseau's imperative of radical autonomy in *l'Inégalité*; Appiah, I think, without quite realizing it.

His agreement with Taylor above notwithstanding, Appiah disagrees with the latter's argument in favor of Quebec's Law 101. But he runs into an aporia that demonstrates the problem children present to liberal thinkers today, just as they did to

---

[18]That view has two variants: the Platonic strand in which language aspires to represent the pre-existent Ideas, and the medieval Christian view of the "world as a meaningful order, or a text." Taylor, *Human Agency and Language*, 223.

Locke, the problem of inevitable dependence. In objecting to the provision of the state's law that requires francophones to teach their children in French, Appiah argues that this practice may not be consistent with the "autonomy of future individuals. In particular families it is often the case that parents want the children to persist in some practice that those children resist. This is true of arranged marriage for some women of Indian origin in Britain, for example" (157). The example that Appiah cites—of parents infringing on a child's autonomy—is not what Taylor endorses, however. The language law, in fact, will have the effect that the state may infringe on the parents' rights and autonomy in raising their children—in the case of francophone, or immigrant, parents who wish to send their children to English schools—as well as on the children's autonomy to decide. The two problematic practices are similar, but not identical. For, in the Quebec example, children exemplify the cultural continuity that the state seeks to preserve against the parents' wishes, if necessary. The nation and the family may come to conflict over differing ideals for children, as we saw in the case of Robespierre.

The problem that children present, I believe, is inevitable, given their biological and mental dependence on their parents (or tutors, or the state). Education presents a paradox to the liberal philosopher concerned with realizing the Enlightenment's ideal of autonomy; every child is a chance to realize autonomy, and a demonstration of autonomy's limitations given the dialogical human condition. Education will always have to be a compromise between indoctrination and freedom. The danger of allegorizing is ever present.

I opened this study with the omniscient Athena, and concluded it with the omniscient narrator. Athena's knowledge integrates Odysseus into his community. Can one say the same for the relation of the omniscient narrator to the reader of his day? What about today? What are the implications of the decline of the omniscient realist novel, at least in Western Europe and the United States? A central focus of the modernist novel of the twentieth century is the problematization of the knowable: questioning the mountain on which the omniscient narrator stands; stressing that the mirror he holds up to the world distorts it. The loss of confidence in the omniscient narrator commences earlier, however. The narrator of Dickens's *Tale of Two Cities*—to be sure, a tale of epistemological obscurity—almost throws up his hands in despair at ability to know the alterity, his subject.[19] This gesture—emblematic of the abandonment of the epistemological project of the realist novel—does not merely raise an aesthetic question, for the omniscient realist novel of the nineteenth century is deeply implicated in the creation of the nation. Is the "failure" of the omniscient narrator/legislator a symptom of the disintegration of the belief in the imagined community of the nation? Or, is it rather an index of the nation's triumph that its guardian narrator can finally unbuckle his aegis?

---

[19]The narrator in Dickens's *A Tale of Two Cities* remarks: "A wonderful fact to reflect upon, that every human creature is constituted to be that profound secret and mystery to every *other*."(emphasis mine).

Index

Harvard Studies in Comparative Literature

24. *The Singer of Tales.* By Albert B. Lord. 1960

25. *Praisers of Folly: Erasmus, Rabelais, Shakespeare.* By Walter Kaiser. 1964

26. *Rogue's Progress: Studies in the Picaresque Novel.* By Robert Alter. 1964

27. *Dostoevsky and Romanic Realism: A Study of Dostoevsky in Relation to Balzac, Dickens, and Gogol.* By Donald Fanger. 1965

28. *The Icelandic Family Saga: An Analytic Reading.* By Theodore M. Andersson. 1967

29. *Roman Laughter: The Comedy of Plautus.* By Erich Segal. 1968

30. *Pan the Goat God: His Myth in Modern Times.* By Patricia Merivale. 1969

31. *The Renaissance Discovery of Time.* By Ricardo J. Quinones. 1972

32. *Grounds for Comparison.* By Harry Levin. 1972

33. *Comparative Studies in Greek and Indic Meter.* By Gregory Nagy. 1974

34. *Mirror on Mirror: Translation, Imitation, Parody.* By Reuben Brower. 1974

35. *The Quattrocento Dialogue: Classical Tradition and Humanist Innovation.* By David Marsh. 1980

36. *Fictions of Romantic Irony.* By Lilian R. Furst. 1984

37. *The Taming of Romanticism: European Literature and the Age of Biedermeier.* By Virgil Menoianu. 1984

38. *Literary Structure, Evolution, and Value: Russian Formalism and Czech Structuralism Reconsidered.* By Jurij Striedter. 1989

39. *Mi-lou: Poetry and the Labyrinth of Desire.* By Stephen Owen. 1989

40. *The Living Eye.* By Jean Starobinski. 1989

41. *Death in Quaotation Marks: Cultural Myths of the Modern Poet.* By Svetlana Boym. 1991

42. *The Challenge of Comparative Literature.* By Claudio Guillèn. 1993

43. *Subjects without Selves: Transitional Texts in Modern Fiction.* By Gabriele Schwab. 1994

44. *The Way of Oblivion: Heraclitus and Kafka.* By David M. Schur. 1998

45. *The Story of O: Prostitutes and Other Good-for-Nothings in the Renaissance.* By Michele Sharon Jaffe. 1999

46. *Original Subjects: The Child, the Novel, and the Nation.* By Ala A. Alryyes. 2001